American Indian Rock Art

Volume 43

With Contributions By

Peter Boyle
Ana Laura Chacón Rosas
Livio Dobrez
Diane Fox
Barbara J. Gronemann
Janine Hernbrode
Daniel Herrera Maldonado
David A. Kaiser
James D. Keyser
David Arturo Muñiz García
José Luis Punzo Díaz
César A. Quijada
Stephanie L. Renfro
Polly Schaafsma
Kimberly Sumano Ortega
Jim Uhrinak
Charlotte Vendome-Gardner

American Indian Rock Art
Volume 43

Edited by Ken Hedges and Mark A. Calamia

American Rock Art Research Association

San Jose, California

2017

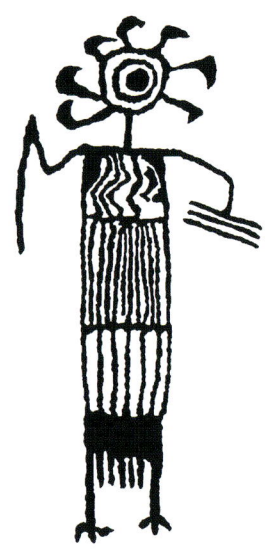

Compilation Copyright © 2017
American Rock Art Research Association

c/o Jack Wedgwood
1884 The Alameda
San Jose, California 95126-1733

This volume is published as a compilation of papers submitted by independent researchers. All rights to the content of individual papers remain with their respective authors.

ISBN 978-0-9888730-4-9

The American Rock Art Research Association is a 501(c)(3) non-profit organization.

Printed and bound in the United States of America.

Editors: *Ken Hedges and Mark A. Calamia*
Copy Editing, Layout, and Design: *Ken Hedges and Anne McConnell*
Editorial Assistance: *Linda Olson*
Cover Layout: *Ken Hedges*
Title Page Photograph: *John Pitts (see page 47)*
Flyleaf Photograph: *Polly Schaafsma (see page 47)*

About the cover:

The front cover is based on a photograph of the Comanche Gap petroglyph site in the Galisteo Basin, New Mexico, by Polly Schaafsma, from her paper beginning on page 47.

Photographs on the back cover are from papers in this volume by these authors (clockwise from upper left): Comanche Gap, New Mexico, by Polly Schaafsma; South Mountain, Arizona, by Barbara J. Gronemann; Rincón del Canal, Durango, by Daniel Herrera Maldonado; Chaco Canyon, New Mexico, by Charlotte Vendome-Gardner; Signal Hill, Arizona, by Janine Hernbrode and Peter Boyle; and Tsagiglalal, Columbia River, Washington, by David A. Kaiser.

Printed by Jostens Commercial Printing
Visalia, California

Table of Contents

Preface vii

Cannibal Woman on the Columbia—Exploring a Mythological Motif
    David A. Kaiser 1

A Horse is a Horse—And They Really Can Tell Us Things
    James D. Keyser and Stephanie L. Renfro 11

Lynx Paw Petroform Alignments to Red Ochre Exposure Below Wisconsin's Niagara Escarpment
    Diane Fox and Jim Uhrinak. 29

Power and Identity: Stability and Change in Pueblo Shield Iconography from the Fourteenth to the Nineteenth Centuries
    Polly Schaafsma 47

The Importance of Landscape-Based Approaches in Rock Art Research
    Charlotte Vendome-Gardner. 67

Broad Distribution of Flower World Imagery in Hohokam Petroglyphs
    Janine Hernbrode and Peter Boyle. 75

Finding the Dog in Arizona Rock Art
    Barbara J. Gronemann 85

The Rock Paintings of Divisadero
    César A. Quijada 93
        Versión en Español 98

Rhythms in the Landscape: The Archaic Pictorial Tradition of Durango, Mexico
    Daniel Herrera Maldonado. 101
        Versión en Español 110

The Woman with Butterfly Hair Whorls in Chalchihuites Rock Art of Durango, Mexico
    Daniel Herrera Maldonado and Ana Laura Chacón Rosas. 117
        Versión en Español 126

Rock Art and Households in Western Mexico: The Case of Chavinda, Michoacán
    Kimberly Sumano Ortega, David Arturo Muñiz García, and José Luis Punzo Díaz 131
        Versión en Español 136

A Universalist Taxonomy for Pictures
    Livio Dobrez 139

Preface

The yearly volumes of *American Indian Rock Art* celebrate our annual conferences with papers submitted for publication as a record of research in rock art conducted by colleagues and presented at our meetings. In addition, ARARA invites rock art researchers to submit independent papers for consideration, and if a paper reflects ongoing work (or if presentation generates additional information or insights), authors can submit papers for future volumes.

ARARA members and guests convened in sunny Las Cruces, New Mexico, for two days of rock art presentations at the 43rd Annual ARARA Conference on May 28 and 29, 2016. This volume contains ten papers submitted from that meeting, supplemented by an independently submitted paper from the Pacific Northwest and a paper that continues research first presented at our international meeting in Albuquerque in 2013.

We present the papers in this volume in geographical order from north to south, beginning with David Kaiser's analysis of the Cannibal Woman motif in rock art along the Columbia River in Washington state, then moving east to the northern Plains, where Jim Keyser, working with Stephanie Renfro, has developed a statistical method of determining the cultural identification of horse motifs. Farther east, Diane Fox and Jim Uhrinak continue their study of Wisconsin petroforms with their analysis of alignments to sigificant landscape features including a major source of red ochre.

We shift focus to the Southwest, where Polly Schaafsma looks at the shield motif in precontact rock art for comparisons to historic shields to explore the nature of social interactions among the Pueblos, the Spanish, and tribes from the Plains. In Chaco Canyon, Charlotte Vendome-Gardner examines the fluteplayer motif from a landscape perspective to provide better understandng of the cultural and natural contexts of rock art.

We move west and south into Arizona where Janine Hernbrode and Peter Boyle continue their analysis of the regional distribution of Flower World motifs in the rock art of the Hohokam. Remaining in Hohokam territory, Barbara Gronemann continues her research on the identification of dogs in Arizona rock art, pointing out that distinguishing characteristics of canine types can be identified in even the most basic animal motifs.

Our colleagues from Mexico were well represented at the conference, and that international participation is reflected in the papers published here. César Quijada reports on a site near Hermosillo with an intriguing anthropomorphic motif, an important addition to this regional Sonoran corpus. Daniel Herrera identifies visual rhythms in the Archaic rock art of Durango in an interesting study examining this rock art in the context of symbolic landscapes. For later Chalchihuites rock art in the same area, Herrera joins with Ana Laura Chacón for a look at a distinctive motif that documents far-reaching relationships between Durango and the American Southwest. Moving farther south in Western Mexico, Kimberly Sumano, David Muñoz, and José Punzo report on their examination of petroglyphs in association with domestic household sites in Michoacán.

The volume concludes with a paper by Livio Dobrez setting forth his pan-geographical approach toward developing a universal taxonomy for pictures by looking at three basic perceptual categories.

The program for the 2016 ARARA meeting in Las Cruces included 28 presentations on rock art research, yet this volume contains only 10 of those papers. As chair of the Publications Committee, I urge you to submit papers when the call is made, and to presenters I urge you to submit your papers for publication. And for all readers, if you have publication-related skills to offer or would like to serve as volunteer editors or reviewers for future AIRA volumes, please get in touch.

I wish to express thanks to my co-editor Mark Calamia for his dedicated efforts to make this a better publication in the face of unanticipated personal demands on his time, to Linda Olson for her editorial assistance, and to our anonymous reviewers.

In producing a book, you never know when little misteaks might creep in here and their, but the Shadow knows, and voila! there are no mistakes in there at all. Once again I express my gratitude to my Shadow editor Anne McConnell, who still insists on not being on the front cover, but without whom this book would have been a vastly more difficult undertaking.

—Ken Hedges

Cannibal Woman on the Columbia—Exploring a Mythological Motif

David A. Kaiser

A handful of mythological motifs have been identified in Columbia Plateau rock art. One of these images is Cannibal Woman. Found in tales throughout the Pacific Northwest, specific ethnographic descriptions have enabled further recognition of her images along the Columbia River. The elements associated with these Cannibal Woman images and their relationship to the landscape help reveal their meaning as well as their importance to the indigenous inhabitants along the river.

Mythological motifs occur in the rock art of many tribal groups on the Columbia Plateau (Hann et al. 2010:19). These images were created "to witness creation" (Cash Cash 2004). Their placement on the landscape where the legends occur commemorate these events and act as mnemonic devices for the recollection of traditional stories.

These motifs were also used by shamans, who created the more elaborate and detailed rock art in the region, to access and proclaim their power. In addition to calling on the spirits of animals and other natural powers, these Indian doctors also petitioned known mythological beings, whose stories would have been known and images recognized by the community.

Distinct constellations of repeated features are key to recognizing such known mythic figures, while ethnography is necessary to identify them beyond their general categories. Progress towards identifying and interpreting some of these mythical beings on the Columbia Plateau has been made (Curtis 1911:ii, 145–146; Hann 2013; Hann et al. 2010:15–18; Keyser 1992:88–89; Keyser et al. 2006:19–23; Keyser et al. 2008:66–69; Keyser and Poetschat 2004:122–126; Keyser and Taylor 2002:iii, 18; McClure 1979; Strong et al. 1930:136; Strong and Schenck 1925:85). Characters of myth such as She Who Watches (Tsagiglalal), Swallowing Monster (Nayshthlá to the Wishram or Itc!i'xyan to the Wasco), Owl, Land Monster, and Thunderbird have been identified in the rock art.

Another mythic being found in the rock art along the Columbia River is Cannibal Woman. Stories were told throughout the Pacific Northwest of a beast who terrorized and ate children or even entire villages. She is sometimes referred to as the Basket Ogress, on account of the basket in which she places her victims. While Cannibal Woman is sometimes considered an important figure in tribal mythological beliefs, often she functions as a "boogeyman" to frighten misbehaving children (Aguilar 2005:228; Trafzer 1998:108–109).

David A. Kaiser
Oregon Archaeological Society

These widespread tales occur throughout the Pacific Northwest, stretching north to British Columbia where a petroglyph of Cannibal Woman has been identified (Meade 1971:28–30). Among the Kwakwaka'wakw (Kwakiutl) the Cannibal Woman is known as Dzunuḵwa (Tsonokwa) and is generally portrayed on totem poles and masks with pendulous breasts and pursed lips. While this petroglyph does not display these typical characteristics, it does show a large-eyed, polydactyl female. Within her torso is the frowning face of what appears to be one of her victims (Figure 1).

On the Columbia Plateau, two huge basalt pillars known as the Twin Sisters overlook the Columbia River in Washington (Figure 2). A Wanapum legend attached to this landscape feature explains that they were once two cannibal women who were turned to stone (Relander 1956:47). Young people were sent to this site to have their vision quests (Relander 1956:306). This must have been an especially frightening prospect after hearing the tales of cannibal women and their proclivity for eating children.

Wanapum elders said that an image of these cannibal women was pictured on the cliffs upstream near Vantage, where there was a large concentration of rock art prior to the damming of the river in the 1960s. Relander (1956:47n5) identifies this image as a pair of anthropomorphs with rayed arcs above their heads (Figure 3).[1] One figure raises an arm, while the other appears to be holding a small human figure by the head. Their large size is emphasized by relation to the smaller human figure. Below them is a downwards curved arc with pendant lines which could be interpreted as a basket. Though the original site is now inundated, this image, along with other salvaged petroglyphs, is now on display at the Ginkgo Petrified Forest State Park.

Paired anthropomorphs, frequently depicted beneath rayed arcs, are a common motif along the Columbia River with a number of possible interpretations (Cain 1950:40; Keyser 1992:77–78; McClure 1981). It is unlikely that all of these twin images are also meant to depict cannibal women. Most commonly, Cannibal Woman is not described in terms of twins, but as appearing on her own, or part of a larger group of sisters. We cannot know whether the Vantage petroglyph was intended by the original artist to depict the two cannibal women, or if it was only later identified as such.

Figure 1. Cannibal Woman petroglyph from British Columbia.

To identify further examples of the Cannibal Woman motif, it is appropriate to examine the ethnography for further identifying characteristics. The Wishram and Wasco have many tales of a cannibal woman called At!at!a'lia (Sapir 1909:34–39, 164–173; 274–286) also known as Tah-tah Kleah to the Yakama (Trafzer 1998:107–109,117–120). She is described as being of immense size, having a striped (or occasionally spotted) body, and often possesses the aforementioned basket in which she carries away her victims. She is married to Owl, whose hooting is a sign that someone will die (Sapir

Figure 2. The Twin Sisters near Wallula Gap. David Kaiser photograph.

Figure 3. Twin Cannibal Women Petroglyph, Vantage Washington. David Kaiser photograph.

1909:39). In fact, At!at!a'lia is not a specific name, but a general word for cannibal women. Several stories tell of five At!at!a'lia sisters, as well as their At!at!a'lia children to which they feed frogs and lizards.

Like the inhabitants along the Northwest Coast, there was at least a limited tradition along the Columbia River of making ceremonial masks (Mercer 2005:34–35). Both the Wishram and Yakama used just such masks of At!at!a'lia/Tah-tah Kleah. The Yakama would wear it while carrying a basket on their back (Trafzer 1998:108). The Wishram mask was striped, and had big eyes and ears (Spier and Sapir 1930:237).

She too is associated with features in the landscape; multiple rocks along the river were said to be her petrified body (Hunn 1996:17; Sapir 1909:286; Spier and Sapir 1930:274). Additionally, there was an island just upriver from the main Wishram village which was known as At!at!a'lia's Furnace, and was said to be the place where she cooked her victims (Sapir 1909:34-39).

Given all these attributes, it is surprising that no clear depiction of At!at!a'lia in rock art has been identified.[2] However, a bone carving of what might be a Cannibal Woman was found downstream at Sauvie Island, where the Willamette River meets the Columbia (Butler 1965:4, 10, 16; Mercer 2005:29). This figure depicts a woman with large almond-shaped eyes and skeletal ribcage. On her back she carries a basket[3] containing a smaller person, also with ribs showing. Zig-zag stripes occur on the larger figure's face and legs.

Besides At!at!a'lia, there is another specific cannibal woman known to the Wishram as Akxa'qusa. She once ate every inhabitant of the main Wishram village of Nixlu'idix, leaving only small bits of bodies and clothing. Discovering this, the daughter of the East Wind piled the pieces together and sprinkled them with paint five times and brought them back to life. This tale is the basis of the name Nixlu'idix, meaning "at once it (your flesh) came together" (Spier and Sapir 1930:164–166).

Akxa'qusa would also seduce all the men who came near, and kill them by throwing them from the cliff where she lived. When Coyote heard of her actions he gathered five stone pestles and five sharp bones and went to meet her. Though playing hard to get, Coyote allowed himself to be led to her home and be seduced. However, when lying with her, he inserted the stone pestles into her which were ground away to nothing; he then inserted the bones which he brought with him. She weakened all the while and was maneuvered to the edge of the cliff where she was pushed over and killed (Curtis 1911:113–114; Strong et al. 1930:101–102; Strong 1956).

The grinding away of the stone pestles and bones is a reference to *vagina dentata* (Strong 1956:410). This is a recurring feature in native legends throughout western North America (Thompson 1929:309n115) and is sometimes depicted in rock art (Keyser and Poetschat 2015:38–39, 183–186; Leen 2017:Section 3C). A petroglyph from Gabriola Island in British Columbia clearly illustrates this motif (Figure 4). Moreover, phallic shaped pestles are a common artifact found along the Columbia River, and may be related to the myth of Akxa'qusa (Strong et al. 1930:101–102).

When Coyote inspected her body, he found that she was made of flint and had shattered into numerous pieces. The spot where she died, or her body itself, was known as Wakemap Mound. Wakemap, (pronounced Wok-em-up), is an anglicized version of the Wishram word Wuq'emap, meaning ogress or old woman (Butler 1957:158; Strong 1959:5). Though now flooded, this artificial mound was large enough to be noted by Lewis and Clark when they passed by. It was a deep midden

Figure 4. Vagina dentata illustrated on a Northwest Coast petroglyph from Gabriola Island. Photographs courtesy of Dan Leen.

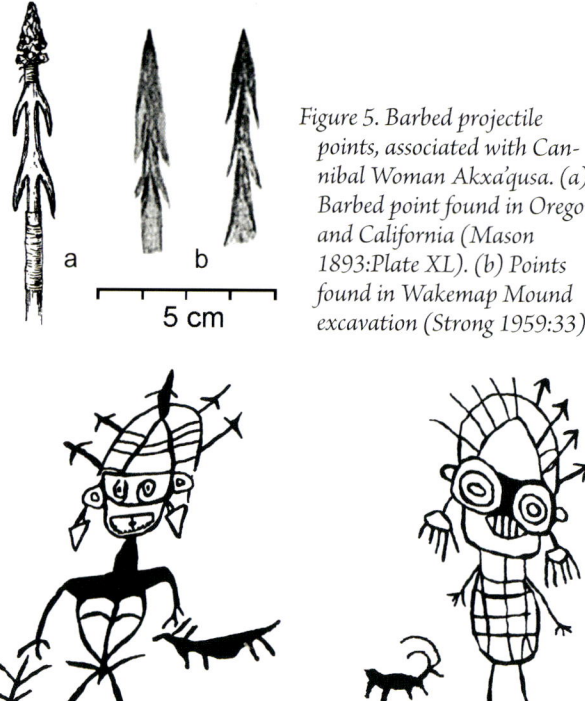

Figure 5. Barbed projectile points, associated with Cannibal Woman Akxa'qusa. (a) Barbed point found in Oregon and California (Mason 1893:Plate XL). (b) Points found in Wakemap Mound excavation (Strong 1959:33).

Figure 6. Two Akxa'qusa images. (a) Blalock Rapids. New tracing from 1967 Lorings photograph, (Loring Collection, Oregon Historical Society). (b) Crawford Point. New tracing from pre-1942 photograph (Marshall Family Photographs, Oregon Historical Society). Mountain sheep added from previous tracing (Keyser et al. 2008), as not visible in photo.

going back a thousand years (Aikens, et al. 2011:180) and was a site where Nixlu'idix villagers would gather flint (Curtis 1911:113–114; Strong et al. 1930:101–102; Strong 1956:410).

Akxa'qusa was also associated with a particular kind of barbed projectile point which was named after the Ogress (Spier and Sapir 1930:199).[4] The point was described as having two to four barbed flint heads, each one nested into the proceeding. The segmented head was designed so a portion would detach and remain in the wound. These points were not used for hunting, but only for war (Spier and Sapir 1930:199).

However, the illustration that Spier and Sapir's informant provided of this Akxa'qusa point appeared to be a multi-barbed bone point, or bone barbs with flint points set in it. They compared it with points illustrated in Mason 1894 (pl. XL fig. 2 and pl. XLIX fig. 5) (Figure 5a). Just such points were later discovered when Wakemap Mound was excavated in the 1950s (Strong 1959:33) prior to its inundation due to dam building (Figure 5b).

These barbed points are key to identifying further Cannibal Woman images, or more properly Akxa'qusa images, in rock art. Two such images have been identified as Cannibal Woman (Figure 6a and 6b) based on their association with projectile points (Keyser et al. 2008:66–68). Each of these images shows a figure wearing a basketry hat, indicative of women in the art of the region. From this hat emerge a series of projectile points. The image from Crawford Point has bear paw or possibly human hand earrings. Similar earrings are also seen on some Tsagiglalal images as well. The figure from Blalock Rapids holds a double barbed point in one of her hands.

A mitigating factor against the Blalock Rapids image being Cannibal Woman (Keyser et al. 2008:81n12) is what appears to be a phallus in the recording by Loring and Loring (1982:109) (Figure 7). Their images were sketched or traced from photographs, and while they provide an invaluable resource for rock art which has been submerged in the waters behind the dams along the Columbia River, their recordings have proved to be inaccurate in the finer details of images. A new tracing (Figure 6a) has been made from the Lorings' original photograph (Oregon Historical Society, Loring Collection, Roll 21, Frame 10). This image is slightly distorted by the parallax of the original 1967 photograph, which is likely why the Lorings sketched it for their publication. However, it shows significantly greater detail. What seemed a possible phallus, now appears to show the figure's body itself being formed as a downwards pointed projectile point. The barbs of the point form an otherwise unexplained horizontal line outside the

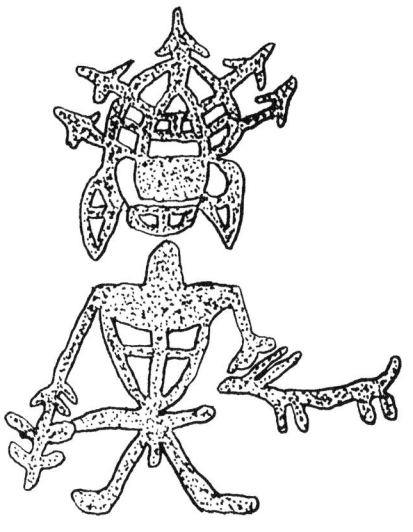

Figure 7. Original Loring and Loring sketch of Blalock Rapids petroglyph.

Figure 8. Four O'clock Rapids. New tracing from original Lorings photograph (Loring Collection, Oregon Historical Society).

Figure 9. Two Cannibal images from John Day Bar. (a) Tracing from pre-1942 photograph (Marshall Family Photographs, Oregon Historical Society). (b) New tracing from original Lorings photograph (Loring Collection, Oregon Historical Society).

figure's lower body in the Lorings' recording.

The further details revealed in the new recording show both images also have prominent ears and earrings, and stripes in their bodies, as well as large eyes and prominent teeth, all traits that are indicative of cannibal women. Both of these figures are juxtaposed with mountain sheep; however, the significance of this is unclear.

Using these defining traits, further Akxa'qusa images along the Columbia can now be identified along the Columbia River (Table 1). While more abstracted, a petroglyph from Four O'clock Rapids shows a human figure, whose head, hands and feet are all made of double-barbed projectile points (Figure 8). As the legend states, her body is made of flint, as seen in the Blalock Rapids figure as well. These projectile points on the Four O'clock Rapids petroglyph are also striped, in keeping with the description of cannibal women. Additionally, two smaller double-barbed points emerge from the head similarly to those seen on the previously identified Akxa'qusa figures.

Two more Cannibal Woman figures are represented by their heads alone (Figures 9a and 9b). Both of these figures come from John Day Bar and each show a mouth full of teeth, large eyes, and a hat on the head.[5] One of the figures (Figure 9a) is surmounted by a downwards pointing projectile point. This image also has a swollen or protruding tongue, like the Blalock Rapids figure. The depiction of the tongue in this fashion was used as a metaphor for death in Northwest Coast art (Wardwell 1996:80-85). This swollen tongue device occurs in stone and bone images of Tsagiglalal (She Who Watches) (Figure 10), who is thought to be associated with a death cult along the Columbia River (Keyser 1990; Keyser et al. 2013:93-95; McClure 1979; Strong 1945).

The other figure from John Day Bar (Figure 9b) has what may be a triangular striped basket hat, or a large projectile point on her head, similar to the image at Four O'clock Rapids. The arc below may likewise be intended to represent the barb on the point. The figure's earrings or braids may also be intended to be seen as a second nested barb. Lines radiate up from this figure's headdress, echoing the earlier compositions with projectile points rising from their hats. The conflation of the triangular hat and the shape of the projectile point

Table 1. Cannibal Woman Elements.

	Blalock Rapids	Crawford Point	4 O'Clock Rapids	John Day Bar - 1	John Day Bar - 2
Projectile Point	X*	X	X*	X	X
Basket Hat	X	X		X	?
Big Ears	X	X		X	
Big Eyes	X	X		X	X
Lines in Body	X	X	X		X
Teeth	X	X		X	X

* Double barbed

Figure 10. Tsagiglalal (She Who Watches). Note the swollen tongue motif. David Kaiser photograph.

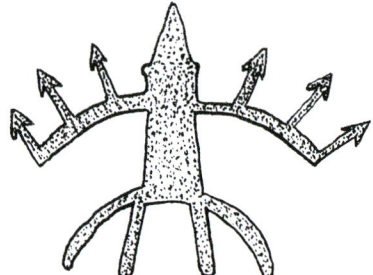

Figure 11. Original Loring and Loring sketch of possible abstracted Akxa'qusa.

is a feature of multiple representations of Akxa'qusa.

The mouth of the John Day River, like Wakemap Mound, was known as a place of intensive, long term projectile point manufacture (Strong et al. 1930:38). The association of both sites with Akxa'qusa, may indicate that her legends were connected with places where flint is found. After all, the source of the flint was her broken body. One Cannibal Woman story begins with two children hunting for flint. One calls to the other, "Hurry and pick up the flints; the At!at!a'lia may come." Sure enough, she immediately appears and captures them, placing the children in her basket (Sapir 1909:274).

Two additional images may also represent Akxa'qusa, though in a much more abstracted form. Another image from Crawford Point shows an anthropomorph in the form of the double-barbed point itself (Figure 11). The body is a triangular form, topped with a distinctive hat or point. Although the figure possesses legs, any arms are only represented by the upper of two curved arcs. Just such double arcs are used to indicate double-barbed points on the Akxa'qusa image at Four O'clock Rapids. This upper arc also has a series of projectile points rising from them in a similar fashion to that seen on the other figures' hats. It is probable that the arcs on this and other Akxa'qusa figures consciously mirror the rayed arc motif found in the region which indicates spiritual power. This image is only documented by an illustration in Loring and Loring (1982:58). Like all the above Akxa'qusa images it is now flooded by the dams. However, its proximity to the other cannibal woman image at Crawford Point supports its identification, just as do the two Cannibal Woman images at John Day Bar.

One final image, originally from Miller Island but now at the Maryhill Museum of Art, may be an even more abstracted representation (Figure 12). However, through comparison with these previous depictions, a tentative identification can be made. The petroglyph consists of a downward pointing triangle below two sideways pointing triangles joined by a zig-zag line. Above this is a row of five upwards pointing lines tipped with barbed points. Encircling the zig-zag and occurring between some of the arrows are rows of dots.

Figure 12. Possible Akxa'qusa image at Maryhill Museum of Art. Image superimposes earlier B-shaped image on the left. David Kaiser photograph.

It is unlikely that this image would have been recognized as a symbolic representation of Akxa'qusa had not the abstracted images at Crawford Point (Figure 11) and Four O'clock Rapids (Figure 8) been identified. Like the image from Four O'clock Rapids, the petroglyph in the Maryhill Museum is composed of connected projectile points. Two points project from each side above a downward pointing triangle. A similar downward pointing projectile point is also seen on the body of the Blalock Rapids figure (Figure 6a). The top of the figure consists of a series of barbed points, similar with other, more explicit, examples. Furthermore, the spots may also indicate the image is related to Cannibal Woman. However, the identification of this image as Akxa'qusa must remain only an intriguing possibility. In addition, the triangles appear to be more recently pecked, possibly suggesting some later adjustment in the visual narrative.

Although tales of various Cannibal Women occur throughout the Columbia Plateau, identified depictions of Akxa'qusa appear concentrated along the middle Columbia River (Figure 13). All of these petroglyphs are carved in the Columbia River Conventionalized style, dated within the last 1,000 years and combining content and styles of the Northwest Coast and the inner Plateau (Keyser 1992:97). In addition to the projectile points specifically associated with Akxa'qusa, she also tends to be depicted with the traits generally attributed to At!at!a'lia cannibal women (Table 1). These traits include a basketry hat, big eyes, ears or earrings, a striped body, and when a mouth is shown it is filled with large teeth indicative of swallowing or cannibalism in the art of the region.

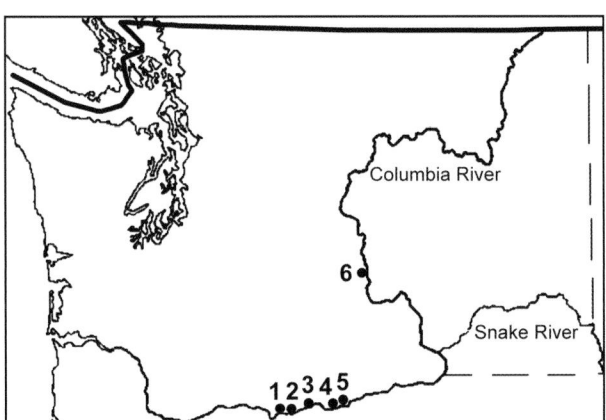

Figure 13. Locations of Cannibal Woman petroglyphs along the Columbia River: (1) Crawford Point, (2) Miller Island, (3) John Day Bar, (4) Four O'clock Rapids, (5) Blalock Rapids, (6) Vantage.

The images of Cannibal Woman, particularly those of Akxa'qusa, show her importance to people who lived in this region. Her tales are also commemorated in place names and a particular kind of projectile point. Unfortunately, only two of the rock art images still exist and neither in their original locations. The remainders are now lost to us due to dam construction and we have only old photographs and illustrations for reference, limiting further interpretation. However, now that a constellation of motifs has been recognized, further examples may still await identification.

Notes

1. Relander cites Cain (1950:27, Figure 34) as showing this image. This figure contains several images from the site, but only Figure 34j would seem to conform to the twin cannibal sisters.

2. Hedden (1957:29, 31) proposed two images along the Columbia that could represent Cannibal Women. One of the figures has a body made up of circular geometric shapes, as well as a phallus, while the other is a face carved on a horizontal boulder. However, he offers no reasoning for either identification beyond the face's large eyes, which he sees as the evil eye that can turn people to stone. This is not supported in Columbia Plateau ethnography, and while large eyes are a trait of Cannibal Woman, they are also found on numerous other Columbia Plateau Conventionalized style images. No other traits attributed to Cannibal Woman are present on either figure.

3. Mercer (2005:29) identifies the object on the woman's back as a cradle, however, its open circular design more closely resembles a basket carried on the back, as seen in Curtis 1911 (Plate 284).

4. A remarkably similar tale is told by the Wind River Shoshone (Shimkin 1947:336-338). Water-Ghost-Woman is a cannibal who is sexually defeated by Uncle Bat. When killed her body breaks into pieces of obsidian. In rock art she is often pictured with a projectile point (Francis and Loendorf 2002:93, 118–119). Likewise, the Shoshone creation story involves Coyote mating with a woman after breaking off the teeth in her vagina using an elk horn scraper (Lowie 1909:236–239). These are just some of the similarities in mythology that show a connection and common influence between the Shoshone and the people of the Columbia River (Lowie 1909:235).

5. A Wishram legend tells of an arrowhead maker who drinks his own blood after cutting himself, and becomes a cannibal. He eats all of his flesh below his

shoulders (Sapir 1909:246–248). This may seem likely interpretation of these images, however the wearing of basket hats appears to be an exclusively female trait in Columbia Plateau rock art. Further details of this legend have been associated with rock art at Picture Gorge in eastern Oregon (Hann 2013), but the cannibal figure is not illustrated.

References Cited

Aguilar, George W., Sr.
 2005 *When the River Ran Wild: Indian Traditions on the Mid-Columbia and the Warm Springs Reservation.* Oregon Historical Society Press, Portland.

Aikens, C. Melvin, Thomas J. Connolly, and Dennis L. Jenkins
 2011 *Oregon Archaeology.* Oregon State University Press, Corvallis.

Butler, B. Robert
 1957 Art of the Lower Columbia Valley. *Archaeology* 10(3):158–165.
 1965 Perspectives On the Prehistory of the Lower Columbia Valley. *Tebiwa* 8(1):21–16.

Cain, H. Thomas
 1950 *Petroglyphs of Central Washington.* University of Washington Press, Seattle.

Cash Cash, Phillip
 2004 To Witness Creation: A Southern Columbia Plateau Rock-Art Ethnography. Report Submitted to the USDA-Forest Service, Pacific Northwest Regional Office, Portland, Oregon, in fulfillment for a "Heritage of Civil Rights" grant.

Curtis, Edward S.
 1911 *The North American Indian,* Volume 8. Plimpton Press, Norwood, Massachusetts.

Francis, Julie E., and Lawrence L. Loendorf
 2002 *Ancient Visions, Petroglyphs and Pictographs of the Wind River and Bighorn Country, Wyoming and Montana.* University of Utah Press, Salt Lake City.

Hann, Don
 2013 Implied Narrative: Rock Art, Landscape, and Myth at Picture Gorge, Oregon. In *American Indian Rock Art, Volume 39,* edited by William D. Hyder, pp. 101–113. American Rock Art Research Association, Glendale, Arizona.

Hann, Don, James D. Keyser, and Phillip Cash Cash
 2010 Columbia Plateau Rock Art: A Window on the Spirit World. In *Rock Art of the Oregon Country: Honoring the Lorings' Legacy,* edited by James D. Keyser and George Poetschat, pp. 1–24. Oregon Archaeological Society, Publication 18. Oregon Archaeological Society Press, Portland.

Hedden, Mark
 1957 Petroglyphs. *Craft Horizons* 12(5):28–31.

Hunn, Eugene
 1996 Plateau Indian Place Names: What Can They Teach Us? *Journal of Linguistic Anthropology* 6(1):3–26.

Keyser, James D.
 1990 Tsagiglalal—She Who Watches: Rock Art as an Interpretable Phenomenon. *Journal of Interpretation* 14(2):S1–S4.
 1992 *Indian Rock Art of the Columbia Plateau.* University of Washington Press, Seattle.

Keyser, James D., and George Poetschat
 2004 The Canvas as Art: Landscape Analysis of the Rock Art Panel. In *The Figured Landscapes of Rock-Art: Looking at Pictures in Place,* edited by Christopher Chippindale and George Nash, pp. 118–130. Cambridge University Press, Cambridge.
 2015 *Seeking Bear.* Oregon Archaeological Society, Publication 23. Oregon Archaeological Society Press, Portland.

Keyser, James D., Livio A. C. Dobrez, Don Hann, and David A. Kaiser
 2013 How is a Picture a Narrative? Interpreting Different Types of Rock Art. In *American Indian Rock Art, Volume 39,* edited by William D. Hyder, pp. 83–99. American Rock Art Research Association, Glendale, Arizona.

Keyser, James D., and Michael W. Taylor
 2002 *Visions On Stone: Rock Art of the Columbia Plateau.* Oregon Archaeological Society, Publication 12. Oregon Archaeological Society Press, Portland.

Keyser, James D., Michael W Taylor, and George Poetschat
 2006 *Talking With the Past: The Ethnography of Rock Art.* Oregon Archaeological Society, Publication 16. Oregon Archaeological Society Press, Portland.

Keyser, James D., Michael W Taylor, George Poetschat, and David A. Kaiser
 2008 *Visions in the Mist: The Rock Art of Celilo Falls.* Oregon Archaeological Society, Publication 23. Oregon Archaeological Society Press, Portland.

Leen, Daniel
 2017 *A Gallery of Northwest Petroglyphs: Shamanic Art of the Pacific Northwest.* Electronic document, http://danielleen.org/petroglyphs.html, accessed March 11, 2017.

Loring, Malcolm J., and Louise Loring
 1982 *Pictographs and Petroglyphs of the Oregon Country, Part 1: Columbia River and Northern Oregon.* Monograph XXI, Institute of Archaeology, University of California, Los Angeles.

Lowie, Robert H.
 1909 *The Northern Shoshone.* Anthropological Papers of the American Museum of Natural History, Volume 2, Part 2, New York.

Mason, Otis Tufton
 1894 *North American Bows, Arrows, and Quivers.* Government Printing Office, Washington.

McClure, Richard H., Jr.
 1979 The Tsagiglalal Motif in Rock Art of the Lower Columbia River. In *American Indian Rock Art, Volume 5,* edited by Frank G. Bock, Ken Hedges, Georgia Lee and Helen Michaelis, pp. 173–189. American Rock Art Research Association, El Toro, California.
 1981 Paired Anthropomorphs of Central Washington. In *American Indian Rock Art, Volume 6,* edited by Frank G. Bock, pp. 36–47. American Rock Art Research Association, El Toro, California.

Meade, Edward
 1971 *Indian Rock Carvings of the Pacific Northwest.* Grays Publishing, Sidney, British Columbia.

Mercer, Bill
 2005 *People of the River: Native Arts of the Oregon Territory.* University of Washington Press, Seattle.

Relander, Click
 1956 *Drummers and Dreamers.* Caxton Printers, Caldwell, Idaho.

Sapir, Edward
　1909 *Wishram Texts, Together with Wasco Tales and Myths*. Late E. J. Brill, Leyden.

Shimkin, D. B.
　1947 Wind River Shoshone literary forms: An introduction. *Journal of the Washington Academy of Sciences* 37(10):329–352.

Spier, Leslie, and Edward Sapir
　1930 *Wishram Ethnography*. University of Washington Press, Seattle.

Strong, Emory
　1959 *Wakemap Mound: A Stratified Site on the Columbia River*. Oregon Archaeological Society, Publication 1. Oregon Archaeological Society Press, Portland.

Strong, William Duncan
　1945 The Occurrence and Wider Implications of a "Ghost Cult" on the Columbia River Suggested by Carvings in Wood, Bone, and Stone. *American Anthropologist* 47:244–261.

　1956 Wakemap: A Columbia River Site Mispronounced. *American Antiquity* 21(4):410.

Strong, William Duncan, and W. Egbert Schenck
　1925 Petroglyphs near the Dalles of the Columbia River. *American Anthropologist* 27(1):76–90.

Strong, William Duncan, W. Egbert Schenck, and Julian H. Steward
　1930 *Archaeology of the Dalles-Deschutes Region*. University of California Press, Berkley.

Thompson, Stith
　1929 *Tales of the North American Indians*. Harvard University Press, Cambridge.

Trafzer, Clifford E.
　1998 *Grandmother, Grandfather, and Old Wolf: Tamánwit Ku Súkat and Traditional Native American Narratives from the Columbia Plateau*. Michigan State University Press, East Lansing.

Wardwell, Allen
　1996 *Tangible Visions: Northwest Coast Indian Shamanism and its Art*. The Monacelli Press, New York.

A Horse is a Horse—And They Really Can Tell Us Things

James D. Keyser and Stephanie L. Renfro

Horses are a key component of Northwestern Plains biographic rock art and scholars have intuitively distinguished Crow and Blackfoot horses based on different neck forms, accoutrements, and typical associations with various humans. Despite this general understanding, no one has formally defined these types of horses or developed a system to quantify their differences. To provide evidence for identifying a Crow "calling card" petroglyph we developed a system to quantify these differences and statistically tested their significance. The resultant identifications enable us to define both Crow and Blackfoot horse styles and use these to better interpret several Plains rock art sites.

The subject matter of Plains Indian biographic rock art—part of a broader biographic art tradition that was also drawn on robes and ledger pages—is primarily horses, humans, weapons, and tipis, which together make up well over 95 percent of the images depicted in that art. Drawn principally as narrative action scenes and coup count tallies that served to document the warrior status of important men (Keyser 1977; Keyser and Klassen 2001; Klassen 1998; Sundstrom 2004), this Biographic rock art occurs from Calgary, Alberta, to the Mexican state of Coahuila and from the Rocky Mountains to the Black Hills and central Kansas (Keyser 2004). Across this broad area, biographic art in its more inclusive sense was drawn and painted by nearly every tribe that occupied the region, and various rock art images have been reasonably attributed to artists from almost a dozen of these groups. Such identifications are based on typical images that are known to be stylistically distinctive, coupled with the location of images within the Historic ranges of these tribes. However, the two groups most commonly identified as the artists of particular rock art sites and images are the Blackfoot and Crow, with more than two dozen sites being specifically identified as the products of each tribe (Conner 1980, 1984; Conner and Conner 1971; Keyser 1977, 2007, 2014, 2015; Keyser and Cowdrey 2008; Keyser and Poetschat 2009, 2012, 2014; Keyser et al. 2012; Klassen 1998; Loendorf 2012; Loendorf et al. 2012; McCleary 2016).

Within biographic rock art, horses account for between 35 and 40 percent of all imagery, reflecting their key importance in the Plains Indian warfare complex, and for both Blackfoot and Crow rock art, horses are stylistically distinct enough that rock art scholars routinely identify examples as being the product of one tribe or another in print (e.g., Loendorf et al. 2012:74–75), and even more often in casual conversation and professional presentations (Keyser 2015). However, such identification is based largely on anecdotal evidence—either their location within Historic tribal territories or the association of spe-

James D. Keyser
Oregon Archaeological Society, Portland, Oregon

Stephanie L. Renfro
Center for Health Systems Effectiveness, Oregon Health & Science University, Portland, Oregon

cific horses with characteristic types of humans—rather than a carefully formulated typological classification. In short, Northern Plains rock art archaeologists usually identify Blackfoot or Crow horses using an intuition-based system rather than a constellation of specific attributes. While scholars are often uncomfortable with such an anecdotal approach, up until now it has been all that is available, and anyone looking closely at the data can see that there are definite differences between horses in one area versus horses in another. As one researcher said to Keyser, "'Crow' horses just look like Crow horses, and 'Blackfoot' horses are clearly different."

The Problem—Defining Crow and Blackfoot Style Horses

As part of a recent research project that led to the identification of a Crow "calling card" petroglyph located right on the boundary of the present-day Blackfeet Reservation (Keyser 2015) it became necessary to formalize the identification and definition of a Crow horse style versus a Blackfoot horse style in order to provide stronger support than simple intuition to the ethnic affiliation of a particular site. Thus, we assembled two samples of horses from sites carefully identified as Crow or Blackfoot and designed a measurement system to quantify the differences that rock art researchers had previously observed. This paper describes that measurement system and shows how it can be used to differentiate Crow and Blackfoot horses from one another and to help identify examples that were depicted at sites far outside these tribes' traditional territories. The value of this method of identification should help future scholars with ethnic identification of other rock art sites, and by expanding this methodology to other tribally distinctive styles it may be possible to better identify horses carved and painted by other tribal artists.

The Intuitive Evidence for Crow and Blackfoot Style Horses

For any scholar familiar with Northern Plains rock art, the abundance of horses found throughout the region is no surprise. And anyone who expends even minimal effort in comparing examples of horses from Writing-On-Stone with those from sites found in the Musselshell, Middle Yellowstone, and Big Horn river drainages quickly comes away with the intuitive impression that Crow and Blackfoot artists drew their horses in significantly different ways (Figure 1). This is particularly true of "mature style" horses (as originally named and defined by Dewdney [1964:26–29] and formalized by Keyser [1977:33–35]), which are common to the Early Biographic rock art style (Keyser 1987). But for Crow horses these distinctions seem also to carry over into their Late Biographic style renderings of this animal. Because Blackfoot artists drew so few Late Biographic style horses, we cannot show this same strong continuity of form.

Blackfoot horses are the classic mature style animals, defined as:

> very "fluid" emphasizing elongated bodies and necks with little attention paid to legs. The nose is usually left open, and often the head is simply represented by the open end of the two curved parallel lines that form the neck…Legs are usually simple stick appendages, and ears and the mane are often depicted. The tail may be long and feathery, or may be shown as a single line. Hooves are rarely depicted, but when they occur they are C or U shaped hooks [that]…depict the idea of the animal's characteristic track [Keyser 1977:33–34].

Several hundred such horse images are found at nearly 50 sites in the greater Writing-On-Stone area (Keyser 1977; Klassen 1998) but others have been noted further afield in Montana and even Wyoming (Keyser 2007, 2015). Typically associated with small rectangular, V-neck, or hourglass body style humans, these horses often have very simple bridle reins indicated, but the only other common horse accoutrement is a type of decorated bridle bit known as the "Thing to Tie on the Halter" (Keyser 1977:43, 1991, 2007:15, 19; Keyser and Mitchell 2001). One characteristic variant of the Blackfoot style horse is the shorthand animal, showing only the front quarters or—more commonly—just the neck and head. Often such shorthand horses are used when large herds of animals are illustrated.

On the other hand, Crow horses—while still meeting the general definition of the mature style for their body and leg form—are considerably different from most Blackfoot horses. These animals typically show a high-arched neck with a head that is usually oriented so that it points strongly downward. Crow horses often show a more elaborate mane and a much wider variety of accoutrements that are usually depicted in much greater detail. Such accoutrements include feather war bonnets, keyhole-shaped face ornaments, zigzag "lightning" reins, and two characteristic types of Spanish chain bridle bit decorations (Keyser 2012; Keyser and Mitchell 2001:200–204; Keyser and Poetschat

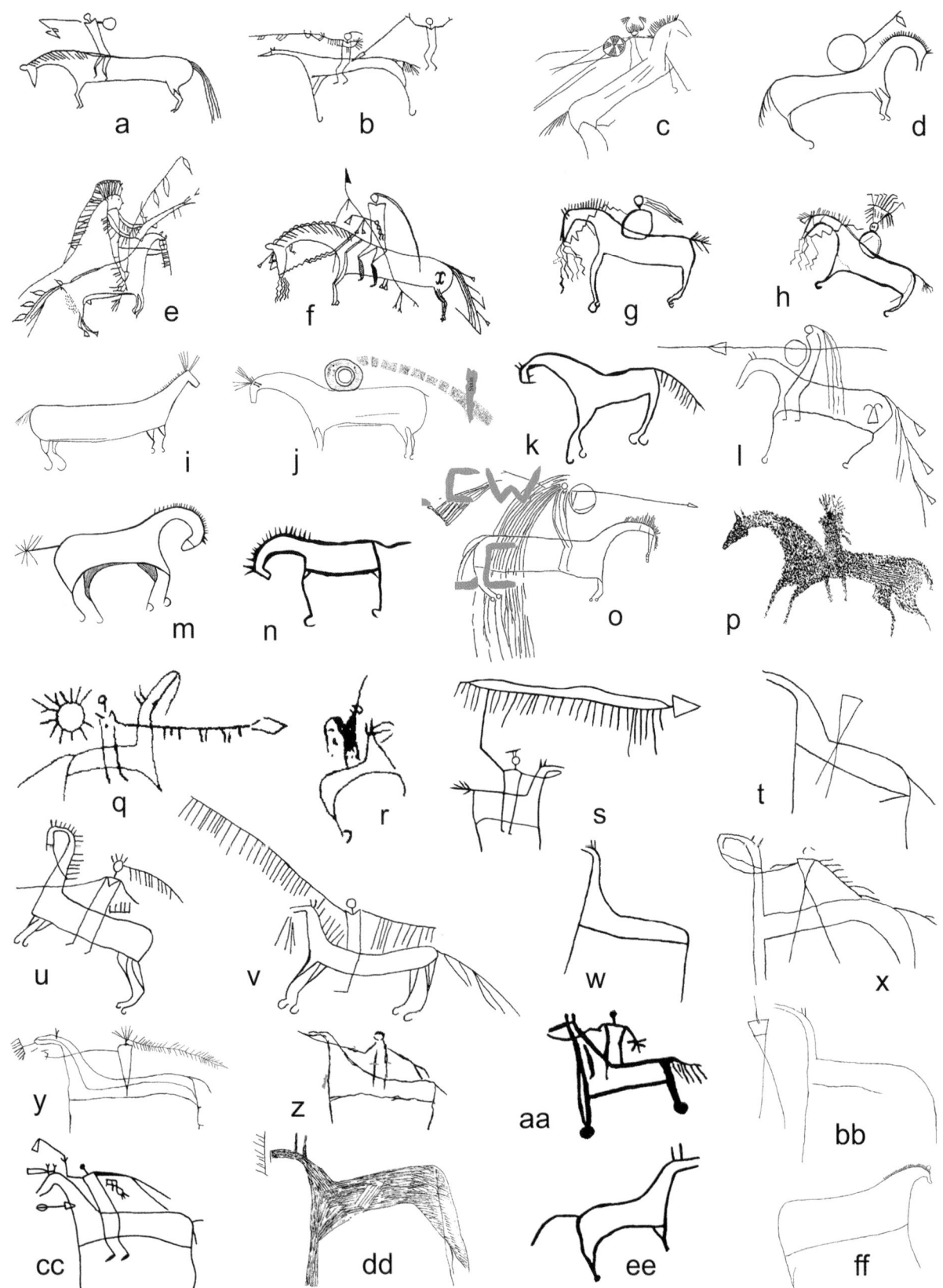

Figure 1. Crow (a–p) and Blackfoot (q–ff) horses in rock art. Grey on j is water stain, on o is vandalism, and on z is red pigment. See Tables 5 and 6 for site identification of each illustration.

2009:30–32). In addition Crow style horses are typically associated with elongate, fluidly graceful human representations that have been described as showing a "strong sense of line alternating between curves and angles" (Brownstone 2001:74). These humans are very different than those typically associated with Blackfoot style horses.

The distinctions intuitively noted for these rock art horses also appear equally consistent in the robe art authored by Blackfoot and Crow artists, and can also be seen in the ledger drawings of Crow warriors. Fortunately for this study, these images provide a sample of illustrations that we can use to test any distinctions that we may discover in the rock art imagery.

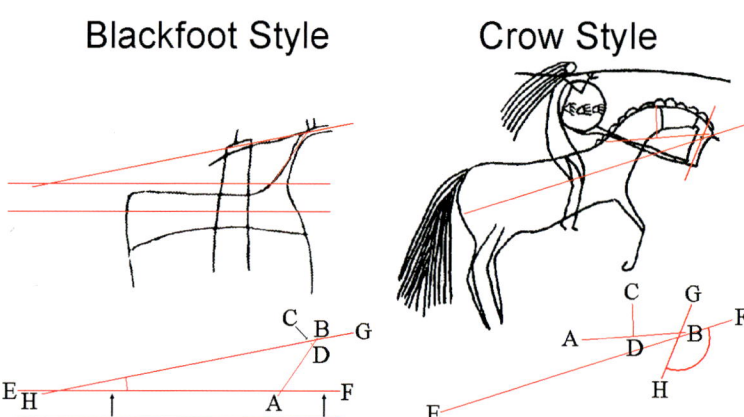

Figure 2. The measuring system for Blackfoot and Crow horses. Chord/sagitta ratio determined using lines A–B, C–D, head position measures the angle formed by lines E–F and G–H. Line through body on horses with shallowly angled head position must be moved up with parallel for easy angle measurement (as shown on this Blackfoot style horse).

However, despite this general understanding among Plains rock art scholars as to the differences between Crow and Blackfoot horses, no one has previously formulated a system to quantify the apparent variation so that ethnic identification of these animals can be more systematic and not the result of cultural or individual biases and intuitive classification systems. For many sites this has not been a problem, since researchers most often attribute imagery within particular tribal territories to artists from the local tribes. However, in recent projects I (Keyser 2007, 2015) have identified rock art sites that can be reasonably assigned to both Blackfoot and Crow artists but which occur far outside their traditional tribal territories. Furthermore, I have suggested that scholars may be missing "calling card" sites because they cannot readily distinguish between ethnic styles with any sense of verifiability (Keyser 2015). Thus, in order to evaluate whether our intuitive identification of Crow and Blackfoot rock art horses can be statistically supported, we have designed a method to measure a series of Northwestern Plains horse images (Figure 2) that can be used to evaluate this problem.

Designing a Measurement System

As a first step in determining how one might quantify the differences between Blackfoot and Crow style horses Keyser assessed what characteristics he personally used to differentiate between them. Limiting this evaluation to the horse itself, since associated imagery is not always present nor can it always be assumed to be contemporaneous, it was evident that the basic characteristics that provide the intuitive impression of these differences were neck shape and posture and the position of the animal's head. These two traits occur on nearly all horses, they could be readily measured and compared within and between samples of images, and they were the most likely to be objectively quantifiable.

Measuring the arc of the animal's neck is the most complex. Using official nomenclature specific to geometry and equine anatomy, this measurement records the amount of arc of the animal's crest (Figure 2). To derive this, one initially draws and measures the chord of the arc that stretches from the poll (the top of the horse's head) to its withers. For rock art depictions we identified the poll as the location of the ears or the obvious angle where the crest changes to the head. The withers were identified as the change in angle from the crest to the body of the animal or, when this was not clearly demarcated, the area directly above the most posterior point where the front legs intersect the trunk.

Once the chord of the arc has been drawn, one measures the sagitta (that is, the height of this arc above the chord—or below it in the case of a recurved crest). The ratio of sagitta length (arc height) to chord length is then calculated and recorded. If the crest closely approximates a straight line then this number is entered as 0 (zero). If the crest of the horse's neck is recurved with respect to the chord line extending from withers to poll, a negative number is used to represent this measurement. In a few instances, when the crest is notably S-shaped so that it extends both above and below the line from withers to poll, 0 was assigned to this measurement.

Measuring the position of the horse's head is somewhat more straightforward. To calculate this a line is drawn through the long axis of the animal's body and a second line is drawn through the long axis of the animal's head. The angle where these two lines intersect is measured with a protractor and recorded as a positive number of radians if the head is angled below parallel with the long axis of the body and a negative number if the head is angled above parallel with the body's long axis. If the lines for head and body are parallel the number is recorded as 0.

Selecting the Images

In order to test the hypothesis that Crow and Blackfoot style rock art horses are morphologically distinctive it was necessary to select samples of horse images that likely represent these two tribal groups. For Crow artists Keyser chose a sample of 52 horses from 21 sites located in the Musselshell, middle Yellowstone, and Big Horn/Wind river drainages (Table 1). This region (Figure 3) is the historic period Crow homeland (Medicine Crow 2000:xx; Voget 2001:696) and there is ample archaeological evidence of Crow occupation throughout this area during Historic times and extending back into the Protohistoric period and the last centuries of the Late Prehistoric period (Frison 1976, 1979, 2007:99–105). In this sample of 21 sites, horse-period petroglyphs at nearly three-quarters of them are likely of Crow origin based on several lines of evidence. These include the association with tall, graceful, Crow style humans, horse bonnets, keyhole-shaped face ornaments, Spanish chain bits, hairstyles with excessively

Table 1. *Measurements for Crow Style rock art horses (site numbers 1–21 correspond to numbers on map, Figure 3).*

	Chord/Sagitta Ratio	Head Angle
1. 48FR2509 Battle Scene (1)	.19	+100
48FR2509 Battle Scene (2)	.26	+106
48FR2509 Battle Scene (3)	.18	+ 94
2. Castle Gardens (48FR108) (1)	.27	+147
3. No Water (48WA2066) (1)	.13	+ 81.5
No Water (48WA2066) (2)	.19	+ 82
No Water (48WA2066) (3)	.12	+ 75
No Water (48WA2066) (4)	.14	+ 85
4. 48BH4275 (1)	.18	+ 83.5
5. Mahogany Buttes (1)*	.17	+ 51
6. 48HO9 (1)	.12	+ 69
7. Cottonwood (24CB1163) (1)	.28	+168
Cottonwood (24CB1163) (2)	.13	+ 88
8. Joliet (24CB402) (1)	.17	+ 98
Joliet (24CB402) (2)	.18	+ 96
Joliet (24CB402) (3)	.09	+ 60
9. Templeman (24YL436) (1)	.21	+117
Templeman (24YL436) (2)	.13	+ 75
10. Razor Creek (24YL578) (1)	.12	+ 54.5
11. Manual Lisa (24YL82) (1)	.29	+130
Manual Lisa (24YL82) (2)	.10	+ 79
12. 24PR2382 (1)	.21	+130
13. Doktordik (24YL417) (1)	.06	+ 78.5
Doktordik (24YL417) (2)	.27	+128
Doktordik (24YL417) (3)	.26	+115
14. Horse House (24YL434) (1)	.06	+ 94
Horse House (24YL434) (2)	.12	+ 70
Horse House (24YL434) (3)	.19	+107
15. Nordstrom-Bowen (24YL419) (1)	.20	+ 80.5
16. Castle Butte (24YL418) (1)	.12	+ 96
Castle Butte (24YL418) (2)	.04	+ 11
Castle Butte (24YL418) (3)	.14	+118
17. Musselshell (24ML1049) (1)	.08	+ 40
Musselshell (24ML1049) (2)	0	+ 50
Musselshell (24ML1049) (3)	.14	+ 84
Musselshell (24ML1049) (4)	.15	+ 46
Musselshell (24ML1049) (5)	.20	+169
Musselshell (24ML1049) (6)	.31	+145.5
Musselshell (24ML1049) (7)	.15	+ 73.5
Musselshell (24ML1049) (8)	.11	+ 41
Musselshell (24ML1049) (9)	.13	+120
18. Kyte Site (1)*	.16	+ 80
Kyte Site (2)	.25	+119
Kyte Site (3)	.11	+ 70
Kyte Site (4)	.33	+101
Kyte Site (5)	.35	+107
Kyte Site (6)	.20	+ 84
Kyte Site (7)	.20	+101
19. Four Dance Cliff (24YL559) (1)	.13	+ 48.5
Four Dance Cliff (24YL559) (2)	.07	+ 55
20. Miller (24YL589) (1)	.08	+ 75
21. H-H (24YL597) (1)	.25	+ 61
21 sites = 52 total horses	* No site number yet assigned	

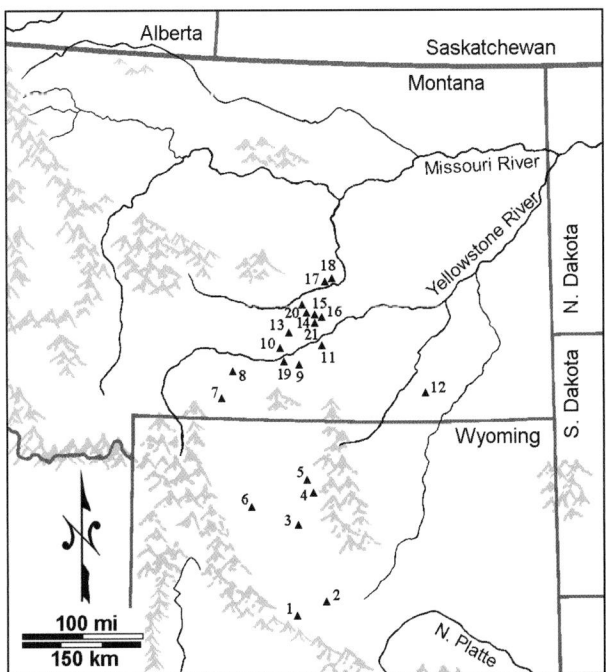

Figure 3. *Rock art sites with Crow style horses used in this analysis. Numbered sites 1–21 are identified in Table 1.*

long locks, a stylistically distinctive way of depicting feathers, and ethnographic information about the site itself as well as items and events depicted in the rock art (Conner and Conner 1971; Keyser 2012; Keyser and Cowdrey 2008; Keyser and Poetschat 2009:95–97; Loendorf 2012; McCleary 2016).

For Blackfoot artists Keyser chose a sample of

Table 2. Measurements for Blackfoot Style rock art horses.

	Chord/Sagitta Ratio	Head Angle
1. DgOv-2 Panel 10	.08	+ 10
DgOv-2 Panel 14 (1)	.05	- 11
DgOv-2 Panel 14 (2)	.08	+ 27.5
DgOv-2 Panel 14 (3)	-.03	+ 6.5
DgOv-2 Panel 16	0	+ 34
DgOv-2 Panel 19	.05	+ 39.5
DgOv-2 Panel 27d (1)	.0	+ 29
DgOv-2 Panel 27d (2)	.13	+ 59
DgOv-2 Panel 27d (3)	.08	+ 57
DgOv-2 Panel 27d (4)	0	- 11
DgOv-2 Panel 27F (1)	.08	- 10.5
DgOv-2 Panel 27F (2)	0	- 1.5
DgOv-2 Panel 27F (3)	-.05	- 20
DgOv-2 Panel 27F (4)	0	+ 10
DgOv-2 Panel 27F (5)	0	- 3
2. DgOv-9	.06	+ 48
3. DgOv-42	.11	- 13.5
4. DgOv-45	0	- 13
5. DgOv-49	0	- 15
6. DgOv-55	.04	- 28
7. DgOv-56	.09	- 10
8. DgOv-57 (1)	0	+ 25.5
DgOv-57 (2)	0	+ 15.5
DgOv-57 (3)	.04	- 46
9. DgOv-63 (1)	.06	- 2
DgOv-63 (2)	.06	+ 19
10. DgOv-69	0	- 19
11. DgOv-79	.08	- 2
12. DgOv-80 (1)	.08	+ 1
DgOv-80 (2)	.06	+ 1
13. DgOv-81 (1)	.04	0
DgOv-81 (2)	.08	- 7
14. DgOv-84	.06	- 11
15. DgOv-130	-.03	- 19
16. DgOw-20	0	+ 3
17. DgOw-27 (1)	0	- 22
DgOw-27 (2)	.06	+ 27
DgOw-27 (3)	.12	+ 29
DgOw-27 (4)	0	- 13.5
DgOw-27 (5)	.08	+ 23
DgOw-27 (6)	0	- 7
DgOw-27 (7)	0	- 28
DgOw-27 (8)	0	- 15
18. DgOw-30	.13	+ 80
19. DgOw-31	0	+ 13
20. DgOw-32 (1)	.06	+ 48
DgOw-32 (2)	.07	0
DgOw-32 (3)	.25	+ 109
DgOw-32 (4)	.03	+ 6
21. DgOw-41 (1)	0	+ 20
DgOw-41 (2)	0	+ 7
22. DgOx-15	.07	0
22 sites= 52 total horses		

52 horses from 22 sites in the greater Writing-On-Stone area (Table 2). Writing-On-Stone is located in the heart of Blackfoot territory, and is known ethnographically and historically to have been heavily used by members of all three tribes of the Blackfoot confederacy (Dempsey 1973; Klassen 1995). In this sample of 22 sites, half of the horse petroglyphs are associated with hourglass body style humans, two others are directly associated with a Blackfoot style capture hand (Keyser and Poetschat 2012), four of the animals wear the characteristic Blackfoot halter decoration known as the "Thing to Tie on the Halter," and one has a rider who carries a Blackfoot style medicine bundle (Keyser and Klassen 2003:12–15). Most of the other horses are associated with rectangular body or V-neck style humans typical of Blackfoot pictography and composed in scenes characteristic of Blackfoot biographic art (Keyser 1977, 1979, 2007; Klassen 1998; Magne and Klassen 1991).

Results of the Analysis

Measurements show distinct differences between the Crow and Blackfoot samples in both attributes (Tables 1, 2; Figures 4, 5). The chord/sagitta ratios are generally much higher for the Crow horses than for the Blackfoot horses, indicating that Crow horses have necks that are significantly more arched. For example, no Crow horse had a recurved neck and only one of 52 had a straight crest, while three Blackfoot horses' necks were recurved and 20 had a straight crest. More generally, more than 90 percent (47 of 52) of Blackfoot horses had a ratio below .09 while 85 percent (44 of 52) Crow horses had ratios above .10 (Figure 4). These two distributions show that while there is limited overlap at the extremes of variation of the two types of horses, the normal ranges of variation are completely separate.

A similar situation is evident for the position of the horses' heads in these two samples (Tables 1, 2; Figure 5). Crow animals' heads point notably downward. In the sample only three horses have heads tilted downward at an angle less than 45 degrees and only one of these—with an angle of 11 degrees—approaches a position approximately parallel to the long axis of the body. In fact, 44 percent of these animals (23 of 52) had their head positioned at an angle more than perpendicular to the long axis of the body. In contrast, heads on Blackfoot horses generally point much straighter ahead. Exactly one half of the sampled animals had their head oriented between 15 degrees below and 15 degrees above the body's long axis, and nine additional animals had heads that pointed up more than 15 degrees. Only six Blackfoot horses have heads that point down more than 45 degrees and of these only two examples are oriented in a nearly perpendicular position to their body's long axis (one at 80 degrees and the other at 109 degrees). When illustrated on a circular histogram (Figure 5) the differences in these two patterns are dramatic and unmistakable.

Figure 4. Histograms showing frequencies of chord/sagitta ratios for Crow and Blackfoot style rock art horses. Note how significantly different the two distributions are from one another.

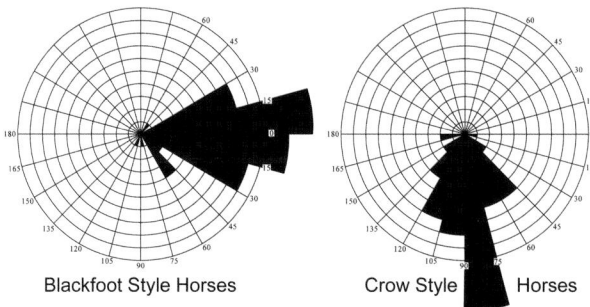

Figure 5. Circular histograms showing frequencies of head positions for Crow and Blackfoot style rock art horses. Note how significantly the two distributions differ. Horizontal line 0 to 180 represents a head position parallel to the long axis of the animal's body.

Mann-Whitney U tests were performed to formally assess the hypothesis that the measurements represent rock art samples drawn from populations with similar distributions versus the alternative—that the measurements characterize two distinct populations. This particular test was selected for its non-parametric nature. It makes no assumptions about the underlying distribution of the measurements (e.g., does not assume a normal distribution). The resulting U-statistics of 207.5 ($p < 0.001$) for the chord/sagitta ratio and 98.5 ($p < 0.001$) for the head angle were both highly significant, providing strong statistical support in favor of these measurements' ability to distinguish between two distinct populations.

A Test with Robe Art Horses

Given the apparent distinction between Crow and Blackfoot rock art horses, we decided to test our result against samples of horses drawn on painted robes known to have been produced by artists from those tribes. We selected six robes from each tribe (one of the Crow specimens is actually a painted war shirt) that spanned the period from approximately 1860 to 1890 (Tables 3, 4) and then randomly selected a sample of 23 horses from each group of six robes. We measured

Table 3. Measurements for Crow Style Robe Art horses.

		Chord/Sagitta Ratio	Head Angle
1.	Charges Strong (1)	.29	+ 92
	Charges Strong (2)	.05	+ 97
	Charges Strong (3)	.11	+ 64
	Charges Strong (4)	.12	+ 57
	Charges Strong (5)	.19	+ 64
	Charges Strong (6)	.08	+ 47
2.	White Swan (1)	.12	+ 54
	White Swan (2)	.07	+ 73
3.	NMAI Shirt (1)	.05	+ 54
	NMAI Shirt (2)	.08	+ 71
4.	NMAI Robe (1)	.10	+ 58
	NMAI Robe (2)	.15	+ 76
	NMAI Robe (3)	.16	+ 62
	NMAI Robe (4)	.11	+ 87
5.	Copenhagen (1)	.13	+ 70
	Copenhagen (2)	.17	+ 68
	Copenhagen (3)	.08	+ 63
	Copenhagen (4)	.20	+ 75
	Copenhagen (5)	.14	+ 87
	Copenhagen (6)	.09	+ 63
6.	Field Museum (1)	.10	+101
	Field Museum (2)	.11	+ 86
	Field Museum (3)	.13	+ 89

6 robes = 23 total horses

Sources for robes:
Charges Strong (Lowie 1956:210), White Swan (Schmittou 1996:42, 50), NMAI Shirt (Brownstone 2001:72), Copenhagen (Brownstone 2001:70), Field Museum (Brownstone 2001:78).

these horses in the same way as the rock art examples and recorded the data in the same manner.

Our analysis of robe art horses provides strong support for the distinctions noted between Crow and Blackfoot rock art horses. Crow robe art horses show all 23 head positions ranging from 47 to 101 degrees below horizontal (Table 3, Figure 6), while four Blackfoot horses' heads were oriented above horizontal and another 11 examples were between 0 and 11 degrees below horizontal (Table 4, Figure 6). In summary, 15 of the 23 Blackfoot animals had their head oriented between 15 degrees below and 21 degrees above the body's long axis, and only three animals had their head angled downward more than 30 degrees. No Blackfoot

Table 4. Measurements for Blackfoot Style Robe Art horses.

	Chord/Sagitta Ratio	Head Angle
1. Deadmond 1	.13	− 21
Deadmond 2	.08	− 07
Deadmond 3	0	+ 4
Deadmond 4	0	− 11
2. Sharp 1	.06	+ 20
Sharp 2	.10	+ 35
Sharp 3	0	+ 4
Sharp 4	0	+ 8
Sharp 5	0	+ 6
Sharp 6	.05	+ 3
Sharp 7	0	+ 8
Sharp 8	.05	+ 11
Sharp 9	.07	+ 19
3. Red Crane	0	+ 11
4. Royal Ontario Museum 1	0	− 10
Royal Ontario Museum 2	.06	+ 40
Royal Ontario Museum 3	0	+ 8
5. Hime 1	.06	+ 27
Hime 2	.08	+ 16
Hime 3	0	+ 22
Hime 4	.07	+ 33
6. Crop-Eared Wolf 1	.08	0
Crop-Eared Wolf 2	0	+ 8

6 robes = 23 total horses

Sources for robes:
Deadmond (Bouma and Keyser 2004), Sharp (Ewers 1983), Red Crane (Grinnell 1896:244), Royal Ontario Museum (Keyser and Klassen 2001:273), Hime (Ewers 1983:56), Crop-Eared Wolf (Barbeau 1960:58).

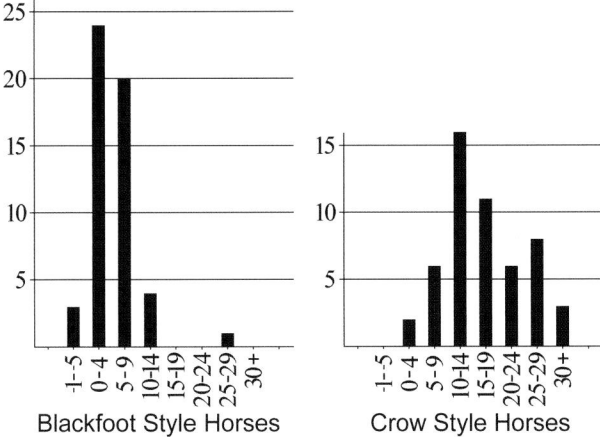

Figure 7. Histograms showing the frequencies of chord/sagitta ratios for Crow and Blackfoot robe art horses. Note how significantly different the two distributions are from one another, but how closely they mimic the distributions of the rock art horses in Figure 4.

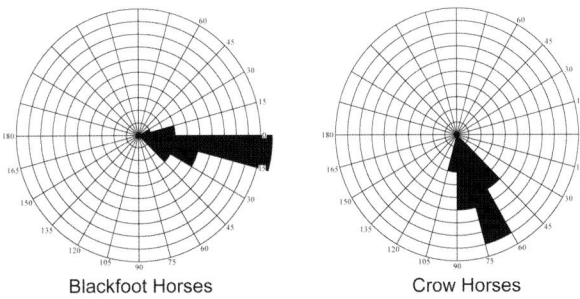

Figure 6. Circular histograms showing frequencies of head positions for Crow and Blackfoot robe art horses. Note how significantly different the two distributions are from one another, but how closely they mimic the distributions of the rock art horses in Figure 5.

example showed a head position as steeply angled as any Crow animal (Figure 6).

A similar situation prevails with the chord/sagitta ratios (Figure 7). For Blackfoot horses 21 of 23 animals have a ratio between 0 and .08, while 16 of the 23 Crow horses have a ratio between .10 and .29. When one compares the histograms of the robe art horses to those of the rock art animals they show essentially the same differences between Crow and Blackfoot samples, and the distributions for robe art animals are essentially identical to those for rock art horses.

Mann-Whitney U tests were also applied to the samples of robe art horses and yielded similar results as for the rock art figures, with p-values less than 0.001 for both the chord/sagitta ratio and head angle measurements (U-statistics 49.5 and 0.0, respectively). These results provide similarly strong support in favor of the measurements representing two distinct populations.

Being able to so clearly distinguish between Blackfoot and Crow horses gives rock art researchers another useful tool for identifying the ethnic identity of Northern Plains rock art imagery. When combined with other ethnically distinctive motifs (such as those referenced in Tables 5 and 6), these two types of horses provide an even more powerful means for identifying Crow and Blackfoot petroglyph and pictograph sites than is now available, and for distinguishing them from one another. Somewhat surprisingly, preliminary examination of data from other sites in Montana, Wyoming, and Colorado suggests that the Crow style of horse defined here may, in fact, reflect a broader stylistic trend of horses with more distinctly arched necks that were also drawn and carved by other tribes who lived south of the Blackfoot, including the Sioux, Cheyenne, and Comanche. Whether horses drawn by artists from these other tribes can be distinguished from those drawn by Crow artists remains to be demonstrated by further research. Interestingly, however, horses iden-

Table 5. Associated ethnic identifiers for Crow Style rock art horses (site numbers 1–21 correspond to numbers on map, Figure 3).

Site/ Horse	Figure Reference	Association*
1. 48FR2509 (1)		1, 5
48FR2509 (2)		1, 2, 5, 7
48FR2509 (3)	Figure 1o	1, 2, 5, 7
2. 48FR108 (1)	Figure 1n	
3. 48WA2066 (1)	Figure 1h	1, 4, 5, 6
48WA2066 (2)		1, 2, 4, 5
48WA2066 (3)		1, 2, 4, 5, 6
48WA2066 (4)	Figure 1g	1, 2, 4, 5, 6
4. 48BH4275	Figure 1k	1
5. Mahogany Buttes	Figure 1p	
6. 48HO9 (1)	Figure 1l	1, 2, 7
7. 24CB1163 (1)		3
24CB1163 (2)		
8. 24CB402 (1)	Figure 1f	1, 2, 4, 5, 6, 7, 8, 9
24CB402 (2)	Figure 1e	1, 5, 8, 9
24CB402 (3)		8, 9
9. 24YL436 (1)		
24YL436 (2)		
10. 24YL578		3, 7
11. 24YL82 (1)	Figure 2	1, 2, 7
24YL82 (2)		1
12. 24PR2382		1
13. 24YL417 (1)		1
24YL417 (2)		1
24YL417 (3)		1
14. 24YL434 (1)		3
24YL434 (2)		2, 4
24YL434 (3)		6
15. 24YL419		1, 7, 8
16. 24YL418 (1)	Figure 1a	1
24YL418 (2)	Figure 1b	1
24YL418 (3)		1, 7
17. 24ML1049 (1)		3, 9
24ML1049 (2)	Figure 1i	3, 9
24ML1049 (3)	Figure 1j	3, 9
24ML1049 (4)		3, 9
24ML1049 (5)		9
24ML1049 (6)	Figure 1m	9
24ML1049 (7)		9
24ML1049 (8)		3, 9
24ML1049 (9)		9
18. Kyte (1)	Figure 1c	1, 4#
Kyte (2)		1, 4#
Kyte (3)		1, 4#
Kyte (4)		1, 4#
Kyte (5)	Figure 1d	1, 4#
Kyte (6)		1, 4#
Kyte (7)		1, 4#
19. 24YL559 (1)		1
24YL559 (2)		1
20. Miller (24YL589)		
21. H-H (24YL597)		
21 sites = 52 total horses		

* Numbers for "Associations" indicate: 1, elongate human; 2, long hair; 3, horse bonnet; 4, keyhole face ornament; 5, Spanish chain bit; 6, "Lightning" rein; 7, "Crow" feathers; 8, Crow ethnography; 9, later Crow rock art.   # The keyhole face ornament at the Kyte site is on another horse that was not measured.

Table 6. Associated ethnic identifiers for Blackfoot Style rock art horses.

Site/Panel/Horse	Figure Reference	Association*
1. DgOv-2 Panel 10		Hourglass 1
DgOv-2 Panel 14 (1)	Figure 2a	
DgOv-2 Panel 14 (2)		Scene/Hourglass 3
DgOv-2 Panel 14 (3)		
DgOv-2 Panel 16		
DgOv-2 Panel 19		"Thing" Halter Decoration
DgOv-2 Panel 27d (1)		Scene
DgOv-2 Panel 27d (2)		Scene
DgOv-2 Panel 27d (3)		Scene
DgOv-2 Panel 27d (4)		
DgOv-2 Panel 27F (1)	Figure 1w	Scene
DgOv-2 Panel 27F (2)	Figure 1s	
DgOv-2 Panel 27F (3)		Hourglass 1
DgOv-2 Panel 27F (4)		Hourglass 1
DgOv-2 Panel 27F (5)		Hourglass 1
2. DgOv-9	Figure 1cc	Blackfoot Medicine Bundle
3. DgOv-42	Figure 1bb	Hourglass 1
4. DgOv-45		Hourglass 1/Scene
5. DgOv-49		
6. DgOv-55		
7. DgOv-56		
8. DgOv-57 (1)		
DgOv-57 (2)	Figure 1r	
DgOv-57 (3)	Figure 1q	
9. DgOv-63(1)		Hourglass 1
DgOv-63(2)		Hourglass 1
10. DgOv-69	Figure 1x	Hourglass 1
11. DgOv-79	Figure 1y	"Thing" Halter Decoration/ Hourglass 2
12. DgOv-80 (1)		Hourglass 1
DgOv-80 (2)		Hourglass 1
13. DgOv-81 (1)		Hourglass 1
DgOv-81 (2)		Hourglass 1
14. DgOv-84	Figure 1dd	"Thing" Halter Decoration
15. DgOv-130		
16. DgOw-20	Figure 1z	Hourglass 2
17. DgOw-27 (1)		Hourglass 1, 2
DgOw-27 (2)		Hourglass 1, 2
DgOw-27 (3)		"Thing" Halter Decoration
DgOw-27 (4)		
DgOw-27 (5)		Hourglass 3
DgOw-27 (6)		Hourglass 1
DgOw-27 (7)		
DgOw-27 (8)		
18. DgOw-30	Figure 1ff	
19. DgOw-31		Hourglass 1
20. DgOw-32 (1)		Blackfoot Capture hand
DgOw-32 (2)	Figure 1t	Hourglass 1
DgOw-32 (3)	Figure 1u	Blackfoot Capture hand
DgOw-32 (4)	Figure 1v	Blackfoot Capture hand
21. DgOw-41 Heffner (1)		Hourglass 1
DgOw-41 Heffner (2)	Figure 1aa	Hourglass 1
22. DgOx-15 Coffin	Figure 1ee	
22 sites = 52 total horses		

* Hourglass 1 = Full hourglass body style human; Hourglass 2 = Triangular body human; Hourglass 3 = Wasp-waisted variant of hourglass body style human; Scene = Distinctive Blackfoot horse-stealing scene.

tified as being of Shoshone authorship at two rock art sites in southwestern Wyoming (Keyser and Poetschat 2005:171–174) are distinctly different than either Crow or Blackfoot style animals, suggesting that other ethnically distinctive styles are likely to be identifiable. Further research along these lines should be undertaken.

Analyzing Other Plains Rock Art Sites

Having shown that Blackfoot and Crow style horses differ so significantly in form, we can use this information to help determine the ethnic origin of certain rock art sites. This is especially true for sites whose imagery seems stylistically "out of place" when compared to that from other sites in the surrounding area. Here we document five examples to illustrate how this information can be used. The sites are DgOw-9/DgOw-51, 24GL1663, the Turner Rockshelter, Panel 22 at 48WA2289, and one small panel at 48LN1640 (Figure 8).

DgOw-9/DgOw-51

Two numbered sites, located only about 200 meters apart on sandstone cliffs on the north side of the Milk River just west of Writing-On-Stone Provincial Park in southern Alberta, contain a set of horses and an associated shield bearer involved as part of a coup count tally scene (Figure 9). All four of these figures are formally quite different than the great majority of horses and shield bearing warriors found at more than 100 nearby sites in the greater Writing-On-Stone/Verdigris Coulee area. Although two horses and the warrior are found at DgOw-9 and the third horse has been given its own site number (DgOw-51) as a solitary animal, both sites are on private land and neither has been carefully recorded since DgOw-9 was originally sketched by Selwyn Dewdney in 1962. Keyser could not obtain permission to visit these sites during his 1976 field work at Writing-On-Stone Provincial Park, but Michael Klassen was able to visit the sites and make limited observations in 1993. The single horse at DgOw-51 (Figure 9b) is sufficiently similar to those at DgOw-9 in both form and technique, and spatially close enough to the others that we have combined the two sites for purposes of this analysis.

All three horses are drawn in the same manner, formed first with a lightly scratched outline, then more or less filled in with very light abrasion. Legs, tail, and probable riders are scratched and abraded. None of the animals has a mane nor do they have hooves although the legs on the two horses at DgOw-9 are reasonably well modeled (Figure 9a). On these same two DgOw-9 animals, forehead decorations are carefully though lightly inscribed and there is a hint of a decorated bridle bit on the animal from DgOw51. In general, the basic technique of using an outline infilled with abrasion is uncommon for horses drawn at other Writing-On-Stone area sites, with only three of the more than 300 horses created in that manner, but it is the strongly arched necks and downward pointing heads, coupled with decorative forehead ornaments that truly set these horses apart from others at nearby sites.

Given the formal differences between these horses and nearly all other horses at nearby Writing-On-Stone area sites, we measured these three animals with the system developed to differentiate Blackfoot and Crow style horses. These horses' measurements for both chord/sagitta ratios and head position put them clearly at the very margins of the ranges for Blackfoot style animals but well within the ranges of Crow style horses (Figures 10, 11, Table 7). We then compared the shield bearing warrior on the panel near the two horses at DgOw-9

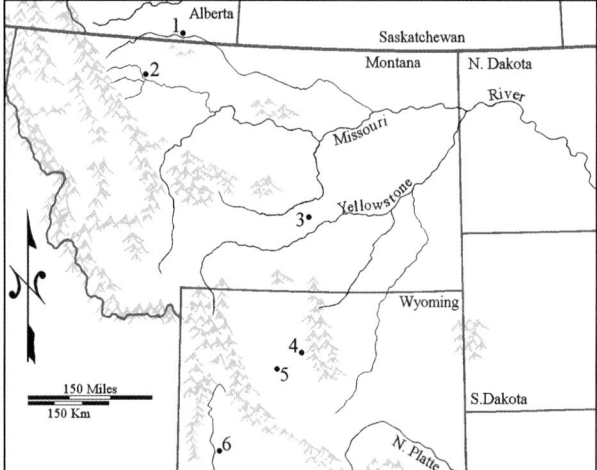

Figure 8. Other Northwestern Plains rock art sites considered in this analysis. 1, DgOw-9 and DgOw-51 in the Writing-On-Stone/Verdigris Coulee site complex; 2, Cheval Bonnet (24GL1663); 3, Turner Rockshelter; 4, Tipi Rockshelter (48WA2289); 5, Legend Rock (48HO4); and 6, La Barge Bluffs (48LN1640).

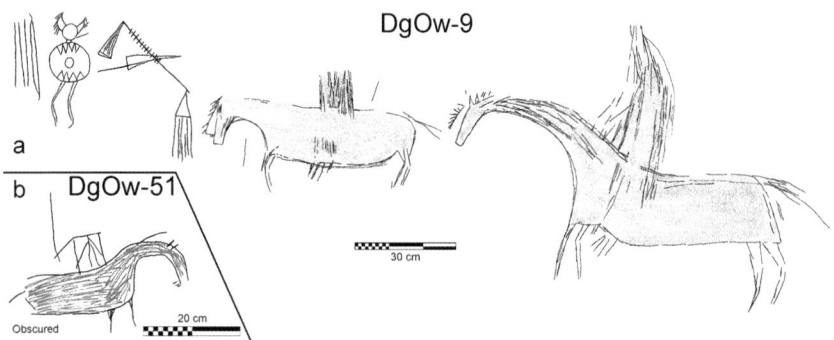

Figure 9. Petroglyphs of interest at DgOw-9 (a) and DgOw-51 (b). Note that shield bearing warrior at DgOw-9 is the object of a coup counted by floating coup-strike tomahawk at right that is being parried by his spear. Captured bow and arrows to left are remainder of tally composition. Grey stipple on horses in a and lines on horse in b indicates light abrasion. Note forehead ornaments on horses in a and compare to similar accoutrements in Figure 1f, h, o.

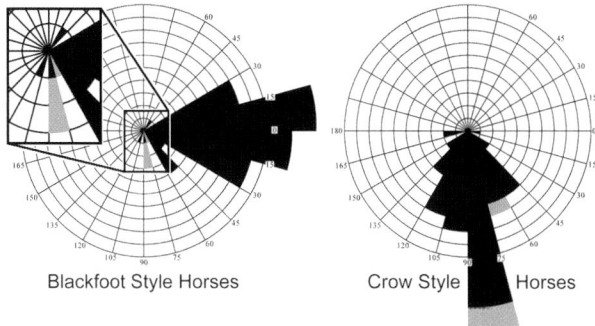

Figure 10. Circular histograms showing frequencies of head positions for Crow and Blackfoot rock art horses (black) with the three DgOw-9 and DgOw-51 horses' measurements added in grey. Note how the measurements are marginal to those of the Blackfoot sample, but clearly fit comfortably within those of the Crow style horses.

Figure 11. Histograms showing the frequencies of chord/sagitta ratios for Crow and Blackfoot rock art horses (grey) with the three DgOw-9 and DgOw-51 horses' measurements added in black. Note that the measurements show a more comfortable fit with the Crow distribution.

Table 7. Measurements for other rock art horses.

	Chord/Sagitta Ratio	Head Angle
1. DgOw-9 (1)	.0	+ 79
DgOw-9 (2)	.16	+ 61
DgOw-51	.17	+ 82
2. 24GL1663 (1)	.30	+ 90
24GL1663 (2)	.07	+ 67
24GL1663 (3)	.16	+101
24GL1663 (4)	- .08	- 1
3. Turner Rockshelter (1)	.0	- 7
Turner Rockshelter (2)	.13	- 11
Turner Rockshelter (3)	.0	- 18
Turner Rockshelter (4)	.14	+ 25
Turner Rockshelter (5)	.13	- 10
Turner Rockshelter (6)	.0	- 29
Turner Rockshelter (7)	- .07	- 10
Turner Rockshelter (8)	.0	+ 3
Turner Rockshelter (9)	.07	- 28
Turner Rockshelter (10)	.09	+ 18
Turner Rockshelter (11)	- .09	+ 8
Turner Rockshelter (12)	.0	0
Turner Rockshelter (13)	- .08	- 1
Turner Rockshelter (14)	.0	- 14
4. 48WA2289 (1)	.0	- 20
48WA2289 (2)	.06	- 16
48WA2289 (3)	.07	0
48WA2289 (4)	.03	- 8
48WA2289 (5)	.08	+ 15
48WA2289 (6)	.0	- 2
48WA2289 (7)	.0	- 1
5. 48LN1640 (1)	- .07	- 16.5
48LN1640 (2)	.06	+ 7
48LN1640 (3)	.17	+ 9
5 sites = 31 total horses		

with others from nearby Writing-On-Stone sites. Initially we observed that the DgOw-9 warrior carries a small, equestrian-size shield, even though he is a pedestrian (Keyser 2010:97–98). Likewise, this figure is not part of the locally common Blackfoot or Verdigris shield bearing warrior styles, but rather is stylistically unidentified (Keyser and Poetschat 2014:108, 141). This is due primarily to leg shape and position and a shield design prominently featuring inward pointing triangles at the shield margins. The warrior's large head is also unlike most—but not all—heads of other Historic period examples of Blackfoot style shield bearing warriors (cf. Keyser and Poetschat 2014:60–61). In short, this shield bearer also appears to be significantly different from most of the others at nearby Writing-On-Stone area sites.

If these four images are not Blackfoot art, can they be reasonably attributed to another group? The horse's measurements put them comfortably within the sample of Crow style animals, but other tribes to the south including the Cheyenne and Sioux also drew horses with arched necks and downward-pointing heads so this alone is not sufficient to confirm such an identification. However, the two horses at DgOw-9 also wear forehead decorations (Figure 9a). One of these is a fringed triangular item identical to others identified as keyhole-shaped face ornaments at sites including Joliet, Montana; No Water, Wyoming; and Box Canyon, Colorado, where they are worn by typical Crow style horses associated with other Crow ethnic identifiers (Keyser and Mitchell 2001:203; Keyser and Poetschat

2009:31). The second item is a fringed forelock ornament that projects out between the animal's ears and extends down over its forehead almost to its nose. This one at DgOw-9 is identical to one pictured on a Crow style horse at 48FR2509 that is associated with Spanish chain bits and Crow style humans with long hair (Figure 1o). No Blackfoot style horse yet recorded in Plains rock art wears either type of such forehead ornament (Keyser 1977).

The marginal triangles and central circle forming the design on the shield bearing warrior's shield have some limited resemblance to shield heraldry of the Timber Creek style, which is thought to have been made by late prehistoric Crow artists (Keyser and Poetschat 2014:18, 36–37, 67, 120–122). Also, the warrior himself is somewhat similar to Crow style human figures at some Crow sites (e.g., No Water), but there is an insufficient amount of his body visible to make a strong case that he is part of that style. On the contrary, marginal triangles and central circles are also occasionally found as shield heraldry for the Late Prehistoric period Castle Gardens style shield bearing warriors and much more frequently for Historic period Cheyenne shields (Keyser and Kaiser 2014:170–171; Keyser and Poetschat 2014:67; Nagy 1994). But this warrior's ethnic identity could certainly be Cheyenne if he was drawn here by a Crow warrior, since he appears to play the part of a defeated enemy in a coup count tally (Keyser and Poetschat 2014:141).

In short, we cannot positively identify these four images as Crow drawings, but we can be reasonably certain that they were not made by local Blackfoot artists—at least any that were following the conventions of their own tribal art styles. And although it is conceivable that these horses and other associated motifs were drawn by some other enemy group entering Blackfoot territory—since we know other groups drew horses with arched necks—the two horse's forehead decorations strongly suggest a Crow origin. A small Crow war party stopping in Blackfoot enemy territory prior to a raid for horses would be a logical candidate for the artists who left these "foreign" images here as a calling card to document their presence for others using the Writing-On-Stone area.

This particular location, at the rear of a relatively heavily treed terrace right at the mouth of a small tributary coulee leading to the level prairie above, would be an optimal place for such a war party to hide out since it is deep in Blackfoot territory but far enough from the more open confines of the main Writing-On-Stone area so a party bivouacking there would be unlikely to be discovered by accident.

24GL1663

Located on Cut Bank Creek in north-central Montana is a small petroglyph site with three panels of scratched imagery showing three unmounted horses and a complex coup count scene (Figure 12a) involving a horse, various weapons, horse hoofprints, human tracks, and two defeated pedestrian opponents (Keyser 2015). Of interest here are the four horses (Figure 12a–c). Two of these, on panel 1, wear feather war bonnets, and the single horse in the coup count scene on panel 3 is associated with exaggeratedly tall, graceful anthropomorphs similar to those identified elsewhere as Crow (Brownstone 2001:74). The fourth horse, on panel 2, is markedly different than the other three in its form, its lack of accoutrements, and its associated V-necked human.

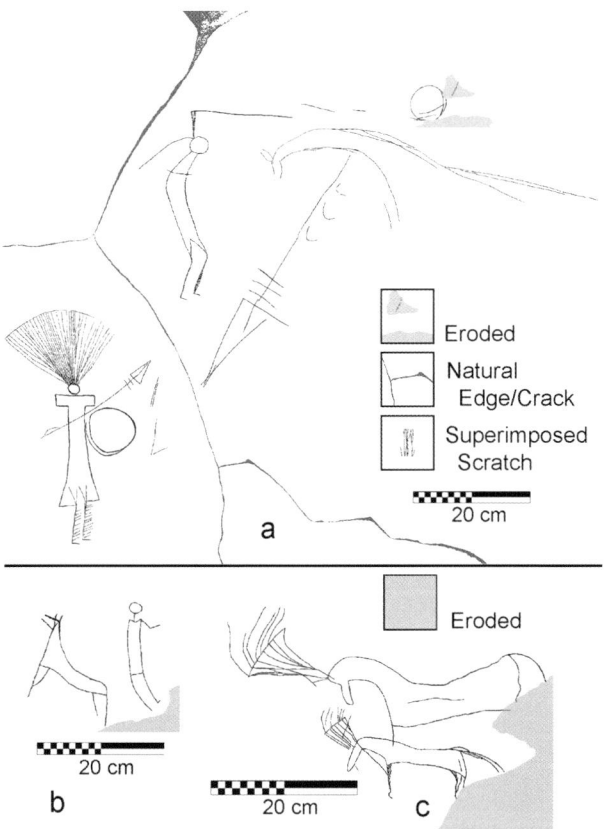

Figure 12. Horse and human images from Cheval Bonnet. (a) panel 3; (b) panel 2; (c) panel 1. All are scratched petroglyphs. Note characteristic associations of tall, linear humans and horse bonnets with Crow horses showing high arched necks and downward pointing heads in a and c, and V-neck human with Blackfoot style horse showing straight neck and forward pointing head in b.

When we measured these horses (Table 7), those on panels 1 and 3 fit clearly into the Crow sample (Figures 13, 14), while the single animal on panel 2 was equally clearly a Blackfoot style horse (Figures 13, 14). These measurements strongly reinforce the identification of three of these horses as Crow art and the forth one as a Blackfoot drawing based on their associated accoutrements and human figures. While the Blackfoot

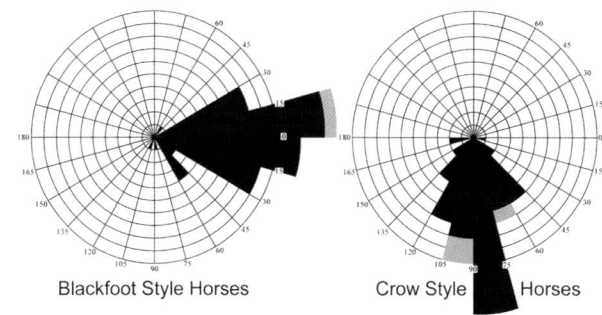

Figure 13. Histograms showing the frequencies of chord/sagitta ratios for Crow and Blackfoot rock art horses (grey) with the four Cheval Bonnet horses' measurements added in black. Note how the one horse clearly fits in the Blackfoot sample, and the other three horses that appear to be Crow style animals (based on other associations) fit well within the Crow sample.

Figure 14. Circular histograms showing frequencies of head positions for Crow and Blackfoot rock art horses (black) with the four Cheval Bonnet horses' measurements added in grey. Note how the one horse clearly fits in the Blackfoot sample, and the other three horses that appear to be Crow style animals fit well within the Crow sample.

compositions illustrating the stories of horse raids, a bison hunt, personal combat, and attacks on fortified war parties (Keyser 2007). Characteristic triangular body style human figures, battle pit fortifications, and a type of decorated bridle bit known as the "Thing to Tie on the Halter" (Figure 15a) were originally used to identify these petroglyphs as the product of Blackfoot artists who had come deep into south-central Montana to raid horses from their Crow enemies.

Visual examination of the fourteen mature style horses drawn at Turner Rockshelter shows that they are very similar to Blackfoot style animals, but when

style animal is obviously within its home territory and almost certainly represents a local artist recording a horse captured as a coup, the Crow horses and coup count scene are best understood as Crow warriors' calling cards, left here to document their presence on horse raids deep into Blackfoot enemy territory (Keyser 2015).

Turner Rockshelter

Located in the open pine parklands country of the Bull Mountains between the Yellowstone and Musselshell river drainages in south-central Montana, Turner Rockshelter is a small petroglyph site with between 50 and 60 small scratched petroglyphs (Figure 15) and three small charcoal pictographs (Figure 15b) arrayed in seven narrative

Figure 15. Petroglyphs and pictographs (the two figures at b) drawn in Turner Rockshelter. The "Thing to Tie on the Halter" is worn by the horse at a, and roughly circular battle pit fortifications (with people, guns, and horses within) are at bottom center, just left of scale. Note the typical Blackfoot style triangular body human figures in all three compositions.

the site was originally reported there was no means by which to differentiate these horses from those drawn by other Northern Plains tribes, so it was necessary to write that "mature style horses [at Turner Rockshelter]…are relatively standardized forms in Plains Biographic rock art" and simply to note that such animals did occur at Writing-On-Stone (Keyser 2007:21). Now, with this newly developed tool we have measured and analyzed the horses at Turner Rockshelter and we note that all of them fit comfortably within the parameters for Blackfoot horses in both the orientation of the head and the chord/sagitta ratios (Table 7, Figures 16, 17). Without doubt these are Blackfoot horses, and their identification as such provides strong support for the previous identification of Turner Rockshelter as a Blackfoot redoubt and the art there as a calling card left by Historic period Blackfoot horse raiders.

48WA2289

On one panel at Tipi Rockshelter (48WA2289) in the Canyon Creek drainage on the west slope of the Bighorn Mountains east of Tensleep, Wyoming, there is a row of seven horses lightly but firmly incised over older, more deeply incised petroglyphs showing tall V-neck human figures and grid-like geometric images (Figure 18). Although somewhat difficult to recognize today because their finely incised lines are weathered and revarnished to essentially the same color as the surrounding cliff surface; when freshly made, these horses would have formed a striking composition easily noted by anyone traveling through the area following the stream drainage. Being on one of at least 20 very visible panels of petroglyphs and pictographs at this site, and incised across clearly evident older imagery, this is an obvious attempt to illustrate these horses in a place where local inhabitants would be extremely likely to encounter them.

These seven horses are distinctly different than mature style horses carved or painted at any other local site. Horses at No Water (48WA2066), 48HO9, 48BH4275, Mahogany Buttes, 48FR2509, and Castle Gardens (48FR108) have all been identified as Crow Horses based on their general shape and/or association with other ethnically distinguishing images (Keyser 2011; Keyser and Poetschat 2009; Loendorf et al. 2012:74–75; this manuscript). Such identification is strongly supported by the measurement system designed and used herein, which shows that these animals have a characteristic posture and neck shape that differentiate them from horses drawn by Blackfoot artists (see above). There are also more than 20 horses carved and painted at the Legend Rock site (48HO4), located about 75 km (50 miles) southwest of Tipi Rockshelter, that range from a single animal shown with a shield bearing rider and a decorated bridle bit to a row of six animals (Figure 19) posed much like those at Tipi Rockshelter (Greer and Greer 2009). However, the Greers note that nearly all the Legend Rock horses have markedly arched necks and downward pointing heads (Greer and Greer 2009:5, 8, 10–11), which are completely unlike the animals carved at 48WA2289. Clearly these Tipi Rockshelter horses are unlike any others so far recorded in the Bighorn Basin.

Measurements of the horses at 48WA2289 show that both the head position and neck shape of these

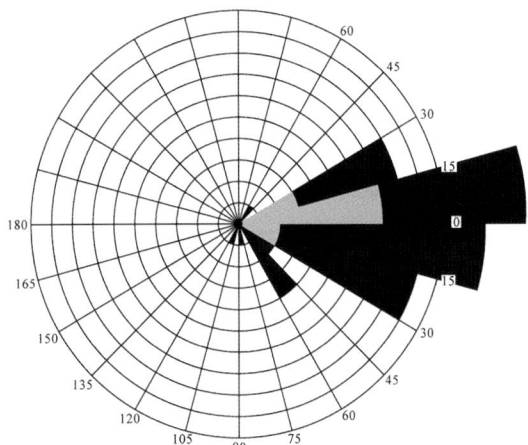

Figure 16. Circular histogram showing frequencies of head positions for Blackfoot rock art horses (black) with the histogram for 14 Turner Rockshelter horses (in grey) superimposed. Note that the two distributions are nearly identical.

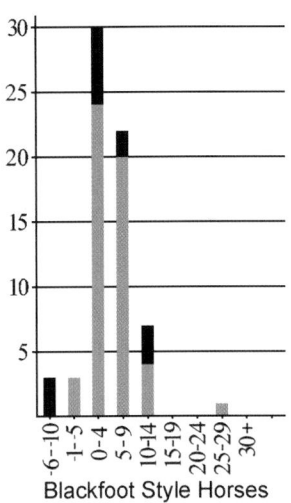

Figure 17. Histogram showing the frequencies of chord/sagitta ratios for Blackfoot rock art horses (grey) with the 14 Turner Rockshelter horses' measurements added in black. Note that the ratios from Turner Rockshelter show the same general distribution as those of the larger sample.

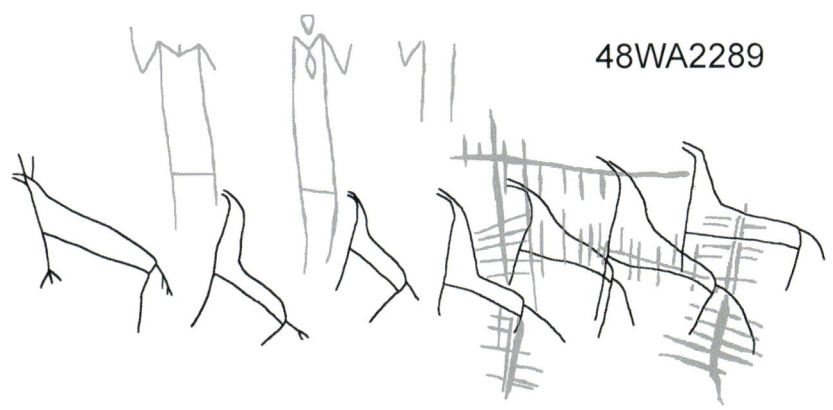

Figure 18. Petroglyphs from 48WA2289. Older, more deeply incised figures are shown in dark grey; row of seven more recent, very lightly incised horses shown in black.

Figure 19. This row of white horses at Legend Rock shows the typical body morphology for horses at that site. Note the arched necks and downward pointing heads. Photograph courtesy of Mavis and John Greer.

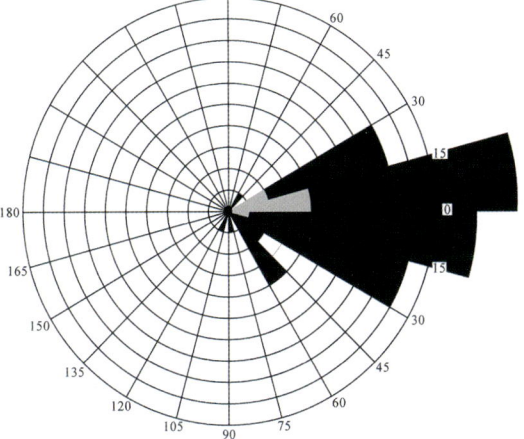

Blackfoot Style Horses

Figure 20. Circular histogram showing frequencies of head positions for Blackfoot rock art horses (black) with the histogram for seven horses from 48WA2289 (shown in grey) superimposed. Note that the two distributions are nearly identical. Also compare to the distribution of Turner Rockshelter horses shown in Figure 16.

tioned in between the main battle scene, which is structured around the capture of the running woman drawn just to the left of the small horses, and the capture of a saddled horse, drawn to their right (Keyser and Poetschat 2005:20, 36–37, 58). These three horses are obvious mature style animals, and are drawn with a heavier line than the scratched train directly above. They contrast markedly in both size and form to the realistic style horses that populate both the main battle animals are within the range of measurements for Blackfoot style horses (Table 7, Figures 20, 21). Clearly the measurements indicate that these animals were not drawn by the Crow artists who were responsible for the numerous horses at nearby rock art sites, nor did the artist who drew these animals use any of the conventions used by the artists who drew the horses at Legend Rock. Given the well-documented presence of Blackfoot war parties coming into this area of Wyoming to raid horses from the Crow and Shoshone, it seems a near certainty that one of these raiders recorded a successful venture here as a "calling card" to taunt his traditional enemies.

48LN1640

Lightly incised on the main panel at La Barge Bluffs (48LN1640) on the upper Green River in southwestern Wyoming is a group of three small, mature style horses. These are situated just below the two railroad trains incised on the panel (Figure 22) and posi-

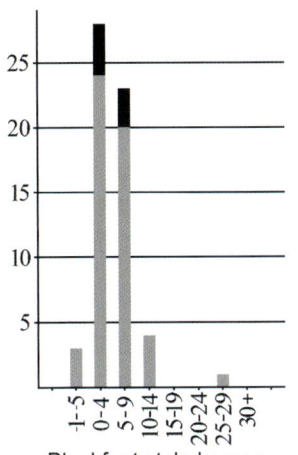

Figure 21. Histogram showing the frequencies of chord/sagitta ratios for Blackfoot rock art horses (grey) with the measurements of seven horses from 48WA2289 added in black. Note that the ratios from 48WA2289 show the same general distribution as those of the larger sample.

Figure 22. Petroglyphs on part of the main panel at La Barge Bluffs (48LN1640). The three mature style horses (shown enlarged in inset at bottom center) are the subject of this study. Adapted from Keyser and Poetschat (2005:Figure 6).

scene and ancillary horse raids and chase scenes on this large panel (Keyser and Poetschat 2005:20, 36, 51). They are so markedly divergent from any other horses at the site that the original investigators suggested they represented a single (presumably foreign) artist's stolen horses, as do similar groups on Historic period painted bison robes (Keyser and Poetschat 2005:59).

Given the significant differences in form between these three horses and any others at this site or nearby sites (Keyser and Poetschat 2005; Keyser et al. 2004), we subjected them to our measurement scheme (Table 7). For both head position and shape of neck these horses fit comfortably within the samples of Blackfoot horses from Writing-On-Stone and elsewhere on the Northern Plains (Figures 23, 24). Like the horses carved at Turner Rockshelter and 48WA2289, these three animals appear to represent stolen horses recorded here as a coup count calling card by a Blackfoot raider who was operating far from home. We know that Blackfoot warriors raided as far south as the headwaters of the Green and Snake rivers, targeting trappers and the Indian tribes who came to trade with them at their yearly rendezvous that were held from 1825 to 1840; and later they even raided travelers on the Oregon Trail (Ewers 1958:55, 196–201). That one of these Blackfoot raiders might well have left a "calling card" petroglyph here at La Barge Bluffs—a site only a few miles from a major Oregon Trail river crossing and "register rock" that was also known to be a place

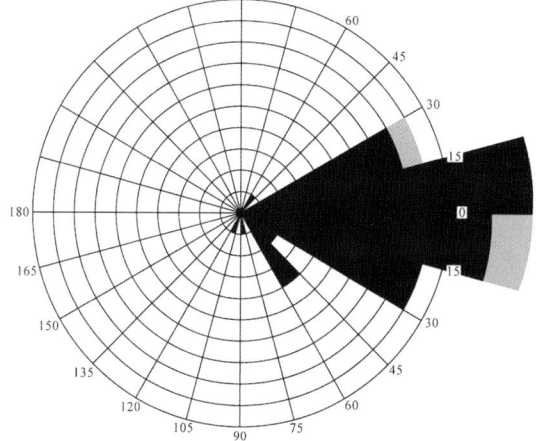

Blackfoot Style Horses

Figure 24. Circular histogram showing frequencies of head positions for Blackfoot rock art horses (black) with the measurements for the three La Barge Bluffs horses added (in grey). Note that the three La Barge Bluffs horses fit well within the distribution of the larger sample.

where local tribesmen registered their presence among the names and dates of overland travelers—is certainly consistent with the historic record. That it was carved among these local tribesmen's drawings strongly suggests that it was left sometime between about 1840 and 1875, when the other petroglyphs were freshly carved on this same panel (Keyser and Poetschat 2005:73).

Conclusion

Scholars have intuitively recognized differences between Crow and Blackfoot style horses for years, but without a means to quantify the variation between them there was no way to support these identifications beyond educated guesswork. By developing and using

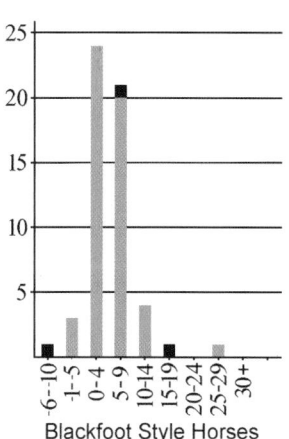

Figure 23. Histogram showing the frequencies of chord/sagitta ratios for Blackfoot rock art horses (grey) with the measurements of three horses from 48LN1640 added in black. Note that the three La Barge Bluffs horses fit well within the distribution of the larger sample.

a measurement system to analyze samples of rock art horses identified as Crow and Blackfoot based on associated imagery thought to be ethnically diagnostic we were able to distinguish two styles of horses whose statistical patterning in the variables we examined was shown to be significantly different for the Crow and Blackfoot samples. We then tested this finding by using the same variables to assess differences in horses painted on Historic period bison robes, which are known to have been painted by those same two tribes. The distributional structures of the variables we used to evaluate these two robe art horse populations were shown to be statistically quite different although nearly identical to the distributional structures of the rock art horse samples, strongly buttressing our identification of the Crow and Blackfoot styles of rock art horses.

After having metrically defined these two styles of horses, we then analyzed four sites with horses whose ethnic identities could provide additional information as to the ethnic origin and function of the imagery carved or painted there. In each case we have been able to show that horses at these sites are almost certainly either Blackfoot or Crow style animals, and depending on the location of the site itself such an identification permits us to suggest how these images functioned for the Historic period artists who carved and painted them. In short, applying our measurement system to these images significantly increases our ability to interpret the petroglyph scenes themselves and to better understand Plains rock art in a broader context.

Acknowledgments. Imagery at these various sites was recorded in the field with help from David Kaiser, George Poetschat, and Mike Taylor. Mike Bies, Michael Klassen, Jack Brink, and Mavis and John Greer graciously provided photographs and tracings of images that were used in this project. Research visits to sites was partially supported by grants from the Oregon Archaeological Society and the late David Easly (through the Indigenous Cultures Preservation Society). Landowners and lessees who allowed access to private property include Tom McCormick, Robert Brubaker, Marie Cantrell, Marvin Kimmet, and the Turner family.

References Cited

Barbeau, Marius
   1960 Indian Days on the Western Prairies. *National Museum of Canada Bulletin* 163.

Bouma, Janis, and James D. Keyser
   2004 Dating the Deadmond Bison Robe: A Seriation Study of Blackfeet Biographic Art. *Plains Anthropologist* 49(189):9–24.

Brownstone, Arni
   2001 Seven War-Exploit Paintings: A Search for Their Origins. In *Studies in American Indian Art: A Memorial Tribute to Norman Feder*, edited by Christian F. Feest, pp. 69–85. European Review of Native American Studies, University of Washington Press, Seattle.

Conner, Stuart W.
   1980 Historic Period Indicators in the Rock Art of the Yellowstone. *Archaeology in Montana* 21(2):1–13.
   1984 The Petroglyphs of Ellison's Rock (24RB1019). *Archaeology in Montana* 25(2–3):123–145.

Conner, Stuart W., and Betty L. Conner
   1971 *Rock Art of the Montana High Plains*. The Art Galleries, University of California, Santa Barbara.

Dempsey, Hugh A.
   1973 *A History of Writing-On-Stone*. Unpublished manuscript on file with Alberta Parks, Edmonton.

Dewdney, Selwyn
   1964 Writings On Stone Along the Milk River. *The Beaver* Winter:22–29.

Ewers, John C.
   1983 A Century and a Half of Blackfeet Picture-writing. *American Indian Art Magazine* 8(3):52–61.
   1958 *The Blackfeet: Raiders on the Northwestern Plains*. University of Oklahoma Press, Norman.

Frison, George C.
   1976 Crow Pottery in Northern Wyoming. *Plains Anthropologist* 21(71):29–44.
   1979 The Crow Indian Occupation of the High Plains: The Archeological Evidence. *Archaeology in Montana* 20(3):3–16.
   2007 Postulated Crow Component at Medicine Lodge Creek. In *Medicine Lodge Creek: Holocene Archaeology of the Eastern Big Horn Basin, Wyoming*, edited by George C. Frison and Danny N. Walker, Volume 1, pp. 99–105. Clovis Press, Avondale, Colorado.

Greer, Mavis, and John Greer
   2009 Horses: Late Aboriginal Use of the Legend Rock Site. Paper Presented at The Legend Rock Petroglyph Site in Time and Space: A Symposium, Annual Meeting of the Wyoming Archaeological Society. Electronic document, http://www.greerservices.com/Assets/publications_pdfs/2009_Greer_WAS_LegendRockHorses.pdf, accessed May 15, 2016.

Grinnell, George Bird
   1896 *The Story of the Indians*. D. Appleton and Company, New York.

Keyser, James D.
   1977 Writing-On-Stone: Rock Art on the Northwestern Plains. *Canadian Journal of Archaeology* 1:15–80.
   1979 The Plains Indian War Complex and the Rock Art of Writing-On-Stone, Alberta, Canada. *Journal of Field Archaeology* 6(1):41–48.
   1987 A Lexicon for Historic Plains Indian Rock Art: Increasing Interpretive Potential. *Plains Anthropologist* 32(115):43–71.
   1991 A Thing to Tie on the Halter: An Addition to the Plains Rock Art Lexicon. *Plains Anthropologist* 36(136):261–267.
   2004 *Art of the Warriors: Rock Art of the American Plains*. University of Utah Press, Salt Lake City.
   2007 Turner Rockshelter: A Blackfeet Redoubt in the Heart of Crow Country. *Plains Anthropologist* 52(201):9–27.

2010 Size Really Does Matter: Dating Plains Rock Art Shields. In *American Indian Rock Art, Volume 36*, edited by Ken Hedges, pp. 85–102. American Rock Art Research Association, Glendale, Arizona.

2011 "My Name Was Made High": A Crow War Record at 48HO9. *The Wyoming Archaeologist* 55(1):10–23.

2012 Northern Plains Horse Bonnets: "His Horse Wore a Magnificent Headdress." *Whispering Wind* 40(5):4–10.

2014 A Crow Warrior's Coup Count Tally at the Ellison's Rock Petroglyphs. *Archaeology in Montana* 55(2):1–15.

2015 Cheval Bonnet: A Crow "Calling Card" in the Blackfeet Homeland. Paper Presented at the 73rd Annual Plains Anthropological Conference, Iowa City, Iowa.

Keyser, James D., and Mike Cowdrey
2008 Northern Plains Biographic Rock Art: Ethnography Written on Stone. *Archaeology in Montana* 49(1):19–34.

Keyser, James D., and David A. Kaiser
2014 Bear Gulch Shield Heraldry: Iconography of a Protohistoric Period Northwestern Plains Warrior Society. *Plains Anthropologist* 59(230):144–181.

Keyser, James D., and Michael Klassen
2001 *Plains Indian Rock Art*. University of Washington Press, Seattle.

2003 Every Detail Counts: More Additions to the Plains Biographic Rock Art Lexicon. *Plains Anthropologist* 48(184):7–20.

Keyser, James D., and Mark Mitchell
2001 Decorated Horse Bridles in Plains Biographic Rock Art. *Plains Anthropologist* 46(176):195–210.

Keyser, James D., and George Poetschat
2005 *Warrior Art of the Green River Basin: Biographic Petroglyphs along the Seedskadee*. Oregon Archaeological Society, Publication 15. Oregon Archaeological Society Press, Portland.

2009 *Crow Rock Art in the Bighorn Basin: Petroglyphs at No Water Wyoming*. Oregon Archaeological Society, Publication 20. Oregon Archaeological Society Press, Portland.

2012 "On the Ninth Day We Took Their Horses:" Blackfeet Horse Raiding Scenes at Writing-On-Stone. In *American Indian Rock Art, Volume 38*, edited by Eric W. Ritter, Melissa Greer, and Peggy Whitehead, pp. 35–52. American Rock Art Research Association, Glendale, Arizona.

2014 *Northern Plains Shield Bearing Warriors: A Five Century Rock Art Record of Indian Warfare*. Oregon Archaeological Society, Publication No. 22. Oregon Archaeological Society Press, Portland.

Keyser, James D., Russel L. Tanner, and David T. Vlcek
2004 Pictures by the Seedskadee: A Preliminary Analysis of the Biographic Rock Art of the Green River Basin, Southwestern Wyoming. *Plains Anthropologist* 49(190):129–151.

Keyser, James D., David A. Kaiser, George Poetschat, and Michael W. Taylor, editors
2012 *Fraternity of War: Plains Indian Rock Art at Bear Gulch and Atherton Canyon, Montana*. Oregon Archaeological Society, Publication 21. Oregon Archaeological Society Press, Portland.

Klassen, Michael
1995 Icons of Power, Narratives of Glory: Ethnic Continuity and Cultural Change in the Contact Period Rock Art of Writing-On-Stone. MA Thesis, Trent University, Peterborough, Ontario.

1998 Icon and Narrative in Transition: Contact-period rock-art at Writing-On-Stone, Southern Alberta, Canada. In *The Archaeology of Rock-Art*, edited by Christopher Chippindale and Paul S. C. Taçon, pp. 42–72. Cambridge University Press, Cambridge, United Kingdom.

Loendorf, Lawrence L.
2012 *Three Rock Art Sites on the Musselshell River, Montana*. Sacred Sites Research, Inc., Albuquerque, New Mexico.

Loendorf, Lawrence, Laurie L. White, and Greg White
2012 *Rock Art Panel Tracing at Castle Gardens: Site 48FR108, Fremont County, Wyoming*. Sacred Sites Research, Inc., Albuquerque, New Mexico.

Lowie, Robert H.
1956 *The Crow Indians*. Holt, Rinehart and Winston, New York. Reprint edition, original publication 1935, Farrar & Rinehart, New York.

Magne, Martin, and Michael Klassen
1991 A Multivariate Study of Rock Art Anthropomorphs at Writing-On-Stone, Southern Alberta. *American Antiquity* 56(3):389–418.

McCleary, Timothy P.
2016 *Crow Indian Rock Art: Indigenous Perspectives and Interpretations*. Left Coast Press, Walnut Creek, California.

Medicine Crow, Joseph
2000 *From the Heart of Crow Country: The Crow Indians' Own Stories*. University of Nebraska Press, Lincoln.

Nagy, Imre
1994 A Typology of Cheyenne Shield Designs. *Plains Anthropologist* 39(147):5–36.

Schmittou, Douglas Allen
1996 A Stylistic Analysis of the White Swan Robe: Crow Representational and Applied Art as Ethnic Markers. MA Thesis, University of Tennessee, Knoxville.

Sundstrom, Linea
2004 *Storied Stone: Indian Rock Art of the Black Hills Country*. University of Oklahoma Press, Norman.

Voget, Fred
2001 Crow. In *Handbook of North American Indians, Volume 13: Plains*, edited by Raymond J. DeMallie, pp. 695–717. Smithsonian Institution, Washington, D. C.

Lynx Paw Petroform Alignments to Red Ochre Exposure Below Wisconsin's Niagara Escarpment

Diane Fox and Jim Uhrinak

The Lynx Paw Petroform and its bisecting stone alignment are aimed toward Neda's Iron Mountain, the highest point on Wisconsin's Niagara Escarpment. This prominence in southern Wisconsin with strong central-place characteristics is at the intersection of American Indian trail routes and natural geographic features. A second alignment introduced by a boulder in the carpal pad position extends toward a perennial headwater spring feeding into Wildcat Creek at the base of Neda's Iron Mountain. Both of these alignments intersect a culturally significant, rare, natural surface exposure of oolitic red ochre in the Neda Ironstone deposit above the springline. Historic mining documents the original accessibility of the ochre.

Petroforms and other American Indian set boulder monuments are well documented in the western Great Lakes area (Steinbring et al. 2003). Revisitation, reuse, and recalibration of these features by subsequent culture groups over long periods of time are evidenced by conical and effigy earthmounds placed in relation to, and in places on top of, previously placed petroform boulders (Steinbring and Bender 2000). In addition, intrusive burials in the earthmounds, culturally modified trees, and modern votive offerings show that historic recognition of some of these sites has been ongoing. This paper is a follow-up to our previous papers documenting directionality in Wisconsin petroforms (Fox 2011) and the configuration and interpretation of the Lynx Paw Petroform (Fox and Uhrinak 2016).

The Lynx Paw Petroform (Figure 1) is a boulder arrangement approximately 1000 times the size of an actual lynx paw based on comparative anatomy of Carnivora in the Great Lakes Region. As a 3-D model, the petroform likely served as a mnemonic device to link personal knowledge of tracking, lynx behavior, and cultural information related to Great Lynx and Underground/Underwater Panther oral traditions (Fox and Uhrinak 2016). The visual similarity of the basic paw formation to the foot pads of a gigantic feline's foot breaking through the surface of the earth from below is the basis for the premise that the rest of the animal's body would be underground. Bliss-Phillips' observations regarding Great Lakes Indian twined bags (Fox and Uhrinak 2016:38) reinforce the idea that lynx and panther (mountain lion) are the two expressions of Underground Panther noted by Skinner (1921:31). Jones, who explored relationships between mountain lion symbolism, sacred paths, and directionality in the Southwestern United States, reported that mountain lion "helpers" point the way for spirit paths or roads (2000:73, 81). In addition, Jones's (1998) conclusions regarding directionality and mountain

Diane Fox
Field Researcher, Niagara Escarpment Resource Network (NERN)
Madison, Wisconsin

Jim Uhrinak
Research Associate, NERN;
Wildlife Ecologist, and Secretary, Milwaukee Audubon Society
Milwaukee, Wisconsin

Figure 1. Elevated view of lynx paw petroform stones with two additional stones along the highlighted alignment line.

boulder (stone A) in the background (Figures 1, 2). This forward alignment matches the nearly universal tendency of cats to walk directly away from a territorial scent mark, allowing cat trackers to anticipate the route of a territory-marking cat without even following the tracks (Rezendes 1999:225). In addition to the metacarpal and toe pads that define the basic pattern of the paw, the lynx has a carpal pad offset and farther back on the paw (Figure 3). In the Lynx Paw Petroform, an additional stone in the carpal pad position (stone M) further strengthens the paw imagery and introduces a second sightline (Figure 3, red line left).

lion symbolism are consistent with our theory that stone alignments through the Lynx Paw Petroform are intentional geographic markers.

The petroform's paw-shaped pattern is easily distinguished both from the random scatter pattern of glacial erratics and from the cobblestone appearance of Archaic, mosaic-like petroforms also found in the area. The purposeful placement of two additional stones creates a sightline vector that evenly bisects the paw form bilaterally between the peak of stone G in the metacarpal position and the peak of the

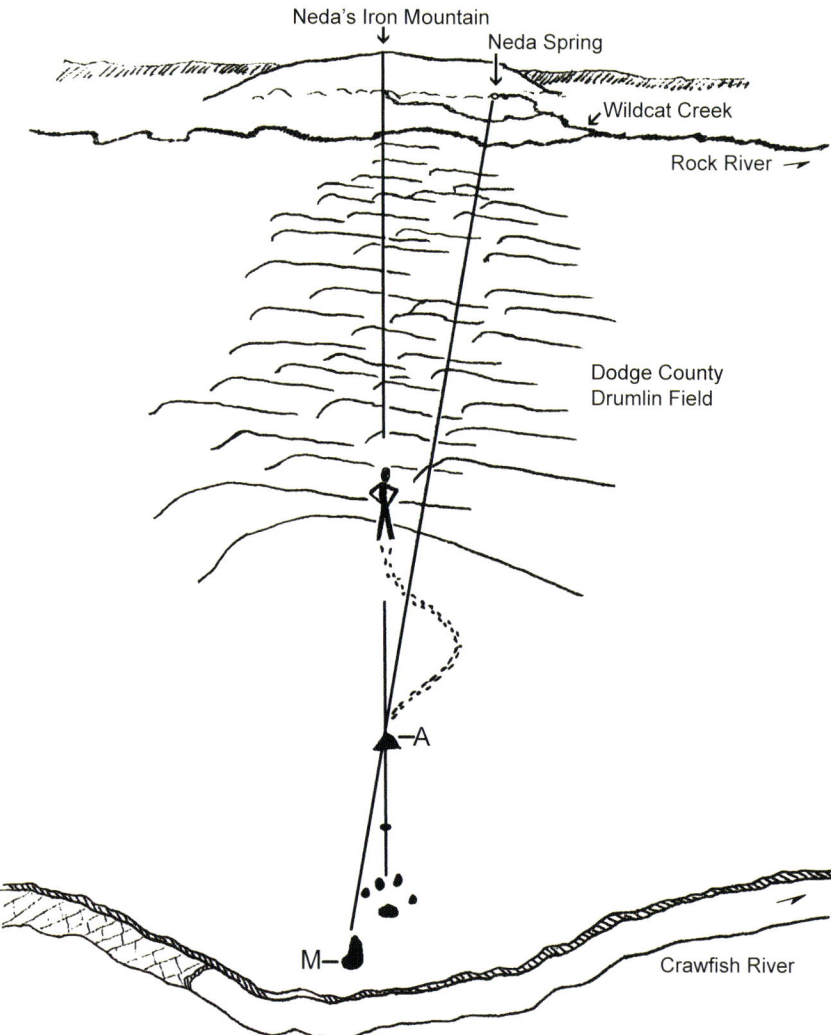

Figure 2: Landscape perspective rendition of relationship of the Lynx Paw Petroform to Neda's Iron Mountain. Foreground to background: Crawfish River, stone in carpal pad position with alignment line to Neda Spring, paw formation with bisecting line to Stone A, meander path through drumlin field, person with sightline across the drumlin field to high point on the Niagara Escarpment at Neda's Iron Mountain, Rock River with Wildcat Creek tributary from Neda Spring, and the Iron Ridge flanked by the Niagara Cuesta.

Figure 3. Juvenile lynx paw showing the relationship of the carpal pad (M) to the metacarpal pad (G) (photo by "Cloudtail the Snow Leopard," used under Creative Commons 2.0 license) with a view of the corresponding petroform boulders. Long red line (left) aligns with Neda spring; short red line (right) bisects the paw and aligns with Neda's Iron Mountain.

wagons may be filled with it by the aid of shovels alone with the same readiness with which they could be from a common sand bank!" (Watertown Chronicle Jan. 30, 1850, in Frederick 1993:63). Whittlesey (1852:449–450) wrote that red ochre covered the limestone like soil. Cassels (1857:505) noted that some of the ore "lies loose and may be shoveled out like loose gravel" but that other beds were compact.

Although it would be easy to say that red ochre is the target of the Lynx Paw Petroform alignments, we propose that it is technically more accurate to say that the two petroform alignments are aimed at two distinct and unique geographic bull's-eyes: Neda's Iron Mountain (the highest point on Wisconsin's Niagara Escarpment) and Neda Spring. These two intersects, a little more than a mile (1.6 km) apart, show the extent of surface exposure of oolitic Neda Ironstone and ochre along the base of the escarpment. Because these two alignments are more precise than would be required to simply find the ochre, it appears that they can be understood as documents of land knowledge (Figure 4).

The four sections of this paper briefly describe: 1) regional setting of the petroform; 2) the significance of red ochre in North American Indian culture; 3) landscape relationships to the petroform alignments; and 4) geometry and the petroform alignments. Our methodology intentionally does not include all details provided for peer review in the interest of protecting this and other related sites. Proposals for additional research follow our conclusions.

The questions that logically follow the alignment discoveries are: 1) Why would this substantial effort have been made to set up and align the petroform to a specific direction? and 2) Is a second sightline (Figures 2, 3) based on a boulder in the carpal pad position an intentional second alignment?

Hypothesis and Intent

One unavoidable geographic feature within the trajectory of the alignment lines is a one and one-half mile section of the Niagara escarpment with an iron, hematite, and ochre-rich exposure at its base. This unusual exposure was described as iron ore "that in many places approaches the surface of the ground, and

Section 1: Regional Setting

A brief overview of the glacial history and physical geography of an area within a 30-mile (48 km) radius of the Lynx Paw Petroform can be helpful in understanding the hypotheses concerning alignments proposed in this paper.

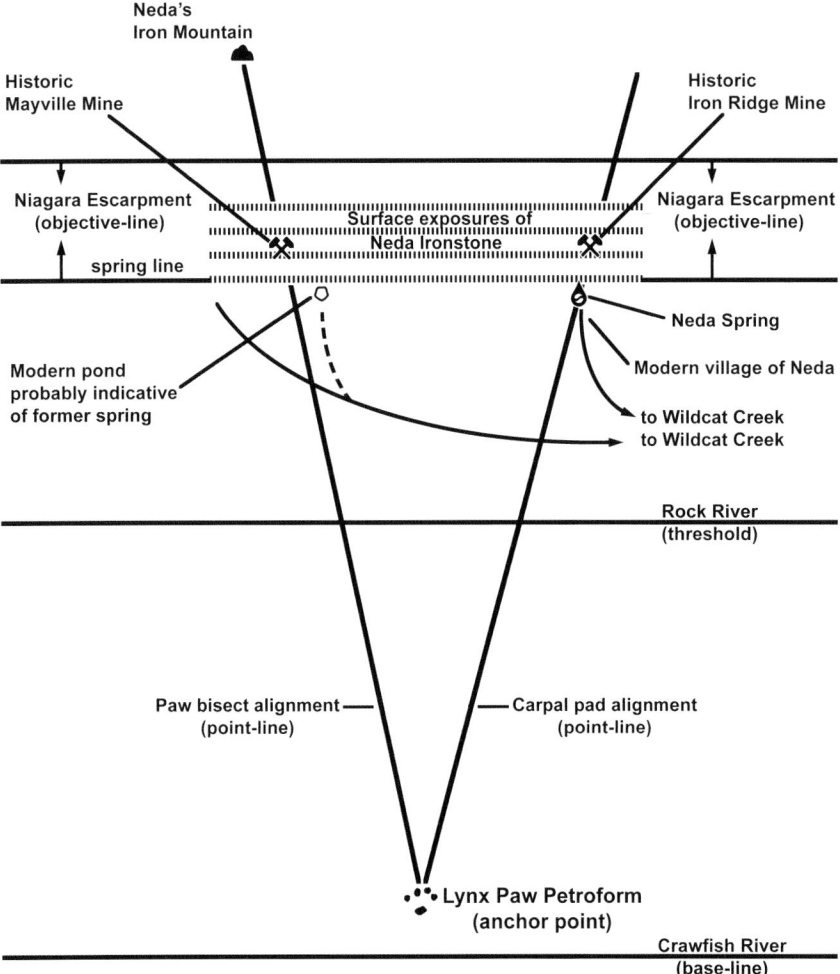

Figure 4. Schematic relationships between Lynx Paw Petroform alignments and a rare surface exposure of Neda hematite and red ochre below the Niagara Escarpment's Iron Ridge. Point-line terminology after Mooers (1972:120–121).

Geologically, the petroform is located within Wisconsin's glaciated area, above sedimentary strata over the Wisconsin arch. Glacial advances have stripped away broad areas of sedimentary layers creating a cuestaform plain and a broad stair-step relationship between the cuestas as shown in Figure 5. The entire area depicted is mantled with glacial deposits with localized exposures of the sedimentary dolomites and shale. Inliers of much older rhyolite, granite, and quartzite surface as visual islands in the predominantly glacial landscape.

Topographically, the western edge of the Silurian cuesta is called the Niagara Escarpment; the western edge of the Sinnipee dolomitic rock is called the Galena-Platteville Escarpment (formerly the Galena-Black River escarpment); and the yet deeper western edge of the Prairie du Chien dolomite group is called the Prairie du Chien Escarpment (formerly the Magnesian escarpment).

Although all three cuestas in Figure 5 are mantled with glacial soils, within the Rock River lowland the Niagara Escarpment is generally most prominent. "As a result of glacial scour, the Niagara Escarpment in eastern Wisconsin, whether buried under drift or exposed, has a cleaner edge than the state's unglaciated escarpments, with fewer salient, indentations and outliers." (Schultz 2004:131) Where the Niagara Escarpment face is clear of glacial soil the structure of dolomite fracturing and slip blocks create tight passages and crevice caves (Figure 6) that provide some of the best wildcat denning structure in Wisconsin (Young and Zuelsdorf 2016). The relationship between tracks and animal living places is such fundamental hunter-knowledge (Brandisauskas 2012:9) that the escarpment would be the logical place to find wild cats in the late winter.

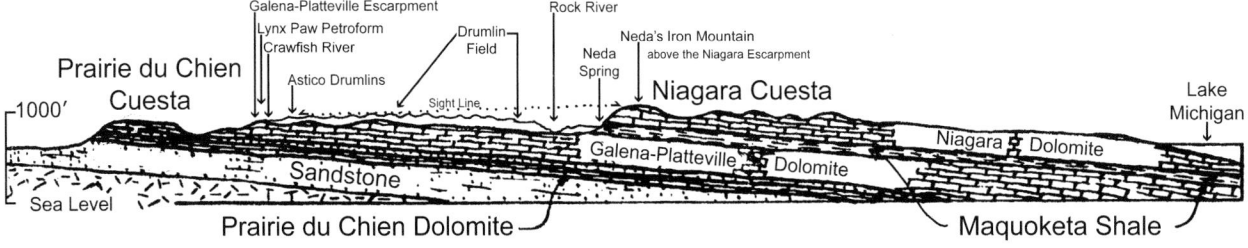

Figure 5. Generalized schematic landscape cross-section of southern Wisconsin's cuestaform plain showing the alignment and sightline relationship of the Lynx Paw Petroform and Iron Mountain based on mutual visibility of high points near the Galena Escarpment and the Niagara Escarpment (not-to-scale schematic by Uhrinak modified from Martin 1965:211).

The Niagara escarpment is a geographic boundary which in some places represents the geologic control for the eastern subcontinental watershed divide separating the Mississippi Basin from the Great Lakes Basin: tributaries flowing east into Lake Michigan and the Great Lakes eventually reach the North Atlantic; those flowing west into the Rock and Mississippi Rivers enter the Gulf of Mexico. One of the escarpment's distinct features is a 3.5 mile (5.6 km) ridge between the towns of Mayville and Iron Ridge which is not part of the subcontinental divide, but rather a distinct section of the escarpment locally known as the Iron Ridge.

Figure 6. Glide block crevices of the Niagara Escarpment in Dodge County, Wisconsin. Jim Uhrinak photo of Delene Hanson on a Milwaukee Audubon Society field trip.

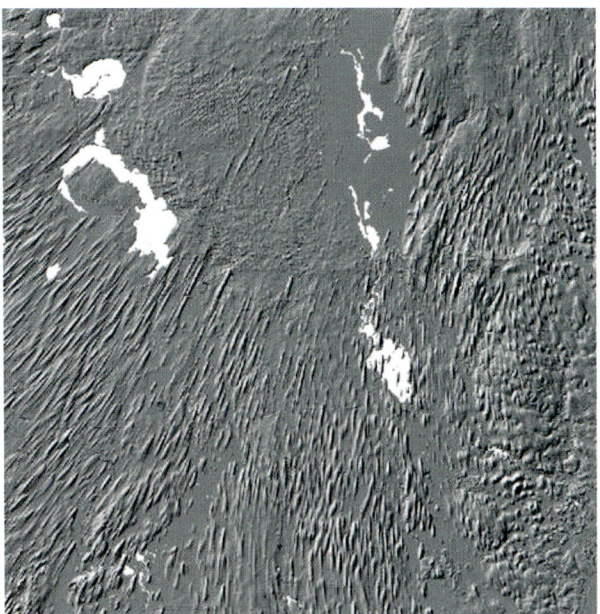

Figure 7. Lidar image of Dodge County, Wisconsin. Drumlin field trending northeast to southwest in southwest corner. Eastern third drumlins on Niagara Cuesta. Southcentral drumlins trend north to south.

The area between the Lynx Paw Petroform and the Niagara Escarpment is a portion of "one of the world's most outstanding drumlin fields" (Schultz 2004:172) known internationally for its density and its orderly trend patterns (Figure 7). The drumlins are elongated in the direction of ice movement and create a washboard-like swell-and-swale topography west of the Niagara Escarpment. In contrast, 30 miles (48 km) to the southwest of the petroform is the maximum extent of the Green Bay lobe of Wisconsin glaciation and the edge of the driftless or unglaciated area of the Midwest. Thirty miles (48 km) to the west/northwest is the eastern end of the prominent Baraboo Hills quartzite, which is almost identical in composition to the Waterloo quartzite outcrop (Schultz 2004:172). Waterloo quartzite was glacially displaced from the bedrock outcrop in a pronounced boulder train trending WSW-ENE with a distinct northern edge aligned with the Iron Ridge.

Original Vegetation

In 1976 Robert Finley used Government Land Office (GLO) survey notes from the 1830s to show that the area between the Lynx Paw Petroform and the Niagara Escarpment was part of a vast anthropogenic bur (*Quercus macrocarpa*) and white (*Q. alba*) oak savanna complex that covered much of the southern third of Wisconsin west of the escarpment (WDNR 2014). The drumlin topography creates between-drumlin valleys that frequently cradle wetlands and control stream flow. This topographic influence on the mapped historic savanna resulted in a prairie-savanna-sedge meadow complex interspersed with pockets of mesic hardwoods including sugar maple (*Acer saccharum*), black maple (*Acer nigrum*), basswood (*Tilia americana*), hickories (*Carya* spp.), ash (*Fraxinus* spp.), and elms (*Ulmus* spp.). Southern Wisconsin oak savanna provided much richer sources of human food than prairie and has high value as wildlife habitat.

The Rock River basin is part of an extensive lowland area extending diagonally across Wisconsin from the Green Bay toward Rock Island, Illinois (Figure 8) (Martin 1965:214, 218, 220; Uhrinak 2012:6). In combination with the Niagara escarpment as a guiding landform, this southwest to northeast trending lowland between the Prairie du Chien and Niagara escarpments is a present-day migratory route for millions of birds that also utilize its vast wetlands. Although the lowland's several original wetlands have been altered and degraded during the history of the state, Horicon is still the largest freshwater cattail marsh in North America and has been recognized by the Ramsar Convention as a Wetland of International Importance. Larry Vine, co-founder of Marsh Haven Nature Cen-

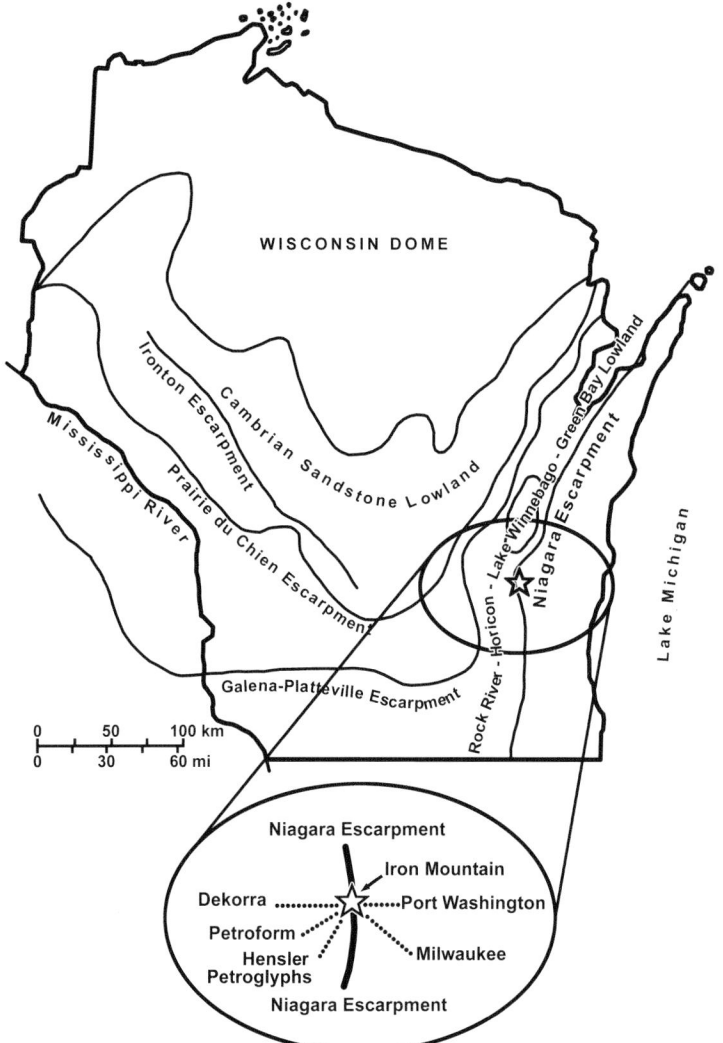

Figure 8. The broad Rock River-Horicon-Lake Winnebago-Green Bay lowland with inset schematic of some central place radial intersects with Neda's Iron Mountain. Base map adapted from Schultz 2004:102.

ter, has said that because of its biological productivity and resources, the Horicon basin has always been a profound resource base for Indian people (personal communication to Jim Uhrinak, 2013).

The greatest concentration of authenticated sites where remains of late-Pleistocene mammals have been found in Wisconsin is located between the Niagara and Prairie du Chien escarpments, including the viewshed from Neda's Iron Mountain (Figure 9 after Schultz 2004:25). The species include woolly mammoth (*Elaphas primigenius*), mastodon (*Mammut americanus*), caribou (*Rangifer terandus*), and giant beaver (*Castoroides ohioensis*). Other late-Pleistocene mammal finds in the area could be added including portions of a wooly mammoth skeleton with apparent cut marks on the bones found along Wildcat Creek east of Neda's Iron Mountain (Figure 9) and now housed at the Dodge County Museum in Beaver Dam.

Documentation of lithic scatter analysis by Loebel et al. (2016) indicates Moline Chert artifacts were found in locations far from the original source material and shows early southwest to northeast hunter movement which may suggest a seasonal round up the Rock River Valley to the Four Lakes and Horicon Marsh area. The straight line distance from Rock Island to the town of Horicon is approximately 170 miles (274 km). Seasonally migrating Paleoindian mammoth hunters with Clovis technology would have moved parallel to the Rock River lowland from sources of Moline chert near the river's confluence with the Mississippi in the vicinity of Rock Island and Moline, Illinois. Later, hunters using Folsom points of Moline chert (Figure 10) extended their travel range further toward Green Bay presumably to reach caribou calving grounds (Loebel et al. 2016).

In broad brush terms, since glaciation the area between the petroform and Neda's Iron Mountain has supported open periglacial mammoth steppe (with no modern analogs) followed by seres, or defined stages, of early successional willow and birch, open spruce forest, boreal spruce forest, and pine forest. Deciduous succession after the white pine maximum was limited by the prairie-favorable altithermal period of the Archaic. After the altithermal climatic effects, the balance between deciduous trees and prairie vegetation was regulated by fire frequencies. Under these climatic and disturbance effects, Wisconsin oak savanna developed with floristic patchiness distinct from either prairie or oak woodland and is not simply a mix of the two.

From a vista and sight-line perspective the three time frames with open plant regimes in the alignment line area would have been 1) mammoth steppe, 2) a long period of prairie advance in the Altithermal, and 3) the establishment of open oak savanna that persisted into the historic period. Despite millions of acres of savanna recorded for Wisconsin in the mid-1800s, Curtis (1959:327) wrote "Beyond question an oak savanna with an intact ground layer is the rarest plant community in Wisconsin today." Rarer yet is a modern open vista of savanna.

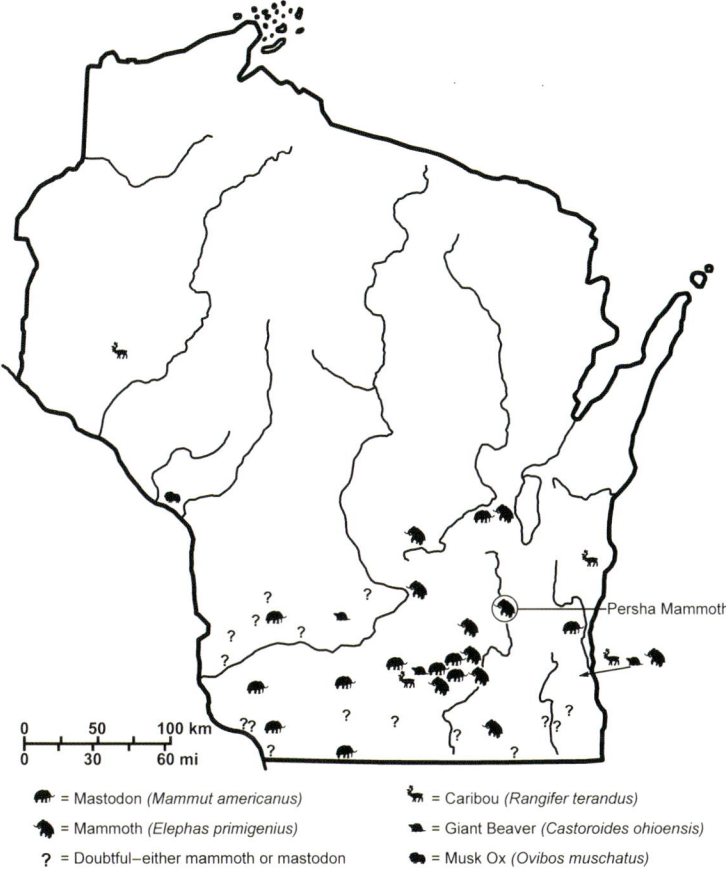

Figure 9. Authenticated distribution of Pleistocene mammal finds in Wisconsin from Schultz (2004:25) with addition of Persha Mammoth.

Figure 10: Folsom and Midland points of Moline chert found in the general area of the Lynx Paw Petroform from material sourced from the vicinity of Rock Island, Illinois.

Defining the Term Neda's Iron Mountain

Numerous historic name changes, combined with mines which do not sequentially correspond to the locations of the towns with which they share names, make it important to be careful and specific in the use of place names. We use the term Neda's Iron Mountain to designate the highest point on the glacial deposits that override the Niagara dolomite near the Niagara escarpment in Wisconsin in contrast to Martin (1965:226) who wrote that the high point was near Iron Mountain, an obsolete name for the present-day village of Neda. This high point near Neda is close to the southern end of Wisconsin's *Horicon Headwaters Divide Unit* of the Niagara Escarpment (Fowle and Uhrinak 2006). Neda was originally known as Sterling Mill. The Iron Ridge Mine, directly to the east, was opened in 1849. "In 1880 the growing village changed its name to Iron Mountain though the railroad depot continued to be known as Nye Station. Neda, the current name for the village, was first used in 1911. The location should not be confused with the present village of Iron Ridge which is about 1.5 miles (2.4 km) south of the original Iron Ridge" (Frederick 1993:2) nor with Iron Mountain, Michigan, nearly 200 miles (322 km) to the north.

In summary, the term Neda's Iron Mountain geographically describes the highest altitude on the Niagara upland above the escarpment in contrast to the village of Neda, Neda spring, and the geologic Neda Ironstone formation hematite exposure (Figures 4, 5). Neda's Iron Mountain is not an independent peak, but rather the highest point on a ridge with a mapped elevation of 1180 to 1200 feet, which Martin (1965:226) listed as 1200 feet (366 m). The central prominence of Neda's Iron Mountain is located southeast of Browns Corner near the center of Sec. 12, T.11N, R.16E. and should not be confused with two slightly higher elevations each approximately 2 miles (3.2 km) east of Neda and Iron Ridge respectively.

Neda Ironstone Formation: Hematite and Red Ochre Within Niagaran Geologic Stratigraphy

The word *Iron* in the term *Neda's Iron Mountain* refers to the Neda Ironstone oolitic hematite formation in the sedimentary bedrock which has natural surface exposure along the base of much of the Iron Ridge. The generic term for the Iron Ridge, the historic name of the Iron Ridge Mine (which is actually at Neda), and the present-day location of the town of Iron Ridge can lead to problems in interpreting texts. Figure 11 shows Silurian age deposits that may be exposed in the Niagara escarpment are above layers within the Ordovician age stratigraphy. At the base of the Silurian stone layers is an occasional deposit of Neda Ironstone. The upper layer of the Ordovician formation is water impermeable Makoqueta shale over Galena-Platteville dolomite. The impermeability of Maquoketa shale often results in the lateral movement of groundwater which feeds seeps and springs.

To the west of the Niagara cuesta, glaciation scoured loose Silurian stone away leaving glacial soils over Galena-Platteville dolomite bedrock. Occasional bedrock exposures can be seen in places where rivers and streams have cut through the glacial soil to reach the dolomite. The Lynx Paw Petroform is located near the edge of the buried Galena-Platteville Escarpment forming the bed of the Crawfish River. The mouth of Wildcat Creek meets the Rock River at the Galena-Platteville bedrock ford at Hustisford near the south end of Lake Sinissippi (Figure 11). Lapham (1848–1849:783–784) noted that lead ore is found in situ at Hustisford.

In historic times the iron ore and paint pigment were produced from the Neda Ironstone. "This oolitic red hematite, in a variety of forms, exists in small localized deposits throughout eastern Wisconsin; however, natural exposures are rare because of its patchy distribution and weak resistance to erosion." (Frederick 1993:3) The Neda Ironstone formation can consist of hard lenticular ore, specular hematite (specularite), or beds of soft granular oolitic hematite that have been described as "shovelable as sand" (Frederick 1993:63).

In 1845 settlers discovered "red dirt" about 4 miles south of Mayville and Chester May laid claim to it (Frederick 1993:54). In 1846 Wisconsin's frontier scientist, Increase Lapham (1846), reported the hematite in Wisconsin: Its Geography and Topography. He later visited the Mayville Mine site and "found a well dug 8 feet deep in the soft ore on the slope of a high limestone bluff. This bluff or cliff [is] sixty to eighty feet high... The rock is bare at the top and much broken by seams and openings...There is however ore enough deposited along the base of this bluff to last many years" (Lapham 1848–1849:727–728). Wisconsin State Geologist Edward Daniels (1858:9, 14) wrote that the ochre at the surface "consists of small grains or concretions, varying in size from a mustard seed to four times as large, quite irregular in shape, but usually slightly oval and flattened to a disc. The color was bright red, with a glistening polished surface, which feels greasy to the touch and stains like red chalk..." Both the Mayville Mine and Neda's Iron Mountain are on the primary alignment line through the petroform. The Mayville Mine area was originally the largest surface exposure. Surface ore also occurred to the south along the escarpment near Neda in an area that became the Iron Ridge Mine. The loose ore at these locations was easily excavated and both surface bodies were mined before stripping or underground operations began (Geological Society of America 1983:6)

Section 2: Significance of Red Ochre in North American Indian Culture

Holmes (1919:155) wrote "Little notice was taken by the early pioneers in any part of America of the aboriginal industries connected with...quarrying and...mining." Since ochre was found at the surface it is

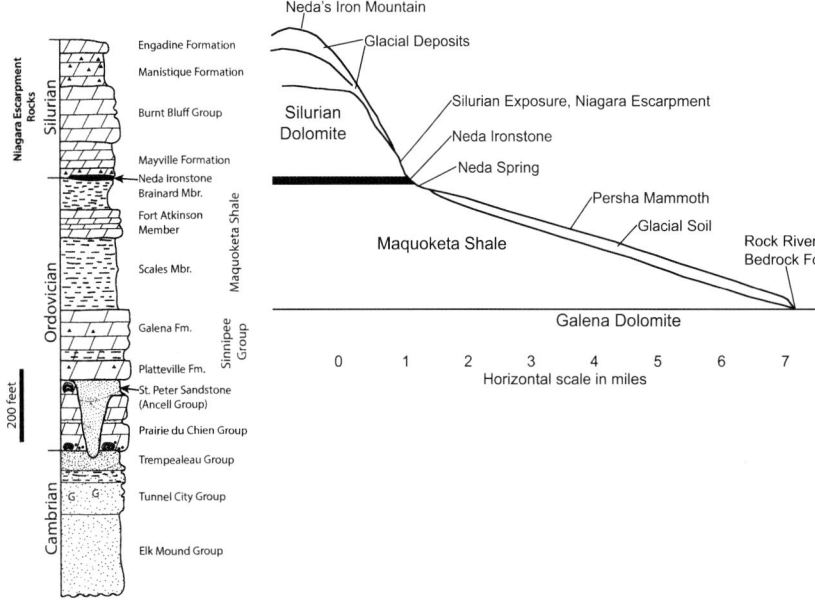

Figure 11. Schematic geologic cross section from Iron Mountain to Hustisford, Wisconsin. Horizontal scale in miles; vertical scale highly exaggerated to match generalized geologic stratigraphic column at left (after Luczaj 2013:6).

possible that earlier shallow digging or working in the paint pit area was disregarded by those claiming discovery. In his exhaustive 735-page mining history of the Iron Ridge, *When Iron Was King in Dodge County, Wisconsin 1845–1928*, Frederick (1993) allowed the following in two sentences: "One legend is that Native Americans pointed out the curious "red dirt" to them [the settlers]" (Frederick 1993:ix). And, "History records that the beds of iron ore were discovered in 1845, however, the existence of the red ochre may have been known even earlier, possibly by the Native Americans who lived in the area long before the first white settlers came" (Frederick 1993:xi). Although prehistoric Indians would have found the granular brown oxide of hematite on the surface as easily as early settlers did in 1845, it is inescapable that the red-stained snow trails of mid-sized mammals moving in and out of burrows in the ochre deposits would have been conspicuous, especially during the winter. Frederick (1993:45) wrote, "... the Neda formation can be seen only in animal burrows below the slump blocks along the east wall." The contrast of blood on snow is similar to the contrast of ochre-stained animal tracks in snow.

American Indian red ochre procurement often preceded historic mining when the original deposits were exposed at the surface. Although modern mining disturbances are often very destructive to the archaeological record, evidence at some sites has been recoverable. The Powars II site located at the Sunrise Iron Ore Mine in Wyoming has yielded many red ochre-covered Paleoindian projectile points, indicating that the "site may have been a rallying point for red ocher procurement by human groups in the area beginning with Clovis and lasting for as long as 5,000 years" (Frison et al. 2014:32). They wrote that "Preliminary work in 2014 adds support to the site being the largest known Paleoindian red ochre mine in North America."

An aboriginal hematite mine in Missouri that yielded hundreds of stone hammers and picks and involved tunneling to depths of 20 feet or more showed the efforts that some Indian people went to in hematite and red ochre procurement (Holmes 1919:226). Based on this report, any evidence of American Indian mine diggings in the Neda formation is likely to have been superseded and erased by the extensive historic mining. However, the relative abundance and ease with which Neda ore was procured with mid-1800s technologies may have buried and protected some original soil surfaces and the artifacts they may contain. The artifact yield of the Powars II site, despite the extensive surface disturbance by modern mining, leads us to believe that buried original land surfaces below modern mine spoils and beneath the earliest railroad grades at Neda could be archaeologically productive.

Old world researchers have attributed very early dates to ochre use in Europe and Asia. Use of the hematite pigment known as red ocher has been documented in North America back to the time of Paleoindians. DNA samples from a "male infant, buried approximately 12,600 years ago with ochre-covered Clovis artifacts belong to a meta-population from which many contemporary Native Americans are descended and is closely related to all indigenous American populations" (Rasmussen et al. 2014:227–228). This data from the Anzick site in Montana was more closely linked to both North and South American Indian populations than to any other population (Rasmussen et al. 2014:229). The widespread distribution of Clovis style points associated with comparable human genetic material and the use of red ocher indicates that ochre was a significant resource for American Indians over a long time span and a large geographic area. Other early examples of ochre use include the Hell Gap sites in Wyoming (Tankersley et al. 1995) and a Folsom occupation at the Lindenmeier site in Colorado (LaBelle and Newton 2010).

Hematite/Red Ochre Use in Wisconsin

Red ochre was recovered from multiple levels during excavations at the Hensler Petroglyph Site attesting to the value and longstanding use of ochre in this region (Steinbring 2012, 2013, 2014). These finds include ochre from low levels correlating to early activity on the site. In addition to ochre nodules at multiple levels, objects covered in ochre were also recovered. It should be noted that high ground features surrounding the Hensler Site are clearly visible from Neda's Iron Mountain, making an open-air exposure of hematite from Neda's Iron Mountain a probable source for some, if not all, of the Hensler ochre finds.

Evidence of early and ongoing human activity within the viewshed of Neda's Iron Mountain is documented through work at the Hensler Petroglyph site. Located on the Waterloo quartzite outcrop, Hensler has yielded a series of petroglyphs pecked into the bedrock that are datable by style and by associated lithic effigies and tools in the naturally deposited soil overburden.

> [I]nitial occupation of the site occurred at least 10,000 years ago. The act of engraving probably started before that time. This is because projectile points, including Hardin

Barbed, the large-Side-Notched Point Tradition, true blades, as well as gravers occur in the lowest level. And, on the rock surface, below these diagnostics, are the remains of petroglyphs already greatly weathered. It would seem that the initial activity at the site was actually engraving itself, and that it occurred before 10,000 years ago. This is entirely consistent with fluted point recoveries at immediately adjacent sites. Fluted points are emblematic of the Paleo-Indian Tradition, the earliest definable culture in North America [Steinbring 2014:31].

Excavations in 2015 uncovered a pecked image of a guanaco, an extinct North American animal related to llamas and alpacas, which has been described as the second professionally recognized ice age mammal image in North America (Steinbring 2015:3–5) after a mammoth image inscribed on bone from Florida (Lister 2014:102).

Use of red ochre in North American burials continued into the Archaic and Early Woodland periods in Wisconsin. "The use of red ocher in a burial at the Gordon Creek Site was radiocarbon dated to 9,750 years B.P. (uncorrected)" (Breternitz et al. 1971:172). Red Ochre burials in Wisconsin, Michigan, Illinois, Iowa, Indiana, and Ohio studied by Ritzenthaler and Quimby (1962:257) were attributed to Late Archaic and Early Woodland periods.

After reviewing red ocher literature published in The Wisconsin Archaeologist beginning with Bubbert (1941) and including the Red Ocher Burial Complex–related papers (Halsey 1972; Niehoff 1959; Overstreet 1980; Ritzenthaler 1965; Ritzenthaler and Niehoff 1958; Ritzenthaler et al. 1957; Van Langen and Kehoe 1971) Kurt Sampson (personal communication with Uhrinak, February 2017) has questioned where the volume of red ochre found with Archaic burials in the band of adjacent counties from Lake Michigan to the area of the Lynx Paw Petroform (Ozaukee, Washington, Waukesha, and Dodge Counties) came from. In one example that Sampson recounted (Ritzenthaler and Niehoff 1958) a bed of ochre 24 x 48 x .75 inches (61 x 122 x 2 cm) over a single burial would have required on the order of 4 gallons (17.6 liters) of ochre.

Hematite/Red Ochre as a Cultural Resource in Wisconsin

The Menominee Indian Tribe of Wisconsin is a federally recognized American Indian Nation which includes descendants of the people often referred to as Menomini in historic accounts from the late 1800s and early 1900s. Traditionally, the Menominee people spoke an Algonquian language and called themselves Mamaceqtaw, the people, and Kiash Matchitiwuk, the ancient ones. The Menominee people claim to be indigenous to Wisconsin and the upper peninsula of Michigan, with origin accounts from the Green Bay area and oral accounts dating back to the last glacial retreat.

One Menominee war bundle origin account attributes red paint as a gift from the "chief of the thunderers" who said: "Take this red paint along, that you may apply it to your men who accompany you when you go to war, and the sight of it will please me. It will put new life into you and your men" (Skinner 1913:99). In addition, "the paint [was] given by the thunderers to cure the wounded" (Skinner 1913:103). The medicines and dreams associated with the war bundle along with the use of red paint and tobacco were believed to relate to pity for the suffering of the people mediated in part by the "swift-flying-birds…the hawks, the swallows, and the hummingbirds" (Skinner 1913:98). Powers and inspiration for travel, protection, longevity, fire, transformation, assistance, foreknowledge, victory, night stealth, the blinding of enemies, cover, the protection of lightning and hail, bundle protection, healing, reward, honor, and power in hunting, as well as the effectiveness of tomahawks and war clubs saturated in powerful medicines, were all promised by the chief of the thunderers (Skinner 1913:99–100).

A number of beliefs regarding the possible meanings or uses of ochre in primitive societies include the idea that ochre-based color represents blood (Linsley 2013), or directional symbolism (Sanger 1973). The Wisconsin Menominee war bundle origin story attributes the original gift of red paint to the Chief of the Thunderers. As the Menominee counted the High Cliff area on Wisconsin's Niagara escarpment as a home of the Thunderers (Turney 2006), it is possible that Neda's Iron Mountain as the highest point along Wisconsin's Niagara escarpment with its source of red ochre was considered the home of the Chief of the Thunderers.

Section 3. Landscape Relationships to the Petroform Alignments

Aveni (2000) described central place attributes as important to understanding human geography with travel routes radiating out from a central place like spokes on a wheel. "The meeting place of two great indian trails was an historic spot, not to be forgotten by the scout, guide or geographer. They were vital points in the country and often became landmarks." (Hulbert 1902:44).

Central Place Characteristics of Neda's Iron Mountain

Figure 8 shows that from a north-south perspective Neda's Iron Mountain is a unique place along the extensive Niagara escarpment which serves as a navigation handrail (Perelman 2015:19) to the trail routes that parallel it below (such as the routes of Highway 67 and Neda Road). Human footpaths often meet or parallel the high ground of the Niagara escarpment throughout its exposures from Wisconsin to New York state, consistent with Parker's (2004:17) trail analysis of the affinity of humans and other animals for edges. Similarly, Hulbert (1902:14–15) noted the North American Indian preference for high ground trails. The advantages included an elevated perspective to view and interpret the topography, locate destinations, and define preferred travel routes. Steinbring (2000:52) observed that eastern Wisconsin petroforms of great antiquity were located on prominences near aboriginal trails making many petroforms mutually visible, enabling the observer stationed on one site to see the next.

The ancient American Indian footpath historically known as the Dekorra Trail crosses the Niagara escarpment through a gap just north of Neda's Iron Mountain. The trail ran halfway across the state from the waterfall of Pigeon Creek in Port Washington on Lake Michigan to the present-day town of Dekorra on the Wisconsin River. Dekorra is just downstream from the continentally important watershed portage at Portage, Wisconsin. The east-west route of modern Highway 33 between Lake Michigan and Beaver Dam follows much of the ancient trail route.

Another pair of Indian trail spokes connected the Milwaukee River-Lake Michigan wild rice estuary with the vast wetland of the Horicon Basin and Lake Winnebago (Uhrinak 2010). The route connects notable landmarks of the Milwaukee River estuary, Menomonee River confluence, Menomonee Falls, Pike Lake, and Powder Hill to Dekorra Trail, Neda's Iron Mountain, and the Horicon marsh. Increase Lapham traveled from Milwaukee to Menomonee Falls and acquired land there. In 1848 he also described Iron ore in abundance at Hartford (near Powder Hill) and proceeded "in a westerly and northerly direction and struck the 'Dekorra Road,' which we followed west" before visiting Mayville Mine below Iron Mountain (Lapham 1848–1849:726–727). Highways 41 and 175 were the approximate route of the Milwaukee-Fond du Lac trail. Highway 33 crosses Highways 41 and 175 near Allenton, formerly the site of a Ho-Chunk village also known as Dekorra. In addition, the historic plank road of 1851 from Mayville to Oconomowoc that followed the west side of the Iron Ridge "was the original Indian trail" (Frederick 1993:64).

As Wisconsin's high point along and above the Niagara escarpment, Neda's Iron Mountain's location at the convergence of multiple trail routes with the northeast/southwest migration corridor of the Rock River basin creates the kind of strongly identifiable place described by Hulbert. Its central-place attributes include its prominence on the Niagara Escarpment, its adjacency to a significant migratory flyway (Schafer 1937) and animal dispersal route, its relationship to a rare surface exposure of red ochre, and its nearness to a strong perennial spring feeding a headwater of Wildcat creek. It is interesting that the Lynx Paw Petroform alignments extend to the headwaters of Wildcat Creek.

Aspects of Mutual Visibility

The viewshed from Neda's Iron Mountain extends west-northwest toward Horicon Marsh and the upper reaches of the Rock River and west-southwest across the lowland in the direction of both the Madison Four Lakes area and the Waterloo Quartzite outcrop. Madison Road running north/south atop the ridge of Neda's Iron Mountain is roughly parallel to Highway 67 and provides an extended viewing area. At a distance of approximately 25 miles (45 km) to the southwest, the highest hilltop near Waterloo is visible between Highway 89 and Jordan Road. Looking in the opposite direction away from the marsh, numerous high ground features within the Northern Kettle Moraine are visible, including Holy Hill 17.4 miles (28 km) away.

Sites sharing mutual visibility can be easily confirmed from unobstructed high ground locations within the broad trans-Wisconsin Rock River lowland. A set of white wind generators located along the ridge between the towns of Mayville and Iron Ridge visually highlight the ridge as high ground. On a clear day the towers are visible from multiple locations. At night, the line of multiple red warning beacons is unmistakable and the radio tower marking the approximate height is easily recognizable. Without doubt, a smoke plume backlit by morning sun (which can look like a neon light) would have made the location unambiguous from a number of viewsites to the west.

Wayfinding and the Petroform Alignments

Mutual visibility between the high ground of drumlin tops near the Lynx Paw Petroform, the Waterloo Quartzite outcrop, and Neda's Iron Mountain makes it easy to see and understand the geographic relationship among these sites. These viewsheds provide a way to comprehend a large landscape. In one use of the memorization technique described as "method of loci" in the Rhetorica ad Herennium written in the first century B.C. (Frakt 2016:A3), familiar locations in a journey are used to facilitate memory. In very simple terms, the viewshed provides the mental images and details of location for several places and their known geographic relationships. These images in turn provide a cognitive cluster (Perelman 2015) or framework on which a person can mentally organize knowledge of the intervening landscape while they are traveling through it. As Mooers (1972:121) wrote "The navigator must always know where he is in relation to something else. (The reverse of that condition is disorientation which of course means that he is lost.)"

In addition, it is possible for an individual to walk between any two of these three destinations in a single day. The alignment line that bisects the Lynx Paw Petroform and crosses the Dodge County drumlin field to Neda's Iron Mountain satisfies several basic tenets of pedestrian navigation (Mooers 1972:120–123). Figures 2 and 4 show that starting with the Crawfish River as a base-line, the Lynx Paw Petroform serves as an anchor point that monuments the direct travel orientations necessary to reach specific objectives (Mooers 1972:121–123). These orientations can be confirmed visually from nearby drumlin tops. The very well ordered NNE-SSW topographic texture of the Dodge County drumlin field (Figure 7) provides recurring topographic reference features (Mooers 1972:150). The Niagara escarpment serves as a findable objective-line. There are several places between the Lynx Paw Petroform and Neda's Iron Mountain from which the escarpment can be seen at a distance allowing route confirmations and/or corrections. Finally, the north/south orientation of the Rock River and Lake Sinissippi provides an unavoidable target several miles wide and serves as a convenient threshold before reaching the objective-line of the Niagara Escarpment (Figure 4).

On crossing the Rock River threshold, a wayfinder could reorient on the height of the ridge immediately east of present day Lake Sinissippi because Neda's Iron Mountain would be visible on a clear day. Even if the objective line of the escarpment was not visible, after crossing the Rock River, a walker would find Wildcat Creek paralleling the river from the north. Following any of Wildcat Creek's north tributaries, a walker would intersect trails heading east to the escarpment, including the Dekorra trail. Following the north and east tributary of Wildcat Creek, the walker would arrive at its head at Neda Springs next to the hematite/ochre exposure at the foot of Neda's Iron Mountain.

This combination of topographic features allows a wayfinder a way to stitch together a series of point-line reckonings between drumlin tops. In contrast, modern lateral errors are introduced by "compass following" (Mooers 1972:123, 149). Point-to-point reckoning can preserve orientation while eliminating the need to beeline across intervening valleys. Just as Polynesian sailors navigated by maintaining tack across ocean waves, having an angular alignment orientation to each succeeding drumlin in a washboard topography would allow a wayfinder to stay on course even when the escarpment destination was out of sight.

The relationship of topographic features and alignments in the area between the Lynx Paw Petroform and the Iron Ridge satisfy Perelman's (2015:13) contention that "solving complex problems requires planning to subdivide the problem space into elements that can each be solved in turn, reducing the agent's cognitive burden…this subdivision requires only two levels, the higher level containing the plan representation, and the low level at which the detailed plan is executed. In both cases breaking up the problem space is designed to overcome memory limitations…" The viewsheds from the area of the Lynx Paw Petroform, Neda's Iron Mountain, and the Waterloo Quartzite Outcrop provide "path planning (i.e., with a bird's eye view)" and the drumlin topography aids on-ground "navigation (i.e., with an egocentric view)" (Perelman 2015:40).

Section 4: Geometry and the Petroform Alignments

Our proposal that two Lynx Paw Petroform alignment lines extend to Neda's Iron Mountain above the Niagara Escarpment and Neda Spring approximately 1.2 miles (1.9 km) to the south are based on the idea that sightlines are geometric observations that do not require mathematical calculations. The present-day main spring flow at Neda is flanked by seep flow to the north and south. Whether defined as the main spring or the seeps, the spring area is a much smaller target than the ironstone deposits. The precision indicates a well formed application of geometry in keeping with the word's Greek origins: earth and measure.

We used simple geometric calculations to cross-check the distance defined by the alignment line intersects at the objective line (the Niagara Escarpment) with the distance between Neda's Iron Mountain and Neda Spring. The certified survey showed that the divergence between our sightings across the stones in the carpal and metacarpal positions to Stone A is 3 degrees, 25 minutes, and 17 seconds or 3.42 degrees. Using the distance from the petroform to the objective line (the Niagara escarpment), the divergence between the alignment intersects is approximately 1.25 miles (2 km) based on the formula 2rπ(3.42/360). This calculation gives a comfortable fit with the current distance between Neda's Iron Mountain and Neda Spring given historic land alterations.

Conclusion

The Lynx Paw Petroform is one part of a larger petroform site and provides a connection to Great Lynx, water lynx, and underground/underwater panther Indian oral traditions that have persisted to historic times (Fox 2011; Fox and Uhrinak 2016). Among other things this petroform serves as an anchor point for two alignments that intersect Wisconsin's Niagara Escarpment toward either end of a rare surface exposure of red ochre. These two alignments are more precise than would be required to simply find the ochre. In combination, it appears that they can be understood as documents of land knowledge that define a paw bisecting alignment both to the highest point on Wisconsin's Niagara escarpment above the largest exposure of red ochre in the area and another potential altered spring site as well as define second alignment to a perennial spring below the historic Iron ridge mine site. We propose that the makers of this petroform related the petroform to the two alignments and the red ochre resource that they encompass in a permanent form that could be easily recognized, described, and utilized. In turn this land knowledge linked into trails, prominent topography, and viewshed connections with other landforms. This leads us to believe that some petroforms could be read like well-crafted documents, particularly in combination with traditional narratives (see Aruneyev in Brandisauskas 2012:13).

The distances and mutual visibility between Neda's Iron Mountain and other high ground such as the Waterloo Quartzite outcrop and drumlin tops near the Lynx Paw Petroform make it entirely feasible for an individual to walk between any two of these three destinations in a single day. We speculate that findable locations such as the Waterloo Quartzite outcrop and the Lynx Paw Petroform near the Crawfish River served as permanent cultural anchor points or base points to redirect toward Neda's Iron Mountain. Guiding landforms and geographic features such as the Rock River, its lowland, the orientation of the Dodge County drumlin field, and high ground of the Niagara escarpment could have been convenient wayfinding landforms for hunters seasonally targeting northern destinations like the Horicon Marsh area.

The high point of Neda's Iron Mountain can be reliably located from mutually visible locations. Drumlins in the area of the petroform provide sufficient elevation for open sightline visibility with Neda's Iron Mountain. Back-sighting from nearby high ground would have allowed orientation of the petroform toward Neda's Iron Mountain. The angular relationship between the petroform and Neda's Iron Mountain could easily be known under steppe, prairie, or open savanna conditions which have existed in this area. Therefore, in practical terms, the Lynx Paw Petroform need only to provide an anchor point to direct a walker the short distance to high ground locations from which Neda's Iron Mountain could be seen. As soon as that linear relationship was experienced and confirmed by a person they could conceivably say, "I don't just see the trail from the Lynx Paw Petroform to the hill, in my mind, I see the whole trail." On the other hand, crossgraining the undulating terrain of a glacial drumlin field would limit long-distance sighting making it much more difficult to find a single, defined point such as a rare surface exposure of red ochre.

The Lynx Paw Petroform alignment makes it possible to place and relocate a geologically and culturally significant natural exposure of red ochre. The use of hematite and red ochre is documented to Wisconsin's Paleoindians. Archaeological evidence shows that humans inhabited this region from a very early time and used red ochre over a long time span (Steinbring 2012, 2013, 2014). A combination of the straight line orientation of the Lynx Paw Petroform understood in the context of Great Lynx oral traditions and the Menominee origin story of red paint provide a strong schematic of land knowledge that is relatively easy to comprehend, recall, and convey.

The natural twenty-mile-long linear north edge of the Waterloo boulder train is aligned with a direct route to Neda Spring and the adjacent source of red ochre. In itself, that long linear edge might not direct anyone to Neda. However, because the large quartzite ledge east-northeast of Waterloo shares mutual visibility with Neda's Iron Mountain, a person could see the direct route from the Waterloo outcrop to Neda's Iron Mountain, walk it, and discover the northeast trending extension of the boulder train. We are not proposing that the boulder train led the way to Neda's Iron Mountain, but that the boulder train accompanied and anchored the direct route in the sense of Parker (2004:16). The original distribution of boulders in the train at the surface would logically have provided readily available stones for petroform and directional markers. The geographic relationships among prominence, natural boulder train alignment, and the resources of spring water and red ochre should stimulate researchable questions. It is possible that the human-made Lynx Paw Petroform alignments took inspiration from other natural boulder train phenomena (Figure 12).

Our assertion regarding the two extended alignments may dovetail into several other ongoing investigations:

1. Lithic scatter analysis of Moline chert sourced from the Rock Island and Moline, Illinois, area southwest of Hensler and the Lynx Paw Petroform indicates human movement from the chert source toward Horicon marsh by Clovis ice age hunters and later movement from the chert source further north toward Green Bay by Folsom hunters (Loebel et al. 2016). The lithic distribution was interpreted as a possible indicator of seasonal round activity between the north and south ends of these respective lithic distributions (Lambert and Loebel 2015). The broad and oversized Rock River valley is a logical SW-NE travelway that runs between Neda's Iron Mountain and Neda to the east and Hensler and the Lynx Paw Petroform to the west.

2. The concentration of authenticated sites where remains of wooly mammoth (*Elaphus primigenius*), mastodon (*Mammut americanus*), and caribou (*Rangifer terandus*) (Schultz 2004:25) south and west of Hensler and the Lynx Paw Petroform show the distribution of animals which support the lithics interpretation of Lambert and Loebel (2015). The recent find of a mammoth jawbone by Kurt Sampson (2016) at the site of the Persha mammoth remains on Wildcat Creek approximately 2.5 miles (4 km) southwest of Neda Spring has allowed Sampson to conclude that the mammoth was a young animal, approximately 12–13 years old. If the cut marks found on one Persha mammoth bone

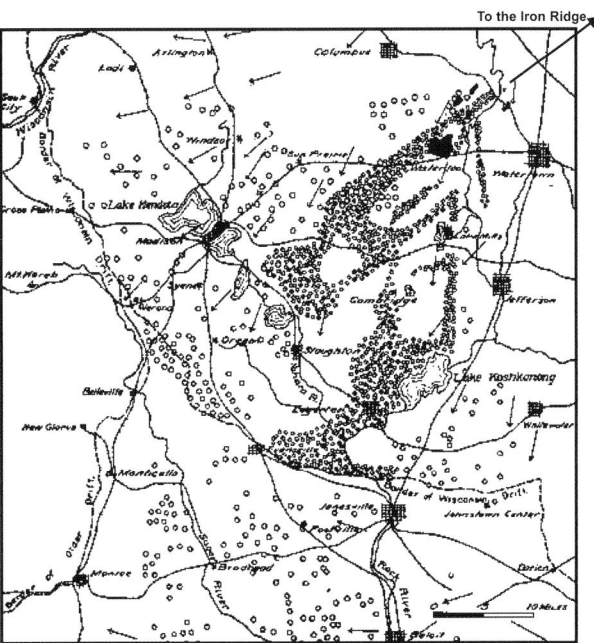

Figure 12. The natural northeast trending north linear edge of the Waterloo boulder train is aligned with the sightline of mutual visibility between the Waterloo Quartzite outcrop and the Iron Ridge. Adapted from Martin (1965:218) with line vector to northeast.

are evidence of human butchering, this puts ice age hunters within an hour's walk of the Neda ochre source. Because Neda Spring is an all-season open-water source there is a near certainty that conspicuous animal trails radiated toward the spring and the salient feature of Neda's Iron Mountain.

3. Documented use of red ochre at multiple excavation levels of the Hensler Site raises the question of whether Neda Ironstone oolite was a source of some of the Hensler ochre.

4. The mutual visibility between the Waterloo Quartzite outcrop and Neda's Iron Mountain suggest that there may be discoverable human use relationships between the two landforms.

5. Frison et al. (2014), Ziemens (2016), and Ziemens and Frison (2015) have described productive archaeological recovery of diagnostic artifacts at the Sunrise Mine–Powars II Clovis red ochre mine site in Wyoming. Findings at Powars II led them to conclude that the "site may have been a rallying point for red ocher procurement by human groups in the area beginning with Clovis and lasting for as long as 5,000 years" (Frison et al. 2014:32). They concluded that "the overall archaeological record demonstrates extensive and varied use of red ocher, much of which appears to be ritualistic."

Proposal for Additional Research

The alignment lines between the Lynx Paw Petroform and the red ochre source of Neda's Iron Mountain/Neda Spring, in light of the five points summarized above, indicate the likelihood that archaeological work in the area of Neda Spring and the Iron Ridge in general could be productive. Holmes (1919:267) and Ziemens and Frison (2015:24) reported complete and finished flint projectile points and blades in the hematite debris at their sites. Frison's conclusion and range of dates can be compared with Steinbring's (2015) conclusions regarding ritual revisitations at Hensler over a 9,000-year time span. The artifact yield of the Powars II site, despite the extensive surface disturbance by modern mining, leads us to believe that buried original land surfaces below historic and modern mine spoils and beneath the earliest railroad grades may be archaeologically productive. Test trenching into the grade aprons could provide a first look. Just as twentieth century mining at the Powars II site did not destroy all prehistoric mining evidence, it is possible that the abundance of ochre at Neda and the limitations of nineteenth century technology have spared some intact original surfaces at Neda. We also recommend X-ray diffraction analysis of the Neda ochre as a potential basis for evaluating ochre found in other areas of the Neda's Iron Mountain viewshed.

In summary the Lynx Paw Petroform monuments the relationship between the petroform and Neda's Iron Mountain as a landmark, a central place at the intersection of trail routes, a year-round source of fresh spring water, and a rare surface exposure of red ochre. Steinbring's conclusion that occupation of the Hensler site occurred at least 10,000 years ago would have provided ample opportunity for the local geography and natural resources to be discovered, understood, and documented in a petroform. The Lynx Paw Petroform is protected on a privately owned, closed site. All research on the site is limited to the core research team with ongoing investigation.

As we work on interpretation of the traditional stories associated with the sites, we have been given encouragement from Menomini descendant Ron Dick and Potawatomi descendant Skip Twardosz, who have worked with us on location. Ben Bearskin Jr., Bear Clan (1952-2013), HoChunk Nation, told us that this work must be written so that future generations will be able to understand the stories. The vast Horicon marsh immediately north of our study area was historically

Figure 13. Burt Greyhair, Wolf Clan (1930-2005), Nishocja haci Hochungara, under the tribal oaks at Winnebago, Nebraska. Photo by Jim Uhrinak.

known as Winnebago marsh. Burt Greyhair (Figure 13), Wolf Clan (1930-2005), from a group displaced from the Wisconsin HoChunk now in Winnebago, Nebraska, told Jim Uhrinak, "at one time we had the ability to see across the curve of the world."

References Cited

Aveni, Anthony F.
2000 *Between the Lines.* University of Texas Press, Austin.

Brandisauskas, Donatas
2012 Making a Home in the Taiga: Movements, Paths and Signs among Orichen-Evenki Hunters and Herders of Zabaikal Krai (South East Siberia). *Journal of Ethnology and Folkloristics* 6(1):9–25. University of Tartu, Estonian National Museum, Estonian Literary Museum, Tartu, Estonia.

Breternitz, David A., A. C. Swedlund, and D. C. Anderson
1971 An Early Burial from Gordon Creek, Colorado. *American Antiquity* 36:170–182.

Bubbert, Walter
1941 *Some Indian Myths About Iron.* The Wisconsin Archaeologist 22(2)9–11.

Cassels, J. L.
1857 Analysis of the Iron Ore of the Iron Ridge. In *Transactions of the Wisconsin State Agricultural Society, Volume IV: 1854-1857.* Atwood and Rublee, Madison, Wisconsin.

Curtis, John T.
1959 *The Vegetation of Wisconsin.* University of Wisconsin Press, Madison.

Daniels, Edward
1858 *Geological Report of 1857: Ores of Iron Ridge—Dodge County.* State of Wisconsin, Madison.

Fowle, Eric, and James Uhrinak
  2006 Physiographic Subunit Divides of the Niagara Escarpment in Wisconsin (map). Niagara Escarpment Resource Network (NERN), on file East Central Wisconsin Regional Planning, Menasha, Wisconsin.

Fox, Diane
  2011 Directional Marking Stones in South Central Wisconsin. *Wisconsin Archaeologist* 92(1):79–81.

Fox, Diane, and Jim Uhrinak
  2016 Lynx Paw Petroform: A Connection to Great Lynx and Underground/Underwater Panther American Indian Traditions. In *American Indian Rock Art, Volume 42*, edited by Ken Hedges, pp. 33–40. American Rock Art Research Association, San Jose, California.

Frakt, Austin
  2016 An Ancient and Proven Way to Improve Memorization. *New York Times*, March 24, 2016, page A3.

Frederick, George G.
  1993 *When Iron was King in Dodge County, Wisconsin 1845–1928*. Mayville Historical Society, Mayville, Wisconsin.

Frison, George, George Ziemens, Dennis Stanford, Marcell Kornfield, and Danny N. Walker
  2014 Paleoindian Red Ochre Mining at the Powars II Site in Southeast Wyoming. *Prehistoric American* 48(4):27–33. Genuine Indian Relic Society, Robinson, Illinois.

Geological Society of America
  1983 The Oolitic Neda Iron Ore (Upper Ordovician?) of Eastern Wisconsin. *Field Trip Guidebook. Seventeenth Annual Meeting North-Central Section Geological Society of America*. University of Wisconsin, Madison.

Halsey, John R.
  1972 The Molash Creek Red Ocher Burial. *The Wisconsin Archaeologist* 53(1)1–15.

Holmes, William H.
  1919 *Handbook of Aboriginal American Antiquities, Part 1: The Lithic Industries*. Smithsonian Institution Bureau of American Ethnology Bulletin 60. Government Printing Office, Washington.

Hulbert, Archer Butler
  1902 *Historic Highways of the Americas, Vol 2: Indian Thoroughfares*. The Arthur H. Clark Company, Cleveland.

Jones, Bernard
  1998 Mountain Lion Images: Metonyms of Directional Symbolism. In *Rock Art Papers, Volume 13*, edited by Ken Hedges, pp. 59–68. San Diego Museum Papers 35.
  2000 Sacred Paths, Mystical Dwellings and Cardinal Directions: Continuing Studies of Mountain Lion Symbolism. In *Rock Art Papers, Volume 15*, edited by Ken Hedges, pp. 73–83. San Diego Museum Papers 39.

LaBelle, Jason M., and Cody Newton
  2010 Red Ocher, Endscrapers, and the Folsom Occupation of the Lindenmeier Site, Colorado. *Current Research in the Pleistocene* 27:112–115. Electronic document, https://www.academia.edu/8773465/Red_Ocher_Endscrapers_and_the_Folsom_Occupation_of_the_Lindenmeier_Site_Colorado_with_Cody_Newton_, accessed March 15, 2017.

Lambert, John M., and Thomas J. Loebel
  2015 Paleoindian Colonization of the Recently Deglaciated Great Lakes: Mobility and Technological Organization in Eastern Wisconsin. *PaleoAmerica* 1(3):284–288.

Lapham, Increase
  1846 *Wisconsin: Its Geography and Topography, Second Edition*. I. A. Hopkins, Milwaukee.

Lapham, Julia Ann
  1848–1849 Typescript of Increase Allen Lapham Journal. Increase Lapham Archives, Wisconsin Historical Society, Madison.

Linsley, Alice C.
  2013 Water and Blood. Just Genesis (blog), April 10, 2013. Electronic document, http://jandyongenesis.blogspot.com/2013/04/water-and-blood.html, accessed March 29, 2017.

Lister, Adrian
  2014 *Mammoths and Mastodons of the Ice Age*. Firefly Books, Buffalo.

Loebel, Thomas J., John M. Lambert, and Matthew G. Hill
  2016 Synthesis and Assessment of the Folsom Record in Illinois and Wisconsin. *PaleoAmerica* 2(2):135–149. Electronic document, http://www.tandfonline.com/doi/full/10.1080/20555563.2016.1174922, accessed March 15, 2017.

Luczaj, John A.
  2013 Geology of the Niagara Escarpment in Wisconsin. *Geoscience Wisconsin* 22(1):6. Wisconsin Geological and Natural History Survey, Madison. Electronic document, https://wgnhs.uwex.edu/pubs/gs22a01/, accessed March 14, 2017.

Martin, Lawrence
  1965 *The Physical Geography of Wisconsin*. The University of Wisconsin Press, Madison.

Mooers, Robert L.
  1972 *Finding Your Way in the Outdoors*. E. P. Dutton, Outdoor Life Books, New York.

Niehoff, Arthur
  1959 Beads from a Red Ochre Burial in Ozaukee County. *The Wisconsin Archaeologist* 40(1):25–28.

Overstreet, David
  1980 The Convent Knoll Site (947-WK-327): A Red Ocher Cemetery in Waukesha County, Wisconsin. *The Wisconsin Archaeologist* 61(1):34–90.

Parker, Troy Scott
  2004 *Natural Surface Trails by Design*. Natureshape, Boulder, Colorado.

Perelman, Brandon
  2015 *A Naturalistic Computational Model of Human Behavior in Navigation and Search Tasks*. Ph.D. Dissertation, Michigan Technological University. Electronic document, http://digitalcommons.mtu.edu/etds/935, accessed March 15, 2017.

Rasmussen, Morten, Sarah L. Anzick, Michael R. Waters, Pontus Skoglund, Michael DeGiorgio, Thomas W. Stafford, Jr., Simon Rasmussen, Ida Moltke, Anders Albrechtsen, Shane M. Doyle, G. David Poznik, Valborg Gudmundsdottir, Rachita Yadav, Anna-Sapfo Malaspinas, Samuel Stockton White V, Morten E. Allentoft, Omar E. Cornejo, Kristiina Tambets, Anders Eriksson, Peter D. Heintzman, Monika Karmin, Thorfinn Sand Korneliussen, David J. Meltzer, Tracey L. Pierre, Jesper Stenderup, et al.
  2014 The Genome of a Late Pleistocene Human from a Clovis Burial Site in Western Montana. *Nature* 506:225–229.

Rezendes, Paul
  1999 *Tracking and the Art of Seeing*. Harper Collins, New York.

Ritzenthaler, Robert
  1965 A Red Ochre Site in Fond du Lac County. *The Wisconsin Archaeologist* 46(2):143–147.

Ritzenthaler, Robert, and Arthur Niehoff
　1958 A Red Ochre Burial in Ozaukee County. *The Wisconsin Archaeologist* 39(2):115–120.

Ritzenthaler, Robert E., and George I. Quimby
　1962 The Red Ocher Culture of the Upper Great Lakes and Adjacent Areas. *Fieldiana: Anthropology* 36(11):244–275. Chicago Natural History Museum. Electronic document, https://archive.org/details/redocherculture03611ritz, accessed March 14, 2017.

Ritzenthaler, Robert, Neil Ostberg, Kirk Whaley, Martin Greenwald, Penny Foust, Ernest Schuh, Warren Wittry, Heinz Meyer, and Edward Lundsted
　1957 Reigh Site Report—Number 3. *The Wisconsin Archaeologist* 38(4):278–310.

Sampson, Kurt
　2016 *Persha Mammoth*. Report on file at Dodge County Museum, Beaver Dam, Wisconsin.

Sanger, David
　1973 *Cow Point: An Archaic Cemetery in New Brunswick*. Archaeological Survey of Canada, Paper No. 12. National Museum of Canada, Ottawa.

Schafer, Joseph
　1937 *The Winnebago-Horicon Basin: a Type Study in Western History*. Wisconsin Domesday Book, General Studies Vol. 4. State Historical Society of Wisconsin, Madison.

Schultz, Gwen
　2004 *Wisconsin's Foundations: A Review of the State's Geology and Its Influence on Geography and Human Activity*. Second edition. University of Wisconsin Press, Madison.

Skinner, Alanson
　1913 *Social Life and Ceremonial Bundles of the Menomini Indians*. Anthropological papers of the American Museum of Natural History 13(1). Electronic document, http://digitallibrary.amnh.org/handle/2246/153, accessed March 15, 2017.

　1921 *Material Culture of the Menomini*. Indian Notes and Monographs Museum of the American Indian, Heye Foundation, New York. Electronic document, https://babel.hathitrust.org/cgi/pt?id=hvd.32044081030090;view=1up;seq=7, accessed March 15, 2017.

Steinbring, Jack
　2000 The Rock Art of Wisconsin. In *American Indian Rock Art, Volume 24*, edited by Frank G. Bock, pp. 49–63. American Rock Art Research Association, Phoenix, Arizona.

　2012 The Hensler Petroglyph Site (47 DO 461): An Early Engraving Site in the North American Mid-Continent. In *L'Art Pleistocene dans le Monde*, edited by Jean Clottes. Actes du Congres IFRAO, Tarascon-sur-Ariege, September 2010, Bulletin de la Societe Prehistorique Ariege, Vol. LXV-LXVI. Societe Prehistorique Ariege-Pyrenees, Tarascon-sur-Ariege, France.

　2013 A Brief Note on Archaeological Superposition at the Hensler Petroglyph Site (47DO461), Dodge County, Wisconsin. *Rock Art Research* 30(1):118-120. Australian Rock Art Research Association, Melbourne.

　2014 Archaeological Investigations at a Wisconsin Petroglyph Site. *Arts* 3:27–45. Electronic document (doi:10.3390/arts3010027) http://www.mdpi.com/2076-0752/3/1/27/htm.

　2015 Another "New" Petroglyph at Hensler. *Mid-America Geographic Foundation Newsletter* 20(2):3–5.

　2016 Form Correspondence in the Assessment of Archaic Cultural Affinities Among Rock Art Sites of the Midwest. *Central States Archaeological Journal* 3(1):38–44.

Steinbring, Jack, and H. E. Bender
　2000 Petroform-Mound Linkage in East Central Wisconsin. *Eastern States Rock Art Research Association Newsletter* 5(2):7–8.

Steinbring, Jack, Jeffrey Behm, and H. E. Bender
　2003. Petroforms in the North American Mid-Continent. In *American Indian Rock Art, Volume 29*, edited by Alanah Woody and Joseph T. O'Connor, pp. 111–120. American Rock Art Research Association, Phoenix.

Tankersley, Kenneth B., Kevin O. Tankersley, Nelson R. Shaffer, Marc D. Hess, John S. Benz, F. Rudolf Turner, Michael D. Stafford, George M. Ziemens, and George C. Frison
　1995 They Have a Rock That Bleeds: Sunrise Red Ochre and its Early Paleoindian Occurrence at the Hell Gap Site, Wyoming. *Plains Anthropologist* 40(152):185–194.

Turney, David
　2006 Lecture notes. First Nations Studies, University of Wisconsin, Green Bay.

Uhrinak, James
　2010 Everyone calls it the Falls. Unpublished presentation for the Friends of Lime Kiln Park, Menomonee Falls, Wisconsin and the University of Wisconsin Field Station Science for Everyone Series, West Bend.

　2012 Introducing a Place Where the Niagara Escarpment and Horizon Marsh Meet. *On the Wing*, Year 115:5–7. Milwaukee Audubon Society, Milwaukee.

Van Langen, Howard, and Thomas F. Kehoe
　1971 Hilgen Spring Park Mound Group. *The Wisconsin Archaeologist* 51(1):1–19.

Whittlesey, Charles
　1852 The "Iron Ridge" and Ore Beds of Dodge County, Wisconsin. Colonel Whittlesey's Report, Chapter I, Section VII. In *Report of a Geological Survey of Wisconsin, Iowa, and Minnesota*, by David D. Owen, pp. 448–451. Lippincott, Grambo and Company, Philadelphia.

Wisconsin Department of Natural Resources (WNDR)
　2014 Finley's Vegetation of Wisconsin in the Mid-1800s. Ecological Landscapes of Wisconsin, Map S2. Digital data prepared by Maribeth Milner and Steve Ventura from vegetation delineations by Robert W. Finley (1976). Wisconsin Department of Natural Resources, Madison. Electronic document, http://dnr.wi.gov/topic/landscapes/documents/statemaps/map_s2_finley.pdf, accessed March 15, 2017.

Young, Rory, and Kurt Zuelsdorf
　2016 *Urban Predator: Lion on the Loose*. Animal Planet episode released May 27, 2016. Electronic document, https://www.youtube.com/watch?v=T2Fww8TjSvE, accessed March 29, 2017.

Ziemens, George
　2016 A Brief Summary of Developments at the Powars II Paleoindian Red Ochre Mine. *Prehistoric American* 50(2):20–21. Genuine Indian Relic Society, Robinson, Illinois.

Ziemens, George, and George C. Frison
　2015 Powars II Paleoindian Red Ochre Mine: the 2014 Field Season. *Prehistoric American* 49(2):23–25. Genuine Indian Relic Society, Robinson, Illinois.

Power and Identity: Stability and Change in Pueblo Shield Iconography from the Fourteenth to the Nineteenth Centuries

Polly Schaafsma

Depictions of Pueblo shields are major elements in precontact Pueblo rock art ca. A.D. 1350–1600. As such they provide a valuable iconographic database with which to compare Pueblo shields from the historic era made during the nineteenth century or earlier. While continuities exist, there are also differences that offer a venue for exploring the nature of the social interactions that took place between the Pueblos, the Spanish, and various tribes from the Plains. Once the changes that occurred are established, suggestions are made as to some of the social processes that account for the differences between precontact and post-contact shields. Conformity, disguise, appropriation of alien power, and a revitalization of identity are considered.

Throughout the world the variable war shield has been a topic of interest for historians and anthropologists, and shields in many cultures take on meanings beyond their physically defensive roles in combat (Tavarelli 1995:7–8), paving the way for their incorporation into ritual and ceremony. Made for use as physical barriers, in the emotional stress of battle shields are frequently viewed as offering magical protection—protection that is attributed to their designs. In some cases, heraldic shield designs and the colors in which they were painted also served social functions. In the heat of conflict, designs might identify a warrior as to army, clan, or as an individual. In other cases, designs and colors were believed to detract the shooter, even blinding and confusing the enemy (Parsons 1939:197; Wallis and Titiev 1945:555; Wright 1976:12).

Due to its very role within contexts of stress and violence, the shield is laden with attributed meanings beyond its utilitarian purposes. Among the Pueblos and a diversity of other cultures worldwide, the shield is viewed as embodying magical forces effective against the enemy, protecting its owner as well as granting him powers in the fight (e.g., Feest 1980:85–86; Tavarelli 1995). The designs themselves, often considered potent, were empowered by explications in oral traditions and origin mythology. Thus they were regarded as more important for protection than the physical shield itself (Mansell 1994). Designs, significant color choices, and other embellishments are perceived as contributing to a shield's power, animating it with spirits and thus enhancing its efficacy, as the powers of the images alone promoted the combative skills of the shield bearer. Acquired as spoils of war, shields and their powers might be transferred from the enemy to the victor.

With such power ascribed to imagery, it follows that a shield's perceived power could be transferred to shield representations. Thus the mere picture of

Polly Schaafsma
*Research Associate,
Museum of Indian Arts
and Culture/Laboratory of
Anthropology*

a shield as rock art in the landscape or near a dwelling could function as an agent of defense (Schaafsma 1992).

In addition to war shields with their attributed magical powers, the shield also had roles in ritual contexts, and a variety of ritual shields were pictured in precontact murals at Pottery Mound (A.D. 1350–1500) (Crotty 2007; Hibben 1975; Schaafsma 2000) and at Awatovi and Kawaika-a at Hopi (Smith 1952). Ethnographically as well, shields were constructed for purely ritual use, including miniature offerings to the War Gods (e.g., Parsons 1939:305). In the kiva murals, shields are portrayed that exceed the limits of reality and practical usage, thus becoming symbols in their own right with allusions to the Sun (Crotty 2007:Figure 6.10; Smith 1952:Figure 52a). Whether as stand-alone icons or in the hands of ritual participants—at times portrayed as combatants—shields bristling with feathers, rimmed with perching birds, or adorned with emerging felines take on metaphorical roles with the power of visual poetry. Portrayals of these shields in prehispanic art alert the modern observer to the fact that the war shield is, in fact, part of a larger conceptual system that merges the material object with the supernatural realm where the shield takes on religious significance.

This paper compares the designs on shields depicted in precontact Pueblo rock art and kiva murals with designs on actual shields from the nineteenth century, with "precontact" defined as ending not with the Coronado expedition in 1540 but in the early 1600s when the missionizing process began in earnest and Pueblo traditions were forcefully discouraged. Beginning in the late A.D. 1300s and following the Pueblo migrations from the Four Corners region of the Colorado Plateau, Pueblo rock art and kiva murals comprise a rich visual legacy that offers a tantalizing iconography pertaining to warfare and its cosmological referents, as well as to the shield's ritual use in late precontact times (also known as the Protohistoric, Classic Pueblo Period, or Pueblo IV, ca. A.D. 1325–1680). While the designs on actual historical Pueblo shields with proposed dates between A.D. 1700 and 1850 (Wright 1976:93) partake of some of the same symbolism, there are notable changes.

The changes addressed here occurred during the unstable and traumatic times following the Pueblo Revolt, a period of colonization and ethnogenesis characterized by dramatic settlement, social, and political changes (Mills 2002) when continuing interaction with the Spanish and equestrian groups from the High Plains impacted Pueblo culture. At some point, selected Plains motifs appear on Pueblo shields, while the traditional iconographic content, figurative styles, and layouts were altered in other ways. However, as Pueblo shield designs were restructured and new icons appeared, Pueblo identity in shield iconography was maintained as it was reinvented.

Precontact Pueblo Shields in Rock Art (ca. A.D. 1250–1610)

Before the concerted Hispanic effort to dominate the Pueblos after A.D. 1611 (C. Schaafsma 1994:122), information on Pueblo shields is largely limited to *representations*. Shield images in the landscape and on kiva walls are numerous between the fourteenth century and the early seventeenth century (Schaafsma 2000).

In the A.D. 1200s in the Four Corners region of the Colorado Plateau, shields were sometimes painted as stand-alone symbols or as body shields on shield bearers on the walls of rockshelters housing defensive cliff dwellings (Crotty 2001; Schaafsma 2000:8–27). On rare occasions they were painted on the exterior of the walls. A rock painting from Defiance House in the Glen Canyon region is an unusual portrayal of combatants confronting each other with hand-held shields and clubs (Schaafsma 2000:title page). Painted in white, large in scale, often around a meter in diameter, these thirteenth century images were and still are highly visible and in their day would have been seen as a warning to intruders. In light of the supernatural attributes known to be associated with later shields and their designs, these paintings indicate that 1) the shield's association with supernatural agency is ancient, and 2) that a shield's supernatural powers also invested their representations, and that these images were made in order to protect these cliff residences. Around A.D. 1280, soon after the portrayal of these images, the Colorado Plateau homeland was evacuated for regions to the south and southeast, an exodus presumably precipitated by adverse economic and hostile social circumstances.

In the centuries that followed, Pueblo rock art production, shield depictions included, proliferated in the Rio Grande valley and neighboring regions (Figure 1). Shield petroglyphs also occur in smaller numbers in the Western Pueblos near Zuni, in the Little Colorado River Valley, and in the vicinity of the Hopi Mesas (Dongoske and Dongoske 2002:123–125; McCreery and Malotki 1994:56, Figure 4.2b; Young 1988:79–81). Shield petroglyphs on Perry Mesa north of Phoenix in central Arizona are probably attributable to a peripheral Pueblo

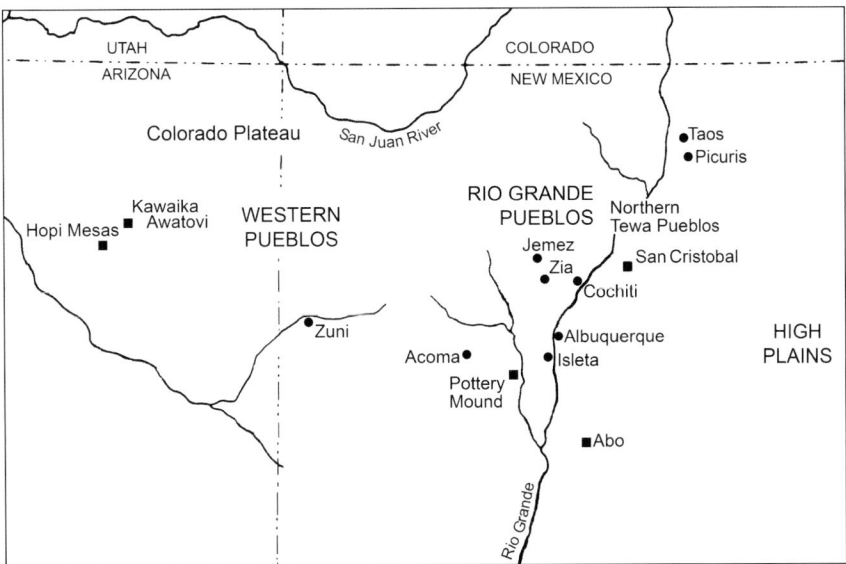

Figure 1. Map of the region.

population occupying this region between ca. A.D. 1290 and 1375 (Russell 2016). Additional shields represented in kiva murals from Hopi and the Rio Grande Valley supplement the rock art data base (Crotty 1995, 2001, 2007; Hibben 1975; Schaafsma 1965, 2000; Schaafsma ed. 2007; Smith 1952).

The Pueblo IV period, during which the precontact shields discussed here were depicted, followed the cultural crisis that precipitated the Pueblo migration from the Colorado Plateau. At that time, Pueblo culture experienced sweeping changes. In the Rio Grande Valley large aggregated pueblos were composed of resident Pueblo populations supplemented by immigrants. These villages represented major adjustments in settlement patterns and social order. New pottery types flourished, and the graphic arts underwent a sea change in style and content, signaling a new religious movement featuring a new cosmology, much of which is still extant (Schaafsma 1980:293–299). An unprecedented complex of warfare iconography characterizes the rock art and kiva murals from this time frame that differs from the limited representations of shields and shield bearers from prior days. The shield designs comprise a much more complex and diverse symbolic repertoire than was known earlier. Metaphorical clusters of intrareferential symbolism prevailed as shield iconography, with explicit references to the Sun, the Morning Star, and animal deities that are still recognized among the Pueblos as protectors and patrons of war. This formalized cosmology associated with conflict indicates that conflict persisted and that organizations pertaining to war such as the ethnographic warrior Opi societies were established at this time. Drawing their memberships from across the village or town, these proposed war societies, like the kachina organization, would have served to integrate the aggregated towns characteristic of Pueblo IV (Adams 1991; Schaafsma and Schaafsma 1974; P. Schaafsma 1994).

In contrast to well known nineteenth century shield representations in Plains rock art and ledger drawings that documented actual military engagements, Pueblo rock art featuring shields and shield-bearing warriors does not appear to be narrative in intent. Warring factions are not represented, while the symbolic powers of the shields and their designs appear to take precedence. Often strategically and prominently displayed, their bold designs are engaging and undiminished in their landscape surroundings (Figures 2 and 3). Commonly large in scale, shield depictions entailed a significant amount of labor. That they were usually very carefully rendered by skilled artisans is consistent with the important functional roles to which they were seemingly assigned. The cosmological powers engaged by the shield designs are not passive, but are believed to attract their likenesses, thereby functioning as active powers that protect the warrior and contribute to his strength and skill in battle (e.g., Schaafsma and Tsosie 2009; Young 1985). In a similar manner, it is proposed that warfare iconography as rock art empowered these Pueblo landscapes, bestowing an element of defense and casting immunity against outsiders and possible enemies.

In a random sample gathered from published sources and personal field documentations and photograph files available for study, 258 rock art shields including those of shield bearers were tallied in the Rio Grande region. Because these data are the summations of a random collection of images, as opposed to spotty, focused surveys, the shields and their designs discussed here are believed to represent general patterns of distribution. In addition, Renaud (1938:Plate 25) illustrates 33 shields or shield-like petroglyphs from north-central New Mexico, five of which can be related to the data presented here. The remaining 28 are not included here as his sketches are somewhat inaccurate and the proveniences cited not always reliable. In the Rio

Figure 2. Panoramic view of Pueblo shield-bearers and related warfare iconography on the Comanche Gap volcanic dike in the Galisteo Basin. Photographs by the author unless otherwise credited.

Figure 3. Large-scale Pueblo shields south of Santa Fe. The shield on the left displays typical Pueblo IV shield iconography. The center shield is a sun shield as noted by its serrated circumference and the Sun's face in the center, accompanied by eagle feathers. Photograph courtesy of Jim Duffield.

Grande valley, the northern Tewa region is heavily represented with a provisional count of 120 shields in the rock art data base under consideration here; it is likely, however, that this number could double. In the southernmost Rio Grande Pueblo sites, petroglyph shields are fewer in number, and in rock paintings shield bearers are small and represented along with other ritual participants.

Numbers alone do not reflect the importance of the imposing shield iconography at many rock art sites. In any number of cases, size, the bold designs, and placement in the landscape contribute significantly to their visual impact. Petroglyph shields measuring around a meter in diameter are common in Northern and Southern Tewa (also known as Tano) rock art as well as in the Towa sites in the Jemez vicinity, where one complicated painted petroglyph shield reaches around two meters across. These large-scale renditions provided more opportunity for details and symbolic information to be included, and their scale insured their visibility at some distance. One concludes that they were highly valued and had a significant communicative role in their landscape settings.

During Pueblo IV, Pueblo shields and their designs varied greatly, although in general they conformed to a few overall static patterns and choices of images. Appropriate symbols were, of course, dictated by adherence to the collective cosmology of conflict, but there were choices, and their presentation on any given shield allowed for a considerable degree of creativity on the part of the individual artist. Because of these allowances, no two shields, or the way their symbols are arranged, are going to be exactly alike.

Shield Designs and Layouts

During the precontact period, bold, abstract patterning that includes sun iconography and the geometric images of stars comprises around 90 percent of all shield designs. Life forms are in the minority. The design layouts on Pueblo IV rock art shield representations commonly include concentric circle schemes, quadripartite divisions, or a vertical or horizontal emphasis established by a line or band that divides the shield more or less in half. These lines or bands thus determine the arrangements of other elements. Beyond this, there remain many idiosyncratic variations.

Some shields feature a dominant central element such as the Morning Star and, much more rarely, the Sun's face (Figures 3 center and Figure 4). Design layouts based on a circular arrangement are very common. These shields may have simply a distinctive band around the circumference, or they may be elaborated with concentric circles.

Among the most distinctive are shields divided into two parts. Horizontal dividing lines or bands tend to fall slightly above the center, leaving ample space for added symbolism below. Horizontally divided shields with large triangular elements projecting downward from the dividing line are characteristic of the Northern Tewa region, where variations on this theme occur

Figure 4. Shield-bearer with arrows. The shield is a sun shield featuring the Morning Star.

Figure 5. Northern Tewa shields with typically static Pueblo IV design layouts.

on 14 percent of the shields in the sample (Figure 5). They are also found elsewhere in notably fewer numbers (McCreery and Malotki 1994:Figure 4.2b), where they may have been "imported" from the Rio Grande. At Awatovi a shield of this type occurs with rock art that includes Rio Grande style horned serpents, all of which may be the work of Tewa immigrants into the Hopi region (Dongoske and Dongoske 2002:Figures 8.2, 8.3). Also among the more "standardized" Pueblo IV shield design layouts are vertically divided shields with downward-curving elements on one side balanced by circles on the other (Figure 3 left and Figure 6). These details vary in number. Unlike the horizontally divided shields just described, these have no regional focus and are found in small numbers throughout the Pueblo realm.

Iconography

The smaller details featured on precontact Pueblo shields in rock art and kiva murals are varied but follow prescribed themes (Schaafsma 2000). Paramount among these are celestial icons such as the Sun and

Figure 6. Shield-bearer on the Comanche Gap dike. The see-through shield shown here, while common on the Plains, is very rare in Pueblo depictions.

Figure 7. A variety of Northern Tewa shields and shield bearers. Ticking around the edge denotes the sun's radience.

Morning Star, the pendant triangles mentioned previously, eagles, paired human heads, bear tracks, and circles. Some symbolism is multivalent with reference to bundled sets of relationships incorporated into a single element. While constituting a well defined iconography, these symbols are arranged in innovative combinations that are unique and non-repetitive.

Solar and Morning Star references in shield iconography prevail above all else. The Sun is the supreme patron of war and a valued source of empowerment for those engaged in combat (Schaafsma 2000:116). Over 30 percent of the representations of Pueblo IV rock art shields display primary sun iconography that includes a rayed circumference indicated by ticking or zigzags, the Sun's face, and eagle symbolism (Figures 3, 4, 7). This percentage would increase substantially were the plain shields and those with concentric circle patterning included, as they too are probably meant to represent a sun shield. In rock paintings and kiva murals, the circumference, often red, may be sprayed on to indicate luminescence, while the disk may be white, yellow, or turquoise in color. Unique to Pottery Mound are ceremonial shields with Sikyatki designs that may incorporate arrows and solar references in the way of the Sun's face (Hibben 1975:Figures 53 and 101).

The sun and the shield comprise an integrated concept as in Pueblo oral traditions, and the Sun Father himself is said "to be present in the spirit of the shield" (Kent 1983:28, citing Stevenson ca. 1882). Alternatively, the sun in the sky may be regarded as the sun's shield being carried across the sky (Parsons 1939:379). A face centered on a shield suggests that the shield represents the Sun deity himself (Figure 3) and, in turn, the sun's face itself is often referred to as a shield or even the sun's mask (Schaafsma 2000:114). The Zia, for example, "did not see the sun himself, but a mask so large that it covered his entire body" (Stevenson 1894:35). The Sun, a sun shield, or a "mask" may be regarded metaphorically as the same thing, thus expanding our concepts of how the supernatural Sun is viewed and represented. Turquoise paint was also used in both pre- and post-contact contexts to represent the Sun. Ethnographic accounts describe ritual sun shields constructed of raw cotton or white buckskin painted with red, yellow, and turquoise (Parsons 1939:240, n2), and these evoke images of the sun shields described in ceremonial scenes in precontact Piro rock art.

Added to the repertoire of the previously described supernatural shields are arrows and even bows pictured in association, sometimes among the feathered radiance (Smith 1952:Figures 52a, 53a). These representations visually confirm the Sun's extended relationships with conflict and, more specifically, war powers. They also visually recall Pueblo oral traditions that describe weapons given as gifts from the Sun to the War Twins during the times of origin. In return for these gifts, weapons are also used as offerings to the Sun (Parsons 1939:136).

Symbolically linked to the Sun as its guardian, the Morning Star is an aspect of Venus, whose symbolic properties may be merged with the War Twins (Young 1992). This star is a frequent icon that often dominates Pueblo IV and historic shields (Figure 4). It is commonly found as an individual figure in association with other war-related content in the rock art of the Rio Grande Valley south of Santa Fe and in Tompiro sites near Abo, as well as in the Pottery Mound murals. While the Morning Star may be indicated by a simple equilateral cross, a more elaborate and also common version is a star with four points expanding around a central circle. A face is often indicated along with a headdress of eagle feathers. In painted examples, this center with or without a face is black. Conflated with the eagle or its supernatural counterpart known as Knifewing (see following), eagle talons are often added to its regalia, and arrows on occasion occur in its headdress.

The Morning Star embodies a complex bundle of meanings related to warfare, as it is tied to the war/fertility complex that demands acts of reciprocity between humans and the supernatural realm in order to assure adequate rainfall, promoting the growth of corn (Schaafsma 2000; 2014;). As such, it is closely related to the Venus/rain/maize complex in its various dimensions in Mesoamerica and in the Pueblo Southwest (Carlson 1991; Mathiowetz et al. 2015; Schaafsma 2000:154–157, 2005; Sprajc 1993a, 1993b), where its presence in the rock art in general refers to the taking of scalps (Schaafsma 2000:154–157, 2005, 2014). Trophy scalps taken in combat, with their rain-bringing powers, firmly establish the presence of the war/fertility complex among the Pueblos. On shields it offered protection as it enabled the warrior in his quest.

Although relatively few in number, images of or symbolic references to animal deities contribute to the supernatural power of Pueblo shield representations. The animals pictured are known for their associations with the directions where they reside and, as guardians of the world, their powers are sought in conflict (Schaafsma 2000:138–144; Young 1988:103). Most common is the eagle. Already mentioned in reference to the Sun and Morning Star, the eagle adds to the repertoire of celestial war powers as a bold shield motif in its own right. Deified as Knifewing, predatory bird of the zenith, it too is a patron of scalping (Schaafsma 2000:146–150). Shield-bearing warriors are sometimes portrayed as human/bird conflations (Figures 2 left and Figure 8).

In Pueblo cosmology, the mountain lion also has ties to the sun, and mountain lion portrayals with eagle tail feathers are visual statements to this effect.

Figure 8. Composite eagle warrior holding a knife. The crosses are a late addition thought to have been made by Spanish sheepherders

Although paws and forelegs of mountain lions, as well as the mountain lion itself, may be depicted in conjunction with shields in Pueblo IV rock art, the theme does not appear on the shield's face itself during this time frame. Absent from the face of the shield, felines may emerge from it, or a shield may function as a magical transformative device uniting a man and feline (Schaafsma 2000:Figure 3.32). Pueblo ethnographies describe the merging of the former office of war priest with the powers of the sun and the mountain lion. Further, the head of the Opi (Warrior) Society, or scalp-takers were known as "Mountain Lion" (Schaafsma 2000:139). The war priest representing the Sun is also regarded as father of the Twins, the latter with parallels to the Evening and Morning Star (Young 1992).

The bear as a war power and guardian of the northwest is represented occasionally on shields by its stylized track or paw (Figure 9) (Parsons 1939:341, 937, 964; Schaafsma 2000:136–138; Stephen 1936:97; Titiev 1944:155). In addition, snakes, guardians of the nadir at Hopi and with directional significance elsewhere (e.g., Parsons 1939:689), also have war powers. Although they are infrequently represented on shields in precontact times, a large, coiled rattlesnake person portrayed on the sun shield in Kiva 8 at Pottery Mound is a dramatic exception (Crotty 2007:Figure 6.10). In addition, mountain lions in kiva murals are depicted with the banded tail of a rattlesnake, a further example of conflating, and thus compounding, animal powers (Hibben 1975:Figure 77; Smith 1952:Figures 71a, 77). Further, there are associations between stars and rattlesnakes in both media (Schaafsma 2000:Figures 3.25c, 3.33a). Today at Hopi, Snake Society members are considered warriors, and Voth (1903:334) identified a militaristic element in summer snake rites, wherein the Snake men were painted like warriors prior to entering the plaza. At Isleta the war chief is a Scalp chief and Snake Society chief (Parsons 1939:926). A likeness between snakes and lightning contribute to the symbolic power of the former, lightning being a weapon of the War Gods.

Animals associated with precontact shields are boldly depicted with a tendency toward geometric stylization. Combined with their large scale, their visual impact is forceful. In this respect they differ significantly from animal representations on the postcontact nineteenth century shields to be described.

Figure 9. Shield with bear paws, Petroglyph National Monument.

As well, it is important to underscore the fact that in Rio Grande style rock art and the contemporary kiva murals, composite beings described here are frequently represented. The visual syntheses of life forms, including humans with snakes, mountain lions, and eagles, are testimony to a belief system lacking the perception of a rigid separation between living beings, having instead a system within which powers are shared. With boundaries blurred, commonality and continuity are recognized between all forms of life, in this case enabling warriors to access the necessary supernatural powers that these animals embody.

It is likely that none of the shield depictions described so far date later than the early 1600s when the Spanish exerted severe pressure on the Pueblos, converting them to Christianity as their population suffered devastating losses (Liebmann 2002). Native religions were forced underground, and society members would have been severely dispersed, making it difficult to maintain the prescribed rituals. With a few exceptions, the near cessation of making rock art related to Pueblo cosmology and religion is thought to have occurred in the first half of the 1600s, ending the many depictions of shields and shield-bearing warriors that proliferated in prior centuries. The latest known kiva paintings of sun shields or shields conflated with animals are from Awatovi (Smith 1952:Figures 47b, 49b, 61b, 71a, 72b,c, 89a,c). According to Smith (1952:316), the rooms in which they occurred date from the first third of the seventeenth century. Importantly, the initiation of the Colonial Period in the early seventeenth century brings us to a chronological break in our knowledge of Pueblo shields. Changes in design systems were to follow.

Historic Pueblo Shields

In 1942 Leslie White (1942:316) observed that "old war shields are still treasured in storerooms" although little remained of the war cult. Pueblo shields as material culture items are found today mostly in museum collections and in the hands of private collectors. Possibly the earliest documented historic Pueblo shield, now in a private collection, is dated at 1843. This date is offered in the original collector's note from 1925 that accompanies a shield from Santa Clara Pueblo. Historic shields in the Fred Harvey Fine Arts Collection at the Heard Museum comprise one of the largest collections of historic Pueblo shields. Wright (1976:93) estimates that the shields in this collection, largely acquired between 1901 and 1910, would have been in use between ca. 1700 and 1850, with two of later date between 1850 and 1900. On the basis of iconography and style, very few petroglyph representations of Pueblo shields can be assigned to the historic period with any degree of confidence. Those illustrated here (Figure 10) from the Rio Grande Gorge near Taos conform closely to layouts and subjects represented on historic shields. One is typically Pueblo, while the other, on the basis of the designs, could just as well be of Plains origin. Technically, however, it conforms to Pueblo standards.

Design changes between precontact shields and historic Pueblo shields are ascribed in part to the social upheavals that ensued during the European conquest. Some iconographic choices appear to have resulted from varied social pressures related to European contacts. The simultaneous displacement of various eastern tribes westward onto the High Plains due to European incursions from the east resulted in increased interaction between Plains groups and the Pueblos, and this, too, is evident in modifications to Pueblo shield iconography.

Historical accounts discuss the complex relationships between Plains groups and the Pueblos from the seventeenth into the early nineteenth centuries (Beck and Trabert 2014; Gunnerson and Gunnerson 1988; Hendricks and Wilson 1996; Jones 1962). In the early historic period, Pueblo/Plains relationships intensified and Spanish oppression promoted Pueblo upheaval, precipitating migrations—although often temporary—away from the Rio Grande valley eastward onto the Plains. Alliances between Plains and Pueblo groups were unstable and shifting. "In the mid to late 1600s, several small groups of Pueblo Indians, especially from Taos, Picuris, San Juan, and Santa Clara took refuge among Apaches in western Kansas to escape Spanish retaliation after a revolt at Taos in 1640 and the larger Pueblo Revolt of 1680" (Gunnerson and Gunnerson 1988:ix). Alternatively between 1751 and 1774, allied Pueblo/Comanche/Spanish forces fought against the Apache, and "Plains war fashions spread" (Parsons 1939:1030). As summarized by the Gunnersons,

> The area west of the eastern foothills of the Rocky Mountains, in south-central Colorado, was dominated throughout the historic period by Utes who joined with Comanche bands after 1706 to make forays onto the plains. The Central High Plains, *per se*, was dominated by Apaches during the 1500s and 1600s, with other tribes crossing or entering the plains only incidentally. In the early

Figure 10. Rare petroglyph shields with designs typical of historical shields, Taos Gorge. Photographs courtesy of John Pitts.

1700s the Apaches continued to dominate the Central Plains but Utes and Comanches moved into the southwestern corner. By the middle of the 1700s, the semisedentary Apaches were forced to abandon their villages, and for the rest of the century Comanches were the dominant force, with other tribes entering the area only occasionally. At the beginning of the 1800s, however, tribes from the north challenged the Comanches and by 1820 Arapahos, Cheyennes, Kiowas, and Kiowa Apaches had spread south to the Arkansas River, and beyond, in substantial numbers. Before and after this date Shoshonis, Blackfeet, Gros Ventres, Crow, Sioux, and Pawnee occasionally entered parts of the Central High Plains, making their presence felt by raiding Spanish installations, and/or New Mexican natives allied with the Spanish [Gunnerson and Gunnerson 1988:ix].

Overall, increasing mobility provided by horses and changing alliances among these groups further complicated the picture between the mid-seventeenth to mid-nineteenth centuries. Pueblo interactions with Plains tribes during this 200-year period of social flux promoted the adoption of cultural features deemed advantageous or powerful, including shield designs. While the revamping of shield designs involved traditional Pueblo iconography, it also included newly borrowed Plains motifs.

Historic shields from the Western Plains present a wide array of designs that are tied to Plains cosmology and regional religious beliefs. Not only do they exhibit a great deal of diversity, but tribal affiliations based on design structure and the elements employed are particularly difficult to organize along ethnic lines. Many are individualistic. Plains rock art of the Ceremonial tradition dating from the Late Prehistoric and Historic periods crosscuts language and ethnic boundaries. "Ceremonial tradition sites in southern Alberta are well within the historic range of the Blackfeet, while sites in western South Dakota are in territory occupied by Mandan, Hidatsa, Sioux, and Cheyenne groups between A.D. 1300 and 1800…Montana and Wyoming sites are in the homeland of the Crow, Shoshone, Kiowa, and Arapahoe" (Keyser and Klassen 2001:212). Perhaps most relevant to this discussion is the fact that the Cheyenne migrated into the Black Hills of South Dakota in the early eighteenth century (e.g., Keyser and Klassen 2001:Figure 51). Later, the Santa Fe Trail opened in 1832, facilitating trade relationships between the Pueblos and various Plains groups. Such interaction with Plains groups, possibly including the Cheyenne, is likely to account for the adoption of some of the changes on Pueblo shields in the historic period.

The Historic Pueblo Shields: Continuities and Change

In general, the dominant layouts, figurative styles, and, to a lesser degree, iconography change in the historic period. While the Pueblos preserved their most salient power images from the past on historic shields, the later shields are marked by changes in design layouts and figurative styles attributable to interactions with the Spanish and probably other Europeans, as well as Plains tribes.

Particularly notable among the new elements are allusions to bison—commonly referred to as "buffalo" in these discussions. At this late date, knowledge of bison was not new to the Pueblos. Bison bones are found in northern Pueblo archaeological sites in the Rio Grande beginning possibly as early as the late eleventh century, indicating hunting practices or trade from the nearby Plains (Harris 1999:127–128; Scheick 2003). It is proposed that buffalo-hide shields are represented at Pottery Mound (Schaafsma 2007:145). Whether or not these buffalo-hide shields had symbolic connotations before ca. A.D. 1500 is not clear. Symbolic references to the buffalo via the depiction of bison horns, however, appear with frequency in iconographic contexts related to the Sun on historic shields.

While this may suggest that bison did not become part of the Pueblo cosmological complex until relatively recently, bison-style horns do occur on snakes at numerous precontact rock art sites in the Rio Grande valley. It is not certain, however, if these representations always involved bison symbolism as such, or whether the horns alone evoked power in a general sense. There are no data to support a linkage between bison and snakes in the Pueblo symbolic or cosmological repertoire.

The recurring bold geometric overall patterns described for the precontact shields are missing on historic shields. Rather they are replaced by a repeated layout consisting of a dark horizontal band, commonly surmounted by paired bison horns, frequently with a rising sun between them (Figure 11). The band itself is punctuated with rectangles or circles painted in different colors, and below a rayed fan suggests feathers, a feature that seems to replace the eagle-tail fans similarly positioned on precontact shield representations. Of the eight shields illustrated by Wright with a version of this layout, five are from Jemez Pueblo, and others with similar paintings are from Santo Domingo, Santa Ana, and Taos (Wright 1976:Figures 36/37, 42/43, 44/46, 47/49, 50/51, 55/56, 69/71). There are numer-

Figure 11. Jemez Pueblo shield featuring the bold, formalized design layout with sun and bison horns typical of the historical era. Various versions of this pattern occur on Pueblo shields from the late eighteenth century to the nineteenth century (adapted from Wright 1976:Figures 47 and 49 with color added according to description in text, p. 59).

ous variations on this widespread theme, and the wide band itself is a significant marker of Pueblo identity on historic shields. Beyond this rather standard layout of the bison/sun complex, the bold patterns of Pueblo precontact shields were largely dropped.

Although the wide, decorative central horizontal band is a regular Pueblo feature, this basic arrangement has been described in reference to Cheyenne shields represented as petroglyphs in the north Cave Hills and southern Black Hills of southwestern South Dakota (Sundstrom 2004:Figure 9.19d, e, f; Sundstrom and Keyser 1998). The South Dakota petroglyph shields are divided horizontally by a line (as opposed to a band) to which inward-curving bison horns are attached. Small triangles are grouped rather irregularly along the circumference and are said to indicate the four directions. Further, this layout is consistent with a vision for a shield design obtained by Whistling Elk, a Cheyenne, as described by Grinnell (1923:196–197). Although limited in number, the petroglyphs described by Sundstrom are of interest since they offer some of the clearest evidence for Plains/Pueblo sharing of shield designs. These may or may not, however, imply specific historic contacts, a topic to which we will return. Other shield petroglyphs from the region, also attributed to the Cheyenne, feature the buffalo head as

a central and dominant subject, a seemingly rare occurrence on Pueblo shields.

The Morning Star prevails as a dominant image (Wright 1976:Figure 38), while the Sun's face as a central icon gains in popularity, and bison horns are added to its symbolic repertoire (Figure 12) (Wright 1976:81). Horned Sun representations also occur in other ethnographic Pueblo contexts (Stevenson 1894:Figure 14). Since horns in themselves are widely

Figure 12. Historic Sandia Pueblo shield featuring horned Sun's face and the horned water serpent (adapted from Wright 1976:Figure 68 with color added according to description in text, p. 78).

regarded as seats of supernatural power (Furst 1998), it is not clear in these representations—nor on the previously mentioned petroglyph snakes—whether the bison itself is symbolically implicated or whether the power implied is limited to the horns alone.

Horned beings are widely represented in Navajo sand paintings as well, in which references to horns is largely to their power as such (Reichard 1963:565). On the other hand, Pueblo women buffalo dancers today wear sun shields on their backs, and Parsons (1939:1032–1033) details further parallels between the Pueblos and Plains in regard to bison and sun symbolism as a complex, indicating that the bison/sun relationship was (is) present in Pueblo ideology. The bison, nevertheless, assumes a much larger role in the cosmovision of Plains tribes (Sundstrom 2004:83–87). In contrast with the historic Plains shields on which the bison is pictured in its entirety and symbolized by its hoofprints, such portrayals are scarce on Pueblo shields.

Inter-regionally shared on historic shields is the practice of picturing small naturalistic icons and details, including the crescent moon, in a seemingly random fashion or with a tendency toward a bilateral organization. Overall, however, the iconographic specifics differ significantly between Plains and Pueblo. Only a small percentage of precontact Pueblo shields have life forms depicted on the face, but on historic shields they are more frequent. Hill (1982:119–120) describes northern Tewa Santa Clara shields as painted in red, yellow, black, or blue, occasionally with a piece of red cloth and feathers on the upper periphery. Patterns are said to include geometric designs or representations of deer, elk, and bear, as well as cosmic phenomena such as the sun and stars, along with the crescent moon. Deer and elk mentioned by Hill are not found in the precontact representations. Life forms are small and naturalistic in contrast with their static prehistoric counterparts, and they appear more like mnemonic notations rather than forceful entities attracting power (Figure 13). (Admittedly, this evaluation is my personal response, and it is unlikely that this was the intention.) Bear paws are represented on both the precontact and post-contact shields, but bears themselves are now represented in addition to the tracks. As mentioned earlier, composite beings including animals and animal/human transformations are absent historically. While these hybrid entities occur only rarely on the faces of shields during Pueblo IV, they were commonly portrayed in close association in the wider pictorial contexts available on the broader "canvases" available on rock faces and kiva walls.

In Pueblo IV murals, mountain lions are associated with shields, but on historic shields they are depicted on them (Figure 14). Paired frontally facing felines, some flourishing their tails, bear a stylistic resemblance to the Spanish regal lion with head in profile on heraldic devices, including the Spanish flag and coat-of-arms (Wright 1976:85, 90), and will be discussed further below. They were also popular in the low-relief carvings on late eighteenth century Hispanic furniture in New Mexico (Taylor and Bokides 1987:Plates 20–22). A frontally facing Spanish lion with a human face and wearing a crown occurs on a silver concho (Mera 1959:Plate 2).

Also new on the historical shields is the traditional horned serpent deity, now with a backward curving horn (Figure 14)—not to be confused with snakes with bison horns mentioned previously. Although present with its horn curved forward in Rio Grande Pueblo iconography by the fourteenth century, this deity does not appear on shields until the historic period. These are also relatively small in scale and may occur in balanced pairs. Horned serpents and other snakes may

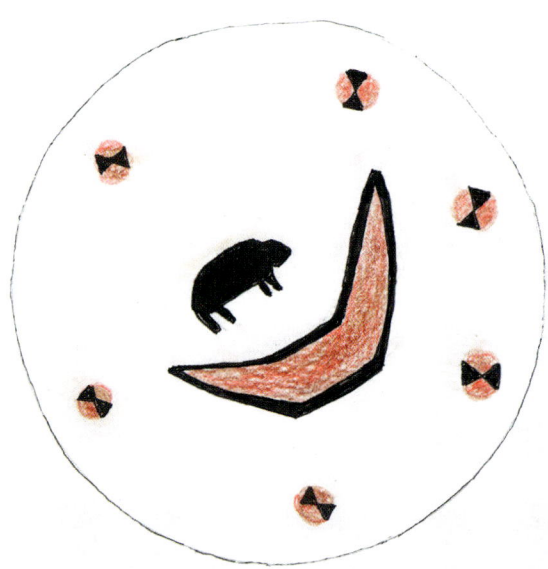

Figure 13. Historic Kewa (Santo Domingo Pueblo) shield with scattered designs including a small bear and crescent moon (adapted from Wright 1976:Figure 16 with color added according to text description, p. 73).

Figure 14. Historic Kewa (Santo Domingo Pueblo) shield with crescent, mountain lions, and horned serpents in a bilateral arrangement. Bird tracks are attached to the circumference. (Adapted from Wright 1976:Figure 28, with color added according to text description, p. 41).

be equated with lightning. In Zuni origin mythology, lightning is said to have emanated from the shields of the War Gods (Hovens 2010:209). Lightning is also portrayed with representations of clouds and rain and even corn plants, suggesting that shields with these motifs may have had a ceremonial link to the war/fertility complex, although no ideological shifts are suggested by their late inclusion. On shields of Pueblo IV origin, this ideological complex is explicit in the Venus symbolism described elsewhere. On the aesthetic front, clouds, lightning, and corn are consistent with the tendency on historic shields to include more small images.

Appropriation, Incorporation, Assimilation, and Revitalization

The described revisions in historical Pueblo shield iconography involved a diversity of responses to diverse situations. Social relationships between the Pueblos and outsiders were unstable and shifting throughout the 1700s and the first half of the nineteenth century when some of the Pueblo shields under discussion—or at least their designs—originated. The social implications of the heretofore described Spanish and Plains symbolism appropriated by the Pueblos after the Pueblo Revolt in 1680 merit further consideration. Among the inevitable results of the appropriation and assimilation of symbolic structures from an alien group is that the newly adopted symbols may undergo changes or modifications in meaning and may contribute to a modified identity of the adoptee, identity being flexible. As Kopytoff (1986:67) states, "what is significant about the adoption of alien objects—as of alien ideas—is not the fact that they are adopted, but the way they are culturally redefined and put to use."

Regarding appropriated objects of power, the well documented reuse of the American flag by the Lakota and other tribes in recent history provides interpretive models for the shield designs discussed here (Herbst and Kopp 1993). As booty of war, a captured flag was regarded by the Lakota as a prized trophy, symbolic of bravery and glory. In addition, according to Howard Bad Hand (1993:12–13), the American flag was used by the Lakota as a means of reinforcing their own warrior tradition and taking on its power. In this context, the alien flag was in a sense confiscated for reuse by the Lakota, symbolizing the prowess of the individual warrior and not American patriotism. In addition, it was not only a symbol of power but an amulet of protection. On the other end of the scale, incorporated into craft objects, largely between 1880 and 1910, the American flag promoted sales to tourists and functioned as a pleasing design for use in mundane objects (Herbst and Kopp 1993:24–25).

From the West: Spain and Beyond

Some changes in shield iconography relate specifically to the Spanish. Relationships between the Pueblos and the Spanish fluctuated over time and even varied between Pueblos. From the early 1700s into the early 1800s, at least some of the Pueblos were allied with the Spanish against raiding Utes, Comanches, and Navajos (Hendricks and Wilson 1996; Jones 1962). There exists the possibility that these Pueblo auxiliaries may have been a select group such as Christianized individuals and did not represent entire villages. In spite of these alliances, the effects of Spanish oppression were lasting, and the "disguises" put in place against the Spanish are still in use (Ortiz 1969; White 1942).

Appropriated foreign elements were subject to manipulation so that they benefited the Pueblos. Apparent new sources of supernatural power that were added to the Pueblo repertoire did not necessarily conflict with the symbolism and cosmology already in place, but instead replaced older iconic forms while the meaning remained essentially the same. Such may be the case with the Spanish-style feline described earlier. Large felines being of utmost importance in Pueblo cosmology, the adoption of Spanish canons of representation in the face of Spanish oppression may have masked their own native regard for this animal as a guardian and war patron. The adopted Spanish form may have been intended to have been viewed by the Spanish as a gesture of acquiescence, while as a disguise, it comprised an act of resistance (e.g., Mobley-Tanaka 2002:79).

Katherine Wells (personal communication 2016) reports that a dozen of these lions with manes are found among the northern Tewa petroglyphs at Mesa Prieta north of the Pueblo of Ohkay Owingeh (San Juan) (Figure 15). Not to be confused with the indigenous hybrid figures described earlier, they turn humanlike faces toward the observer and flourish their tails, details well outside traditional Pueblo representational canons. Significantly, Mesa Prieta is within the general vicinity of the first Spanish capital in New Mexico. Established at San Gabriel in 1598, it persisted for 12 years until it was moved to Santa Fe in 1610. Assuming that the petroglyph lions were manufactured by the Tewa during the seventeenth century, it is possible that in the public domain they signaled acquiescence to Spanish rule, while simultaneously asserting the tra-

Figure 15. Northern Tewa petroglyph of a Spanish-derived lion. Various versions of this lion are carved on wooden trucks of Hispanic origin and on jewelry. Photograph courtesy of Jim Duffield.

ditional powers ascribed by the Tewa to large felines across their landscape. Similar lions also appear on the historic shields described here (Figure 14). Meanwhile, absconding with a little of the power of the Spanish empire might have been included in the appropriation, although this is merely speculation.

The appropriation of the Spanish lion is part of a wider context of adaptation to Spanish introductions. Other examples of Pueblo incorporation of Spanish symbolism and cultural practices are described by Leslie White (1942:256–270, 351) and Alfonso Ortiz (1969:161–162). Personifications of the Spanish Santiago and the rooster pulls among the Keresan Pueblos (White 1942:263–267) include ritual events that reinterpret Spanish traditions, harmonizing them with Pueblo interests in rain-bringing rituals. In the Spanish-originated "gallo ritual," or rooster pull, lathered sweat generated by the running horses is likened to clouds, and the rooster sacrifice resulting in the scattering of blood and feathers is deemed to bestow blessings for rain, the growth of crops, and the well-being of livestock. In this case, Spanish activities, reinterpreted in terms of native rain rituals, served as a means of empowerment as they were added to the usual annual calendar of rainmaking ceremonies. Meanwhile, the Spanish were placated by the outward form of the event. In addition, Ortiz (1969:161–162) describes the adoption of a Spanish-style mask to disguise Tewa supernaturals so they can perform in plaza rituals without condemnation.

In addition to Pueblo appropriation of alien symbolism, we find the more general modifications in stylistic norms. As noted, life forms on historic shields underwent changes that reflect the naturalistic norms introduced by the West, supplanting the highly stylized portrayals that characterize the precontact images. This shift indicates nineteenth century Native American emulation of Western aesthetic standards. Depending on the date of a shield, boarding schools during the late nineteenth century would certainly have contributed to the changes in drawing styles between the precontact period and the representations on the shields in question. Conformity to Western standards of representation may have been regarded as prestigious, and it is likely that this was an inclusive change on any and all media.

Other modifications included an indigenous re-evaluation of the use of traditional Pueblo symbolic content and may have more profound implications. The adoption of Western stylistic norms does not explain the absence of the composite figures that feature so prominently in the precontact art. This lack of hybrid figures in the historic Pueblo depictions is worthy of note because it is underlain by major differences in fundamental values and worldviews between the West and indigenous Americans.

In order to grasp the meaning of the composite human/eagle or human/lion figures in precontact Pueblo rock art and other media, it is helpful to review ideas among the Pueblos on humanity's place in the cosmological scheme of things. A conceptual hierarchy of living things is well defined by the Zuni (Tedlock 1979:499; Young 1988:127–129). Within this hierarchy life forms are arranged on a continuum of beings from "raw" to "cooked" or "finished," with "raw" beings as the most powerful and "finished" beings having the least power of all. Humanity is in this latter category. "Rawness here seems to imply closeness to the world of the myth and the events that transpired then, and it is those beings for whom this rawness is an attribute who have the ability to effect change in the physical world" (Young 1988:128). As Walker (1979:510) states, "…it is extremely unlikely that any Zuni prior to European contact could have conceptualized humans as opposed to animals…for the categories *human, animal, nature,* and *man* are all alien to the native Zuni classification of the universe insofar as this is known to linguists." All these entities are linked under the category of *beings*. Young (1988:128–130) goes on to note that since humans have little influence themselves they must rely on the raw beings as mediators between themselves and the most powerful beings. These mediators include the kachinas, the animal gods of the directions, and a myriad of other forms of life. Since mediation is often effected by means of visual representations of the mediators, depictions of these images are a means for humanity to acquire the power to effect the desired changes in the universe. Importantly for this discussion, the eagle warriors in rock art or the images of human lion syntheses in kiva murals have agency, attracting the powers represented—in this case war-related.

While the multivocal composite figures from Pueblo IV are understandable from this perspective, it is easy to suggest that they would have been regarded negatively by Europeans who had a dim view of native beliefs. There are documented instances among the Maya in which Europeans denied the ability of Native Americans to think metaphorically or abstractly (Blume 2006:355). In such cases, it is likely that such portrayals, especially those of hybrid humans and animals, would have been viewed by the dominant culture as acts of witchcraft. In this environment, these visual statements of combined supernatural powers would, of necessity, have been eliminated, while natural representations of animals, like those in a naturalist's notebook, would have gone unchallenged.

From the Plains

Pueblo/Plains social encounters involved alliances and trade, as well as hostilities, and contacts involved diverse Plains groups (Lange 1979). Some changes to historic Pueblo shields include selected iconography and design layouts shared with Plains shields. Depending on the situation, the appropriation of Plains shield designs by the Pueblos had potentially variable social significance. Before addressing the social implications of these shared elements and layouts, a brief overview of historic Plains shields provides additional perspective on the shared Pueblo/Plains designs.

Cheyenne shield iconography is described in detail by Nagy (1994a, 1994b), and these specifics likely had wider tribal relevance among Plains tribes (e.g., Keyser and Klassen 2001). The layout on many shields tends to be bilaterally symmetrical. Elements frequently denote the four directions or the resident spirits thereof, and these marks may be triangles, arcs, small circles, or other abstract notations situated at or removed from the edge of the shield (Nagy 1994a:Figures 4 and 14). Other typical elements are moon crescents, fork-tailed birds, buffalo tracks, snapping turtles, eagles, the buffalo itself, horned anthropomorphs, and the *hetanehao*, a symbol for male power. Additional typical elements are dragonflies (the blue dragonfly offering protection from death) that, like sacred birds—thunderbirds, magpies, crows, ravens, flickers, and butterflies—carry messages to spirits at the zenith (Nagy 1994a:13–19). These and other symbolic notations animate Cheyenne shields, the life forms serving as spirit helpers to the shield bearer. Other details represent winds, the sun, the moon, and divisions representing day and night (Irwin 1994:231). On Cheyenne shields, the crescent moon, an antagonist of darkness and death, is mimicked in shape by claws and animal horns, all of which on shields are protection against violent death. Even the snapping turtle may be pictured with horns (Nagy 1994a:Figure 13). Of particular note here is the fact that the horns and horn-shaped objects, due to their shape alone, may assume protective power without reference to the buffalo. This situation was discussed previously in regard to the depiction of horns on historic Pueblo shields. Such abstraction is common in symbolic "lexicons."

On the Plains, the choice of what is to be represented on one's shield is revealed during a vision quest. It is useful here to include a quote that elucidates in great detail the vision that resulted in the symbolism of Whistling Elk's shield, Whistling Elk being a Cheyenne tribal member:

> On the morning of the fourth day, a buffalo raised its head above the water and sang a song, directing Whistling Elk to make this shield and describing how it should be made.
>
> The painting on the shield consists of a pair of long, slender, upward-directed horns, a little above the center of the shield; below them is a large disc surrounded by dots; between the horns is a red disc also surrounded by dots, and there are four dark discs evenly distributed near the border of the shield. These discs on the outer rim represent the four directions; the disc below the horns is the moon; the red disk between the horns, the sun; and the dots are stars. The horns represent the animal that took pity on Whistling Elk and taught him how to make this shield. The moon is the spirit that during the night protected the brave who carried the shield, and the sun protected him during the day. The upper round spot to the left of the horns represents the wind which comes

from the setting sun. The upper spot at the right of the horns represents the wind from the north, the lower spot on the right, the wind from the east, and the lower spot on the left, the wind from the south. The spirit which controls the south wind is supposed to have the greatest power when prayed to for help [Grinnell (1923:196–197].

Although each vision is individual, the content of a vision is also determined by the cultural framework of the times. While the Plains worldview differs from that of the Pueblos, a design complex shared to this extent poses challenging questions. Since a wide cultural system prevailed among Plains groups (Keyser and Klassen 2001:59), it is perhaps advisable to not focus tightly on a Cheyenne source described here for the Pueblo sun/bison shield layout.

The Pueblo shields with this basic structure and iconography were collected early in the twentieth century, and the petroglyphs from South Dakota likely date from the latter half of the nineteenth. It is reasonable to propose that Whistling Elk's vision occurred in the 1800s and was, therefore, roughly contemporaneous. The symbols in this design are those of a unified Plains cosmology that include multiple sacred powers embracing the earthly and celestial realms, all of which contribute to the effectiveness of the shield. On Pueblo shields, bison symbolism and especially that of bison horns with the sun is the primary borrowed symbolism. Many of the other characteristic symbols on Plains shields are absent. With the major exception of the bison/sun complex, borrowing was selective and conformed for the most part to established Pueblo beliefs. This basic layout, with the addition of the horizontal band marking Pueblo identity, replaced the bold layouts described on the precontact petroglyph shields. In doing so it also represents a new aesthetic solution to Pueblo identity.

As for shields themselves, a consideration of the social "biographies of things" (e.g., Kopytoff 1986) may elucidate the social mechanisms accounting for the spread of shield motifs. On the Plains, the only person empowered to make a shield was the visionary himself. Shield-making, as with the manufacture of other sacred objects, was undertaken to the accompaniment of prayers, offerings, and song and other rituals followed before a shield was carried into a conflict (Irwin 1994:232). How, therefore, did a shield design, retaining its power, get passed around? On the Plains there were various practices in place by which one could "obtain a shield." One could ask someone who had a vision shield to share its power, or ask a shaman to fast for him and then make the shield; or one could fast and make one's own shield independently (Irwin 1994:232). Through a vision quest, spirit helpers were sought, later to be pictured on an individual's shield. Owners of these designs could give them away or sell them (Nagy 1994b:78–82).

Does the popular patterning on historic Pueblo shields, closely adhering to Whistling Elk's vision, represent Pueblo appropriation and emulation of Plains war powers? Was the Plains source at the time an enemy or an ally? If an ally, did the appropriation and assimilation of this design express solidarity and alliance building with skilled Plains warriors, possibly against the Europeans (e.g., Liebmann 2002:133)? Was this design transferred or sold to the Pueblos by a Plains visionary, the rightful owner of the design? Alternatively, was the bison/sun complex appropriated from a shield acquired by the Pueblos as a trophy in a battle against a Plains group? Once the design was reconfigured with the wide band denoting Pueblo identity, by what means was it shared among the Pueblo towns? Lacking more historical information and chronological specificity, one can only make suggestions about the social processes that led to this acquisition in the first place.

The trophy shield captured in conflict is a final consideration. In many parts of the world trophy-taking is not only a means of flouting one's power over the enemy and success in battle (Chacon and Dye 2007), but also a means of acquiring the enemy's power. Capturing enemy shields, like capturing the American flag, was one means of stealing the enemy's power and the designs in which power resided.

A historic shield from Tesuque, a northern Tewa village, is a case in point. The central motif is a large, imposing bison head in black that superimposes an earlier painted bison head (Figure 16). Among other visible original elements is a series of zigzag lines ending in circles, a common Plains motif, situated below the upper circumference (Nagy 1994b:369). Over these and the horns of the original bison is superimposed a typically Pueblo horned serpent. The dominant design feature today, the black head of a bison, is the final addition. For Zuni rock art, Young (1988:185) suggests that superimposition may augment the power of the images and the place where they appear, and in Pueblo view the layering of accumulated imagery similarly may have enhanced a shield's power. The bison head,

Figure 16. Shield from Tesuque Pueblo ca. 1850 showing various stages of repainting. Beneath the black head of the bison is another, along with wavy lines ending in circles, typical of Plains shields, here superimposed by the Pueblo horned serpent (adapted from Fields and Zamudio-Taylor 2001:Figure 30).

rare on Rio Grande shields but reported also at Cochiti Pueblo (Lange 1990:166), is a Plains motif.

Beyond the trophy shield and its iconography are parallel examples that illustrate a pattern of trophy-taking and power acquisition between the Pueblos and their enemies. At Santa Ana, for example, the fallen enemy's power was acquired from his confiscated clothing (White 1942:318). Likewise, enemy scalps obtained by Pueblos in successful battle were carried home and ritually brought into the village, where they were subjected to initiation to make them "friends." In this way their powers as rain fetishes could be used for Pueblo benefit (Bunzel 1932:679, 1933:33; Mathiowetz et al 2015; Schaafsma 2000:149, Stephen 1936:97). In other words, the enemy was not only vanquished but his powers were assimilated by the victors.

Final Comments and Conclusions

This paper has explored some of the traditions and changes that led up to Pueblo shield iconography in historic times. Writing within the context of the calmer days of the twentieth century, Hill (1982:120) states that at Santa Clara, a northern Tewa Pueblo, the choice of shield designs was based on "a personal whim," but he also notes that the same designs rendered as body painting or on the shafts of war clubs contributed to a warrior's protection and prowess. As described in this paper, it is clear that the apparent "whim" was not a casual choice but one carefully made, based on sources of power where life and death are at stake.

How selections were made for representations used by individuals painting Pueblo shields is not explicit. There is little ethnographic information on how new ideas were acquired or why others were dropped, although some suggestions are offered, taking into consideration the specific historical contexts within which these changes occurred. As opposed to the information available for the Plains, we have little information on the ritual procedures that accompanied the painting of Pueblo shields. As far as we know, individual vision questing, a widespread means on the Plains for seeking protective imagery for shields, was not practiced by the Pueblos. At least it is not documented. According to Wright (1976:12), ritual practitioners were not involved in painting Pueblo shields. Nevertheless, protection and enablement continued to be sought in traditional powers. Among the Pueblos, criteria for individual selections may have deep roots within societal knowledge, privy only to members of warrior societies. One is also impelled to inquire further and ask whether or not additional social affiliations may have dictated the appropriate protective elements to be represented in line with the membership of a shield's owner in a given clan or other sodality. Should this be the case, it would indicate the precedence of Pueblo societal relationships as determining factors in an individual's choice of a shield design and its content.

Within the broader cultural framework, in addition to appropriating the enemy's power in the course of victorious battle, emulation, alliance-building, and disguise are among the factors that may be marshalled to account for many of the iconographic and layout changes on Pueblo shields during the historic period. Appropriated alien symbolism that notably gave endorsement to the bison was, nevertheless, very selective, and numerous icons such as the American flag, regarded somewhat later in time as powerful by Pueblo adversaries, are absent on Pueblo shields. During the violent social and cultural disruptions that characterize this period of history, the Pueblos maintained their fundamental relationships to their own deities, who played key roles in the ideologies of conflict. The primary images of the Sun, Morning Star, and predatory animal guardians are sustained throughout despite stylistic and other changes. Borrowed design layouts were somewhat reconfigured and Pueblo identity on their historic shields, although altered, was retained.

On a final note, this study is regarded as an initial foray into the study of Pueblo shield iconography to which more data and observations can be added, providing guidance and directions for future investigations.

Acknowledgments. This paper would not have been possible without assistance of numerous friends and colleagues. Allison Colborne, librarian at the Museum of Arts and Culture/Laboratory, has been most helpful in locating references. John Pitts and Jim Duffield generously have made their photographs of shield representations in rock art available for study, and their contributions to the illustrations in this paper are gratefully acknowledged. Thanks also to Duane Anderson, Toby Herbst, Will Russell, and Hoski Schaafsma for providing additional material. Toby has offered support throughout this research contributing his extensive knowledge on historic Pueblo shields and providing guidance on sources of information. Finally my profuse thanks and gratitude to Curt Schaafsma for his patience as he rescued me from the numerous computer snags that continuously beleaguer these endeavors.

References Cited

Adams, E. Charles
  1991 *The Origin and Development of the Kachina Cult.* University of Arizona Press, Tucson, Arizona.

Bad Hand, Howard
  1993 The American Flag in Lakota Traditions. In *The Flag in American Indian Art,* edited by Toby Herbst and Joel Kopp, pp. 11–13. New York State Historical Association, Cooperstown, and University of Washington Press, Seattle.

Beck, Margaret E., and Sarah Trabert
  2014 Kansas and the Postrevolt Pueblo Diaspora: Ceramic Evidence from the Scott County Pueblo. *American Antiquity* 72(2):314–336).

Blume, Anna
  2006 Animal Transformations: The Imagery of Maya and European Fantasy and Belief. In *A Pre-Columbian World,* edited by Jeffery Quilter and Mary Miller, pp. 343–362. Dumbarton Oaks, Washington, D.C.

Bunzel, Ruth
  1932 Zuni Ritual Poetry. *Forty-Seventh Annual Report of the Bureau of American Ethnology,* 1929–1930, pp. 611–835. Smithsonian Institution, Washington, D.C.

  1933 *Zuni Texts.* American Ethnological Society Publications 15. Stetchert and Co, New York.

Carlson, John B.
  1991 *Venus-regulated Warfare and Ritual Sacrifice in Mesoamerica: Teotihuacan and the Cacaxtla "Star Wars" Connection.* Center for Archaeoastronomy Technical Publication 7. College Park, Maryland.

Chacon, Richard J., and David H. Dye, eds.
  2007 *The Taking and Displaying of Human Body Parts as Trophies by Amerindians.* Interdisciplinary Contributions to Archaeology. Springer, New York.

Crotty, Helen K.
  1995 *Anasazi Mural Art of the Pueblo IV Period, AD 1300–1600: Influences, Cultural Adaptation and Cultural Diversity in the Prehistoric Southwest.* Ph.D. Thesis, University of California, Los Angeles. University Microfilms, Ann Arbor, Michigan.

  2001 Shields, Shield Bearers, and Warfare Imagery in Anasazi Art, 1200–1500. In *Deadly Landscapes: Case Studies in Prehistoric Southwestern Warfare,* edited by Glen E. Rice and Steven A. LeBlanc, pp. 65–83. University of Utah Press, Salt Lake City.

  2007 Western Pueblo Influences and Integration in the Pottery Mound Painted Kivas. In *New Perspectives on Pottery Mound Pueblo,* edited by Polly Schaafsma, pp. 85–107. University of New Mexico Press, Albuquerque.

Dongoske, Kurt E., and Cindy K. Dongoske
  2002 History in Stone: Evaluating Spanish Conversion Efforts through Hopi Rock Art. In *Archaeologies of the Pueblo Revolt,* edited by Robert W. Preucel, pp. 114–131. University of New Mexico Press, Albuquerque.

Feest, Christian H.
  1980 *The Art of War.* Thames and Hudson, London.

Fields, Virginia M., and Victor Zamudio-Taylor.
  2001 Aztlan: Destination and Point of Departure. In *The Road to Aztlan: Art from a Mythic Homeland,* edited by Virginia Fields and Victor Zamudio-Taylor, pp. 38–77. Los Angeles County Museum of Art, Los Angeles.

Furst, Peter T.
  1998 Shamanic Symbolism, Transformation, and Deities in West Mexican Funerary Art. In *Ancient West Mexico: Art and Archeology of the Unknown Past,* edited by Richard F. Townsend, pp. 169–189. Art Institute of Chicago, Chicago.

Grinnell, George B.
  1923 *The Cheyenne Indians: Their History and Ways of Life.* Volume 1. Yale University Press, New Haven, Connecticut. Facsimile reprint edition 1972, University of Nebraska Press, Lincoln.

Gunnerson, James H., and Dolores A. Gunnerson
  1988 *Ethnohistory of the High Plains.* Bureau of Land Management, Colorado State Office, Denver.

Harris, Arthur H.
  1999 The Nonavian Fauna from Picuris Pueblo. In *Picuris Pueblo Through Time: Eight Centuries of Change at a Northern Rio Grande Pueblo,* edited by Michael A. Adler and Herbert W. Dick, pp. 127–139. William P. Clemens Center for Southwest Studies, Southern Methodist University, Dallas, Texas.

Hendricks, Rick, and John P. Wilson
  1996 *The Navajo in 1705: Roque Madrid's Campaign Journal.* University of New Mexico Press, Albuquerque, New Mexico.

Herbst, Toby, and Joel Kopp
  1993 The Grandfather's Flag. In *The Flag in American Indian Art,* edited by Toby Herbst and Joel Kopp, pp. 15–26. New York State Historical Association, Cooperstown, and University of Washington Press, Seattle.

Hibben, Frank C.
  1975 *Kiva Paintings of the Anasazi.* KC Publications, Las Vegas, Nevada.

Hill, W. W.
    1982 *An Ethnography of Santa Clara Pueblo, New Mexico*. Edited and Annotated by Charles H. Lange. University of New Mexico Press, Albuquerque.

Hovens, Pieter
    2010 *The Ten Kate Collection 1882–1888*. American Indian Material Culture, Museum of Ethnology, Leiden. ZKF Publishers, Friedburg, Germany.

Irwin, Lee
    1994 *The Dream Seekers*. University of Oklahoma Press, Norman.

Jones, Oakah L., Jr.
    1962 Pueblo Auxilliaries in New Mexico, 1763–1821. *New Mexico Historical Review* 37(2):81–109.

Kent, Kate Peck
    1983 *Pueblo Indian Textiles: A Living Tradition*. School of American Research Press, Santa Fe, New Mexico.

Keyser, James D., and Michael A. Klassen
    2001 *Plains Indian Rock Art*. University of Washington Press, Seattle and UBC Press, Vancouver.

Kopytoff, Igor
    1986 The Cultural Biography of Things: Commoditization as Process. In *The Social Life of Things: Commodities in Cultural Perspective*, edited by Arjun Appadurai, pp. 65–91. Cambridge University Press, Cambridge, United Kingdom.

Lange, Charles H.
    1979 Relations of the Southwest with the Plains and Great Basin. In *Handbook of North American Indians, Volume 19: Southwest*, edited by Alfonso Ortiz, pp. 201–205. Smithsonian Institution, Washington, D.C.
    1990 *Cochiti: A New Mexico Pueblo, Past and Present*. University of New Mexico Press, Albuquerque.

Liebmann, Matthew J.
    2002 Signs of Power and Resistance: The (Re)Creation of Christian Imagery and Identities in the Pueblo Revolt Era. In *Archaeologies of the Pueblo Revolt*, edited by Robert W. Preucel, pp. 132–164. University of New Mexico Press, Albuquerque.

Mansell, Maureen E.
    1994 *By the Power of Their Dreams*. Chronicle Books, San Francisco.

Mathiowetz, Michael, Polly Schaafsma, Jeremy Coltman, and Karl Taube
    2015 Darts of Dawn: the Tlahuizcalpantecuhtli Venus Complex in the Iconography of Mesoamerica and the American Southwest. *Journal of the Southwest* 57(1):1–102.

McCreery, Patricia, and Ekkehart Malotki
    1994 *Tapamveni: The Rock Art Galleries of Petrified Forest and Beyond*. Petrified Forest Museum Association, Petrified Forest, Arizona.

Mera, Harry P.
    1959 *Indian Silverwork of the Southwest, Illustrated*. Volume 1. Dale Stuart King, Globe, Arizona.

Mills, Barbara J.
    2002 Zuni Ceramics, Social Identity, and the Pueblo Revolt. In *Archaeologies of the Pueblo Revolt*, edited by Robert W. Preucel, pp. 85–98. University of New Mexico Press, Albuquerque.

Mobley-Tanaka, Jeannette L.
    2002 Crossed Cultures, Crossed Meanings: The Manipulations of Ritual Imagery in Early Historic Pueblo Resistance. In *Archaeologies of the Pueblo Revolt*, edited by Robert W. Preucel, pp. 77–84. University of New Mexico Press, Albuquerque.

Nagy, Imre
    1994a A Typology of Cheyenne Shield Designs. *Plains Anthropologist* 39(147):5–36.
    1994b Cheyenne Shields and Their Cosmological Background. *American Indian Art* 19(3)38–47, 104.

Ortiz, Alfonso
    1969 *The Tewa World: Space, Time, Being, and Becoming in a Pueblo Society*. University of Chicago Press, Chicago.

Parsons, Elsie Clews
    1939 *Pueblo Indian Religion*. 2 volumes. University of Chicago Press.

Reichard, Gladys
    1963 *Navajo Religion: A Study of Symbolism*. Bollingen Series XVIII. Princeton University Press, Princeton, New Jersey. Reprint edition, original publication 1950, Pantheon Books, New York.

Renaud, E. B.
    1938 *Petroglyphs of North Central New Mexico*. University of Denver Archaeological Survey, 11th Report. Denver, Colorado.

Russell, Will G.
    2016 Cultural Diversity and Social Identity Atop Perry Mesa. *Archaeology Southwest Magazine* 30(2):19–20.

Schaafsma, Curtis F.
    1994 Pueblo Ceremonialism from the Perspective of Spanish Documents. In *Kachinas in the Pueblo World*, edited by Polly Schaafsma, pp. 121–137. University of New Mexico Press, Albuquerque.

Schaafsma, Polly
    1965 Kiva Murals from Pueblo del Encierro (La 70). *El Palacio* 27(3):7–16.
    1980 *Indian Rock Art of the Southwest*. School of American Research, Santa Fe, and University of New Mexico Press, Albuquerque.
    1992 War Imagery and Magic: Petroglyphs at Comanche Gap, Galisteo Basin, New Mexico. In *Archaeology, Art, and Anthropology: Papers in Honor of J. J. Brody*, edited by Meliha S. Duran and David T. Kirkpatrick, pp. 157–174. Archaeological Society of New Mexico Papers 18.
    1994 The Prehistoric Kachina Cult and its Origins as Suggested by Southwestern Rock Art. In *Kachinas in the Pueblo World*, edited by Polly Schaafsma, pp. 63–80. University of New Mexico Press, Albuquerque.
    2000 *Warrior, Shield, and Star: Imagery and Ideology of Pueblo Warfare*. Western Edge Press, Santa Fe, New Mexico.
    2005 Feathered Stars and Scalps in Pueblo IV. In *Current Studies in Archaeoastronomy: Conversations across Time and Space*, edited by John W. Fountain and Rolf M. Sinclair, pp. 191–204. Carolina Academic Press, Durham, North Carolina.
    2007 The Pottery Mound Murals and Rock Art: Implications for Regional Interaction. In *New Perspectives on Pottery Mound Pueblo*, edited by Polly Schaafsma, pp. 137–166. University of New Mexico Press, Albuquerque.
    2014 The Morning Star/Rain/Maize Complex in the American Southwest. In *Astronomy and Ceremony in the Prehistoric Southwest Revisited: Collaborations in Cultural Astronomy*, edited by Gregory E. Munson, Todd W. Bostwick, and Tony Hull, pp. 19–28. Maxwell Museum of Anthropology Anthropological Papers 9. University of New Mexico, Albuquerque.

Schaafsma, Polly, and Curtis Schaafsma
　1974 Evidence for the Origins of the Pueblo Kachina Cult as Suggested by Southwestern Rock Art. *American Antiquity* 39(4):535–45.

Schaafsma, Polly, and Will Tsosie
　2009 Xeroxed on Stone: Times of Origin and the Navajo Holy People in Canyon Landscapes. In *Landscapes of Origin in the Americas,* edited by Jessica Christie, pp. 15–31. University of Alabama Press, Tuscaloosa.

Scheick, Cherie L.
　2003 *Archaeological Investigations of a Middle to Late Developmental Period Site Adjacent to Fort Marcy Hill, Santa Fe, New Mexico.* Southwest Archaeological Consultants Research Series 454d, Santa Fe, New Mexico.

Smith, Watson
　1952 *Kiva Mural Decorations at Awatovi and Kawaika-a with a Survey of Other Wall Paintings in the Pueblo Southwest.* Papers of the Peabody Museum of American Archaeology and Ethnology 37. Peabody Museum, Harvard University, Cambridge.

Sprajc, Ivan
　1993a The Venus-Rain-Maize Complex in the Mesoamerican Worldview, Part I. *Journal of the History of Astronomy* 24(1–2):17–70.
　1993b The Venus-Rain-Maize Complex in the Mesoamerican Worldview, Part II. *Archaeoastronomy* 18:S27–S53. Supplement to *Journal of the History of Astronomy* 24.

Stephen, Alexander M.
　1936 *Hopi Journal of Alexander M. Stephen.* Edited by Elsie Clews Parsons. Columbia University Contributions to Anthropology 23. Columbia University Press, New York.

Stevenson, Matilda Coxe
　ca. 1882 *Dress and Adornment of the Pueblo Indians.* Bureau of American Ethnology, Manuscript #2093. National Anthropological Archives, Smithsonian Institution, Washington, D.C.
　1894 *The Sia.* Eleventh Annual Report for the Bureau of American Ethnology for the Years 1889–1890, Smithsonian Institution, Washington, D. C.

Sundstrom, Linea
　2004 *Storied Stone: Indian Rock Art of the Black Hills Country.* University of Oklahoma Press, Norman.

Sundstrom, Linea, and James D. Keyser.
　1998 Tribal Affiliations of Shield Petroglyphs from the Black Hills and Cave Hills. *Plains Anthropologist* 43(165):225–238.

Tavarelli, A.
　1995 *Power and Display: Shields of the Islands of Southeast Asia and Melanesia.* Boston College Museum of Art, Boston.

Taylor, Lonn, and Dessa Bokides
　1987 *New Mexican Furniture 1600–1940: The Origins, Survival, and Revival of Furniture Making in the Hispanic Southwest.* Museum of New Mexico Press, Santa Fe.

Tedlock, Dennis
　1979 Zuni Religion and World View. In *Handbook of North American Indians, Volume 9: Southwest,* edited by Alfonso Ortiz, pp. 499–508. Smithsonian Institution, Washington, D.C.

Titiev, Mischa
　1944 *Old Oraibi: A Study of the Hopi Indians of Third Mesa.* Papers of the Peabody Museum of American Archaeology and Ethnology 22(1). Peabody Museum, Harvard University, Cambridge.

Voth, Henry R.
　1903 *The Oraibi Summer Snake Society.* Field Columbian Museum, Anthropological Series 3(4). Chicago.

Walker, Willard
　1979 Zuni Semantic Categories. In *Handbook of North American Indians, Volume 9: Southwest,* edited by Alfonso Ortiz, pp. 509–513. Smithsonian Institution, Washington, D.C.

Wallis, Wilson D., and Mischa Titiev
　1945 Hopi Notes from Chimopavi. *Papers of the Michigan Academy of Science Arts and Letters* 30:523–555. University of Michigan Press, Ann Arbor.

White, Leslie A.
　1942 *The Pueblo of Santa Ana, New Mexico.* American Anthropological Association Memoir Series 60.

Wright, Barton
　1976 *Pueblo Shields from the Fred Harvey Fine Arts Collection.* Northland Press, Flagstaff, Arizona.

Young, M. Jane
　1985 Images of Power and the Power of Images: The Significance of Rock Art for Contemporary Zunis. *Journal of American Folklore* 98:3–48.
　1988 *Signs from the Ancestors: Zuni Cultural Symbolism and Perceptions of Rock Art.* University of New Mexico Press, Albuquerque.
　1992 Morning Star, Evening Star: Zuni Traditional Stories. In *Earth and Sky: Visions of the Cosmos in Native American Folklore,* edited by Ray Williamson and Claire R. Farrer, pp. 75–109. University of New Mexico Press, Albuquerque.

The Importance of Landscape-Based Approaches in Rock Art Research

Charlotte Vendome-Gardner

In many studies a solely shamanistic approach to rock art has been used, creating a discourse which fails to acknowledge the context created by the cultural and natural features which surround it. While purely symbolic interpretations which arise from the use of this approach often propose open-ended and continuous answers, in short there is, and will be, no clear answer. By using a landscape-based approach and re-siting the image back into its original context we can begin to establish factual evidence regarding its cultural environment over periods of time. This will allow us to see the many instances in which rock art can be found, and how it may have interacted with past peoples in a variety of situations and ways. This paper seeks to discuss the importance of the use of a landscape-based approach in rock art research, using the fluteplayer as an example of its application.

It has become apparent through my research, although still in its relative infancy, that there is a resounding reliance on the use of symbolic interpretations to study and understand rock art sites. This awareness was apparent through my previous academic studies (2013), but was further propelled by a recent visit to the Creswell Crags in England (Figure 1), home to Britain's oldest rock art site. Our tour guide, a trained and knowledgeable archaeologist, stated that although there was no firm evidence to suggest the symbolic function of the images, she was of an opinion that they were the result of both hunting magic and a neurophysiological altered state of mind. If this was a way to engage people with the rock art, it was doing it an injustice. Further discussion revealed that the cave had once been inhabited, and then later abandoned in favour of another on the opposite side of the valley, directly opposite the old cave. For me, there was more information to be held in the understanding of the site from that small piece of information relating to the cultural landscape. It should not be disputed that my British ancestors held an ideology and connection with the earth in ways which we will never understand, but that was just it: we will never know. Symbolic interpretations should primarily be reserved for those indigenous cultures whose ancestors directly created the rock art, such as the Native American peoples. These cultures still hold a connection to and understanding of their past which many Europeans now do not, and as such they are well informed to interpret the images in such a way. In contrast to this, western peoples, such as myself, have lost most, if not all, knowledge of the ideologies held by our ancestors. We instead understand our past through evidence, documents, and archaeological remains, which we can interpret and study. At the Creswell Crags, the habitation movement and understanding of the landscape would provide more knowledge about the peoples who created and interacted with the rock art than focusing specifically on the image itself, as it could at any site. For these

Charlotte Vendome-Gardner
University of Exeter, England

Figure 1. Creswell Crags. This limestone gorge is home to England's only known Ice Age rock art.

reasons I feel it is appropriate to discuss why I believe symbolic interpretations are problematic, specifically in relation to prehistoric sites, and often hinder rock art study, and why we should begin to adopt the use of landscape-based study on a wider scale within the discipline.

Rock Art and Symbolism

It is important that I start this discussion by outlining the definition of symbolism. It is listed in the dictionary as follows: "1. The use of symbols to represent ideas or qualities, 1.1 Symbolic meaning attributed to natural objects or facts" (Oxford Dictionaries 2017). The latter of these definitions within the discipline of rock art is frequently used as an approach in its study. This symbolic approach often focuses on proposed neurophysiological and shamanistic properties of prehistoric rock art image or panel. The rock art is associated with a magical sphere, its purpose to aid and comprehend survival in the world surrounding the rock art location. It is an approach which focuses on the image itself. It can often rely on questionable, secondhand, ethnographic sources to interpret prehistoric rock art. Chippindale and Nash (2004:14) have stated that "practically no rock-art traditions continue into the present, and there are precious few of which there is a good ethnographic or enthnohistoric record...so for much prehistoric art, we have no basis for informed knowledge." In addition to the uncertainty which these sources offer, they will not reflect the rock art's changing past. Angus Quinlan (2000:101) has remarked, in response to a particular aspect of David Whitley's research, that "the uncritical use of ethnography to interpret prehistoric materials... seems to have portrayed Native American societies in North America as remarkably static" and that applying the same symbolic function to an image over vast periods of time creates the impression of a static culture, and one which would have held the same "...function and interpretation throughout that time." Images evolve and change to fit altering ideologies and worldviews, and often symbolic interpretations do not reflect this dynamic. The discourse of this can be seen with fluteplayer images, specifically in the American Southwest. Despite being a key element in rock art, and other media, for a significant period of time, the commonly associated function of this image is that of a fertility symbol (Slifer 2007:103–109). Other options are explored, such as the notion that he was a trader from Mexico or South America or an individual with spinal deformity (Slifer 2007:103; Slifer and Duffield 1994:18), but these are dismissed in favor of the idea that fluteplayer imagery in fact represents fertility. This idea has further been propelled by the mis-association with the kachina Kokopelli (Malotki 2000) and the deity's growing popularity. The fluteplayer could have represented many ideas over its vast time period, and implying that it is a fertility symbol limits its cultural significance and its ability to change to fit altering ideologies.

As a result of these altering ideologies, it becomes increasingly difficult to ascertain the original symbolic function of a rock art image, as seen with fluteplayer imagery. The changing symbolic functions will result in many meanings held by many different people, particularly from the descendants whose ancestors created the rock art. When commenting on the incorporation of rock art created prior to the formation of the Zuni tribe, Young (1988:239) identifies the complexity of expressions of Zuni ideology, stating that "... this by no means points to a neat network of common cultural meanings; the diversity of interpretations of imagery and reasons for the production of rock art reveal considerable individual variability of meaning as well." All rock art interpretations are subjective to the viewer and can be based on personal experiences which are reflected onto the image. This may result in multiple functions for a single image.

Young's research focuses on an indigenous culture, and as a result many ethical issues arise from the inquisitive questions which seek to establish a symbolic function. The subject matter may be sensitive in nature, or perhaps even sacred or religious. Although Young (1988:xv) was invited by the Zuni Tribal Council and Zuni Archaeological Program to conduct fieldwork, "...opinions within the community towards giving aid to outsiders vary considerably, and no one wants to be known as 'the person who said the wrong thing about Zuni'...I have heard strong criticism of those who have offered information to other 'Anglos'..." (Young 1988:xviii). The information which we seek may be sensitive in nature, and even if this knowledge is shared in confidence and trust, should we then publish it? Furthermore, researchers from differing cultures will not be able to truly understand the knowledge which they are given, as Donald Fixico has discussed. He states that western and Native American people think in opposing ways, linear and circular. Linear minds focus on rationalizing how something originates at different points, as intuition is omitted in favour of problem-solving and philosophy. It cannot deal with abstract thought (Fixico 2009:15). Circular is a broader way of thinking and "...assures that everyone understands, and that all is considered, thereby increasing the chance for harmony and balance in the community and with everything else" (Fixico 2009:15–16). As a result of these opposite ways of thinking, symbolic interpretations can become misunderstood, appropriated, and mis-associated as the rock art images become metaphorically removed from their original contexts.

Symbolic interpretations are primarily image-specific, and often this research fails to acknowledge the landscape, the cultural and natural features which surround a site and establish a context. This does not mean that the study of the rock art images themselves becomes invalid, as I will discuss later. There are instances where the surrounding area, often the immediate vicinity, is incorporated into the study of a site within an approach that focuses on symbolic interpretations. Again, Quinlan has noted this in his research, stating that "even when rock art and settlement co-occur, it is argued that the rock art was made by shamans when settlements were not in use by others..." (Quinlan and Woody 2003:374). In many cases the landscape is then viewed in relation to the proposed neurophysiological or shamanistic properties of the rock art sites, and in turn becomes associated with these functions. Focus should be given to the surrounding cultural landscape, which should then be assessed in relation to rock art sites without any prior assumptions or interpretations about proposed symbolic functions. This will allow an unbiased study of sites.

As rock art researchers we seem to want to know what these often ancient images mean. There is a sense of mysticism and allure which drives us to seek meaning—why it was created and to what purpose. Approaches within any discipline depend on the questions that one might wish to be asked and answered, and within rock art research we endeavor to know more about the images which present themselves to us. Symbolic approaches do not often answer these questions with enough strong evidence to support theories, and are subject to varying cultural perceptions. Symbolic interpretations are a direct, but often problematic, way of achieving this, and as a result they propose more open-ended than concluded answers.

Rock Art and Cultural Landscape

Rock art is a cultural element still found, in many situations, within its original site location. Although the landscape itself has altered and changed over periods of time, evidence can still be found of past cultures who once inhabited the area, and left imprints of their family, life, and society in many forms. As a result of this we can re-site rock art images back into their original context, establishing factual evidence regarding the placement of a site within a certain culture. Context is a key approach as it enables us to understand "the situation within which something exists or happens, and that can help explain it" (Cambridge Dictionary 2017). It allows us to understand the contributing factors surrounding the object of study, including the cultural landscape. Myrtle Shock has suggested that each context provides various social roles for the rock art. As a result, "...it is not possible to assign one global role to the art; rather, the specific contexts must be explored" (Shock 2007:86). Landscape approaches identify the surrounding cultural and natural features within the area of a rock art site and thus allow a context to be identified. The cultural landscape is key to providing an accurate study of rock art sites. Rock art itself is an element which forms part of the cultural landscape, and as such the formal properties of rock art should be assessed in relation to its environment, and not just as a single entity. Chippindale and Nash (2004:14) believe that this type of formal information, as they term it, can be obtained by looking at the images themselves, and their relationship to each other, the landscape, and any associated archaeological features. In particular, with my own study of rock art fluteplayer imagery, I am keen to establish whether there is a pattern of placement between certain features and types of fluteplayer depiction. In turn this may allow us to understand why there are altering variations in fluteplayer imagery. Recent research has found that some rock art references plants and animals found within the site's location

(Bailey 2016:135), further evidence of the connection between the image and landscape. The study of the image itself is not an invalid approach, but a focus on the form, the style, and features of rock art, which is then contextualized within the cultural landscape, will allow a broader and unbiased study.

Due to natural erosion, vandalism, and human recycling of materials, many cultural features are now no longer visible to the naked eye. Whole communities can be hidden beneath the surface of the earth, while a cave dwelling may not exhibit obvious signs of human habitation. Chaco Canyon as visitors see it today appears as a peaceful and tranquil location, dominated by the substantial, and stabilized, Great Houses of the Ancestral Puebloan era. During its occupation by the Ancestral Puebloans, however, the canyon was also filled with smaller habitation sites, fields, roads, shrines, and many other cultural features. Fajada Butte (Figure 2) once overlooked a whole community (Huang 2013) with a Great Kiva and road located nearby (Van Dyke 2008:23, Figure 2.4), all now not immediately visible. The locations of these cultural features need to be established so than an accurate context can be represented. Due to the notoriously difficult nature of dating rock art, establishing a precise date and thus placing it within a specific context can prove problematic.

Rock Art is difficult to date: there is no simpler way of saying it. Although it has been possible to establish general dates for some sites, efforts for others have been unsuccessful, both scientifically and stylistically. As a result, we are unable to determine whether the rock art is contemporaneous with its surrounding cultural landscape or pre- or postdates it. Rock art is, however, often incorporated into its changing landscape and so, "...even if rock art predates settlement activity it could still have been incorporated in the ritual practices of subsequent groups whatever their cultural relationship to the art's original makers. Monuments of the past are often reused and given novel cultural meanings and social roles despite discontinuities in use" (Quinlan and Woody 2003:376). Unless firm dating evidence is presented which will make this notion void, rock art would have been incorporated into the changing cultural landscape. The perhaps altering contexts will reflect the placement of rock art within changing ideologies.

Contexts will allow for each image to be treated individually and to ascertain its placement in society and the audience with which it was intended to communicate (Quinlan and Woody 2003:374). Quinlan's Great Basin research has demonstrated an association between rock art and habitation sites, and as a result "this domestic association opens the possibility that rock art's intended audience and use was not restricted to hunters or vision questers; potentially a large section of the cultural group viewed and interacted with it regularly" (Quinlan and Woody 2003:375). Rock art was, and is, a form of communication. Although we will never know its symbolic functions, we can view how it was placed within a culture to interact with the surrounding cultural landscape and the peoples who inhabited it.

Establishing individual contexts for rock art sites will allow us to begin to see how it was placed to interact with its cultural landscape and peoples. It will not limit our understanding of the image by applying one universal function to them all; instead, it will broaden our knowledge and allow us to view the many instances in which rock art can be found.

Cultural Landscape: Fluteplayers and Chaco Canyon

As previously discussed, fluteplayer imagery has been interpreted as a fertility symbol and as such it has been assumed that its primary task was to function in relation to this role. This paramount association has hindered the study of the fluteplayer image, including those depicted in rock art, limiting its cultural significance. Initial research from publically available sources place three fluteplayer depictions in Chaco Canyon in three varying contexts. It must be stressed that research is still ongoing and as a result conclusive an-

Figure 2. Fajada Butte in Chaco Canyon.

swers have yet to be drawn, but it is being used here to illustrate the use of a landscape approach. In addition, for the protection of the sites I will not disclose place names of locations, either through text or supporting photographic figures.

One site consists of four fluteplayers at various locations on the panel, two of which are shown in Figure 3. They are all depicted with a humpback, one with a headdress (I am using the term headdress to describe the varying depictions of adornments found on the heads of fluteplayers). They are located at the top of a talus slope in a south rincon, placed high upon the cliff face. The cliff supported the structure of a small house site (Figure 4) which consisted of approximately twenty ground floor rooms and three kivas (Lister and Lister 1981:251). It has been dated from the late eleventh century to mid twelfth century, a period crossing into the Late Bonito period (Van Dyke 2004:414). During this period Chaco Canyon was renewing its importance as a center place after droughts and competition from locations such as Aztec had led to the Chacoan people losing faith in the established leaders (Van Dyke 2004:413–414). The incorporation or creation of the fluteplayers during this Late Bonito phase reflects its inclusion and placement within the altering ideology. The placement of the rock art panels is evidence that the fluteplayers were either located above the roof line or inside the house, and were placed in direct relation to the inhabitants who were following the altered ideology in the canyon. Although accessible to the inhabitants, the placement of the fluteplayer in such close proximity to the house initially suggests a restricted communication solely with the occupants, as opposed to the wider community.

Another site located on the south side of the canyon, near the mouth of a rincon, comprises numerous fluteplayers located over three primary boulders. Six fluteplayers can be found on a large boulder (Figure 5) situated behind a lower one. They are located high upon the boulder face, all depicting humped backs and headdresses which resemble the tail feathers of a bird. The boulder immediately in front depicts two fluteplayers at opposing ends. Each is shown with a headdress similar to those mentioned above. The smaller fluteplayer on the left (Figure 6a) has a hump, while the larger one to the right (Figure 6b) also has a hump but is eroded from the waist down. Other fluteplayer images have been recorded, but were not visible during the fieldwork, and as such I cannot comment on their relationship with the landscape. An additional boulder to the right of the location depicts one fluteplayer (Figure 7), also with a humped back and headdress. Small house sites can be found on the ridges and hills surrounding the mouth of the rincon (Vivian and Hilpert 2012:291–292). It has also been suggested that dune farming may have possibly been undertaken (Vivian and Hilpert 2012:119). The dunes are visible directly from the site, as is a view south through the rincon. The precise location of the small house sites and the dating still need to be determined, but these fluteplayers are located within a landscape with potential agricultural affiliations. As before, they are placed within the location of small house sites; however, they do not seem to have been placed in a direct manner, initially suggesting that their placement was not primarily for the occupants of one house, but for a wider community.

In some instances, a certain feature of importance may suggest restriction on a site, as opposed to a direct

Figure 3. Detail of the panel above the small house site, showing two of the four fluteplayers.

Figure 4. The small house site at the base of the cliff.

Figure 5. The large fluteplayer panel (detail). Four of six fluteplayers are visible in this view.

Figure 6. Fluteplayers on the smaller boulder.

to the importance of the solstice marker and absence, as so far determined, of small house sites within the area. A Late Bonito Great House can be found in close proximity, but it is unknown if its construction was ever completed (Van Dyke 2008:218). Pecked basins and a bedrock grinding feature are located on the west side of the boulder; both are similar to those found in Mesa Verde (Malville 2008:68–69). The metate does not necessarily suggest a domestic use for the site, as it may have been used to grind paint pigment or food for other activities. Ritual and domestic activities were embodied as one, and as such there was no distinction between the two (personal communication, Ruth Van Dyke 2013). The associated cultural features at this site suggest a degree of restriction, at least during part of Chaco Canyon's Ancestral Puebloan occupation. The fluteplayer, if this theory is proven correct, would have communicated within a restricted area with socially select peoples.

All three of these fluteplayers, although defined by their characterizing features, reveal varying contexts and placements within Chacoan society. Further research will build upon these and allow us to see the further instances in which the fluteplayer can be found. Is it, for example, found in groups, pairs, or a single depiction by certain features? Our three examples show that scattered group depictions may be found in relation to habitation structures, while the single depiction may have been void of these. Is there a specific feature with which the image is frequently found? Do the flutes themselves point towards specific features which may suggest further interaction? By building an accurate understanding of fluteplayer cultural placements we can begin to establish the varying situations in which it might be found. This will highlight the individuality of each rep-

physical barrier. One fluteplayer is located to the east on a boulder (Figure 8) that depicts a solstice marker on a northeast face (Malville 2008:65). The marker has a direct line of sight to the solstice marker on Fajada Butte and may have aided the depiction of the larger spiral there (Malville 2008:66–67). Although there is no direct physical barrier, I currently think the area may have been restricted to all but a few people due

Figure 7. Fluteplayer on the third boulder in the complex.

Figure 8. Fluteplayer on a separate boulder that also features a solstice marker, possibly indicating a restricted area.

resentation and its wider relationship to the Chacoan people and culture.

Conclusion

Symbolic interpretations which seek to establish the functions of rock art images are problematic, and hinder the study of the subject. The approach often uses ethnographic sources to support theories on prehistoric and ancient rock art, for which there are few, if any, reliable sources. It also presents the idea of a static culture when the same symbolic function is applied to a rock art image over vast periods of time. The living descendants from indigenous cultures are most likely to have a deeper connection to and understanding of their past, and are well informed to provide explanations based on symbolic interpretations. The importance of these should not be dismissed, but should be approached with respect from western scholars with an awareness of the ethical issues and cultural understanding surrounding them. Primarily, however, symbolic interpretations fail to acknowledge the landscape surrounding a site. Rock art is still situated in its original location, and by recreating the context of these landscapes we can see the contributing factors surrounding its placement. Rock art is an element within the cultural landscape, and as such it should be viewed in relation to it. Symbolic functions limit the understanding of rock art images by applying one universal function to them all. Landscape approaches allow the images to be viewed individually, and in doing so we broaden our knowledge of their placement within society and the cultural landscape. Knowledge on fluteplayer images in Chaco Canyon, for example, already offers a greater understanding of their placement and interaction as a result of looking at their cultural contexts. Although this paper has focused on examples based in North America, it can, and should, be used at sites worldwide. Its application at locations within America is used to provide examples for the greater knowledge it can provide.

References Cited

Bailey, Jonathan (ed.)
  2016 *Rock Art: A Vision of a Vanishing Culture*. Johnson Books, Boulder, Colorado.

Cambridge Dictionary
  2017 Cambridge Dictionary (online dictionary). Cambridge University Press, Cambridge, United Kingdom. Electronic document, http://dictionary.cambridge.org/dictionary/english/context, accessed April 4, 2017.

Chippindale, Christopher, and George Nash
  2004 *The Figured Landscapes of Rock-Art: Looking at Pictures in Place*. Cambridge University Press, Cambridge, United Kingdom.

Fixico, Donald L.
  2009 *The American Indian Mind in a Linear World*. Routledge Press, Abingdon, United Kingdom. Reprint edition, original publication 2003, Hawthorn Press, Binghamton, United Kingdom.

Huang, Jennifer K.
  2013 Assessing Relationships Between the Rock Art Imagery and Architecture of Fajada Butte, Chaco Canyon. In The Dynamic Duo of Chaco Rock Art: Papers in Honor of Jane Kolber and Donna Yoder, edited by Rex Weeks Jr. and Jennifer Huang, pp. 66–68. *International Federation of Rock Art Organizations 2013 Abstracts*, Section 8. American Rock Art Research Association, Glendale, Arizona.

Lister, Robert H., and Florence C. Lister
　1981 *Chaco Canyon: Archaeology and Archaeologists.* University of New Mexico Press, Albuquerque.

Malotki, Ekkehart
　2000 *Kokopelli: The Making of an Icon.* University of Nebraska Press, Lincoln.

Malville, J. McKim
　2008 *Guide to Prehistoric Astronomy in the Southwest.* Revised edition. Johnson Books, Colorado.

Oxford Dictionaries
　2016 Oxford Living Dictionaries: English (online dictionary). Oxford University Press, Oxford, United Kingdom. Electronic document, https://en.oxforddictionaries.com/definition/symbolism, accessed April 3, 2017.

Quinlan, Angus R.
　2000 The Ventriloquists Dummy: A Critical Review of Shamanism and Rock Art in Far Western North America. *Journal of California and Great Basin Anthropology* 22(1):92–108.

Quinlan, Angus R., ed.
　2007 *Great Basin Rock Art: Archaeological Perspectives.* University of Nevada Press, Reno.

Quinlan, Angus R., and Alanah Woody
　2003 Marks of Distinction: Rock Art and Ethnic Identification in the Great Basin. *American Antiquity* 68(2):372–390.

Shock, Myrtle P.
　2007 A Regional Settlement System Approach to Petroglyphs: Application to the Owyhee Uplands, Southeastern Oregon. In *Great Basin Rock Art: Archaeological Perspectives*, edited by Angus R. Quinlan, pp. 69–91. University of Nevada Press, Reno.

Slifer, Dennis
　2007 *Kokopelli: The Magic, Mirth, and Mischief of an Ancient Symbol.* Gibbs Smith, Salt Lake City, Utah.

Slifer, Dennis, and James Duffield
　1994 *Kokopelli: Flute Player Images in Rock Art.* Ancient City Press, Santa Fe, New Mexico.

Van Dyke, Ruth M.
　2004 Memory, Meaning and Masonry: The Late Bonito Chacoan Landscape. *American Antiquity* 69(3):413–431.
　2008 *The Chaco Experience: Landscape and Ideology at the Center Place.* School for Advanced Research Press, Santa Fe, New Mexico.

Vendome-Gardner, Charlotte
　2013 *The Fluteplayer of Chaco Canyon.* MRes Dissertation, University of Plymouth, United Kingdom.

Vivian, R. Gwinn, and Bruce Hilpert
　2012 *The Chaco Handbook: An Encyclopedic Guide.* Second Edition. University of Utah Press, Salt Lake City.

Young, M. Jane
　1988 *Signs from the Ancestors: Zuni Cultural Symbolism and Perceptions of Rock Art.* University of New Mexico Press, Albuquerque.

Broad Distribution of Flower World Imagery in Hohokam Petroglyphs

Janine Hernbrode and Peter Boyle

Examination of rock art at eight substantial sites in Southern Arizona indicates a widespread presence of imagery associated with the Flower World, an ancient Uto-Aztecan metaphor dating back thousands of years. We examined data and photographs from our recording projects at Tumamoc Hill, Sutherland Wash, and Cocoraque Butte as well as at five additional sites recorded by others. The Flower World Complex is clearly evidenced at five of the sites. It is either not present or is equivocal at the three other sites. The five sites with Flower World imagery are all in the greater Tucson area, whereas the other three sites are distant from Tucson. Taken together, the data suggest a broad presence of the Flower World Complex among the Hohokam in Southern Arizona, but its expression varies across the landscape.

We recently reported that Flower World imagery is present among the Hohokam petroglyphs at two sites near Tucson, Arizona, the Sutherland Wash Rock Art District (Hernbrode and Boyle 2013) and Cocoraque Butte (Hernbrode and Boyle 2016). This finding is significant because previous work suggested that there is little archaeological evidence for the presence of Flower World imagery among the Hohokam prior to A.D. 1300 (Hays-Gilpin and Hill 1999). Hays-Gilpin and Hill (1999) examined the material culture data for the American Southwest and concluded that Flower World imagery is widespread in the Southwest after A.D. 1300, but prior to that was limited to the Mimbres area, Chaco Canyon, and a few Kayenta sites, all of which are outside the Hohokam culture area. As was emphasized by Jane Hill (1992) in her original paper regarding the Flower World, it is surprising that evidence of Flower World imagery is lacking among the Hohokam because the Flower World is a component of the belief system of their modern descendants, the O'odham.

Based on datable surface ceramics, we believe both the Sutherland Wash and Cocoraque sites predate A.D. 1300. Specifically, ceramics at Sutherland Wash date primarily to the middle Rincon Phase of the Hohokam Sedentary Period (A.D. 950–1000). Most ceramics at Cocoraque Butte date to the Tanque Verde Phase of the Hohokam Classic Period (A.D. 1150–1300). The purpose of this study was to assess the pervasiveness of Flower World imagery in petroglyphs at Southern Arizona rock art sites prior to A.D. 1300.

Background

The Flower World is an ancient and enduring component of a belief system that is still present in the songs of 30 tribes ranging across a wide area from Panama on the South, encompassing Mexico and the American Southwest to near San Francisco and the Puebloan areas of Arizona and New Mexico (Hays-Gilpin and Hill 1999; Hill 1992). Estimates for its antiquity, based

Janine Hernbrode
Independent Researcher

Peter Boyle
Independent Researcher

on linguistic commonalities within the Uto-Aztecan language family (Hill 1992), suggest that the belief may be as old as 7,000 to 9,000 years.

Songs about the Flower World describe a vibrant, sparkling, intensely chromatic spiritual landscape with flowers, brilliantly colored and particularly iridescent birds, butterflies, and dragonflies, as well as rainbows and sparkling features on the landscape (Sekaquaptewa and Washburn 2004; Hays-Gilpin with Sekaquaptewa 2006). People can bring forth this centered and peaceful place through prayer and hard work; simply viewing a flower or other beautiful chromatic display can evoke the Flower World (Hays-Gilpin with Sekaquaptewa 2006). Although evidence for the Flower World exists primarily in songs, it is also a complex of visual imagery, defined as images of chromatic elements like flowers, birds, butterflies and rainbows that are depicted on ceramics and other material culture, including Kiva murals and petroglyphs. These images, collectively termed the Flower World Complex, serve as visual metaphors for the Flower World (Hays-Gilpin and Hill 1999; Sekaquaptewa and Washburn 2004, 2006, 2010).

Although there are commonalities in how the Flower World Complex is represented across cultural groups, there are interesting variations in the cultural associations. The Flower World is widely perceived as a chromatic spiritual landscape, but in some cultures it has more specific associations as well. For example, in some cases it is also connected with specifically male activities such as warfare among the Aztecs and hunting among the O'odham and the Yaqui (Hays-Gilpin and Hill 2000).

We were interested to learn if the presence of Flower World Imagery in the Hohokam area prior to 1300 was unique to the two sites we had studied previously or was more widespread, perhaps suggesting that the Flower World was an important component of Hohokam ideology. We have approached this by examining photographs, drawings, and recorded data from a number of Hohokam petroglyph sites. We examined a total of eight sites; our analysis of the total data set suggests to us that the Flower World Complex was present at a number of sites in Southern Arizona but not all Hohokam petroglyph sites.

Methods

The present paper examines the rock art at eight sites that span much of the Hohokam culture area spatially and temporally. We were personally involved in the recording of three of the sites: Sutherland Wash (Hernbrode and Boyle 2013), Cocoraque Butte (Hernbrode and Boyle 2016) and Tumamoc Hill (Hartmann and Boyle 2013). The other five sites were recorded, or at least photographed, by others; reports are available for three of these (Martynec and Martynec 2008; Wallace and Holmlund 1986; Wright 2011, 2014). We personally examined photographs, drawings and raw data, both published information and other sources that were made available to us by the researchers who studied the sites. These five sites include: Picacho Point (Henry Wallace); South Mountain (Aaron Wright); Charlie Bell Well (Rick and Sandy Martynec); Signal Hill (Allen Dart); and Webb Petroglyph Site (Robin Rutherfoord). We used this information to assess the presence of the Flower World Complex at each of the five sites studied by others, using the same methodology we used at the sites we recorded personally (details in Hernbrode and Boyle, 2016). Site numbers are listed in the end note.[1]

Following Hays-Gilpin and Hill (1999), we quantified the incidence of images that realistically depict flowers, images of related chromatic elements like butterflies and birds, and abstract images thought to represent flowers based on ethnographic information. Representational images of flowers include three major forms: circles with zigzag edges, concentric circles with spokes, and images with obvious petals. Also included in representational flowers are images at several sites that appear flower-like but do not fit neatly into these categories. The other representational imagery relating to the Flower World quantified in this study included images of birds and butterflies. Abstract images of flowers suggested by the ethnographic literature (Hays-Gilpin and Hill 1999) that were quantified in this study include rayed circles, rayed circles with a central dot, and asterisks.

We chose the above list of element types as core imagery, i.e., imagery that we believe most unambiguously and consistently is indicative of the Flower World and also is discernable in petroglyphs. We chose not to include certain images associated with the Flower World by Hays-Gilpin and Hill (1999) because they are less clearly associated with the Flower World in rock art contexts. Rainbows are part of the Flower World Complex enumerated in the analysis by Hays-Gilpin and Hill (1999). This works well in kiva murals, for example, where rainbows are depicted as arcs, concentric circles, and sometimes as parallel lines where they are recognizable because of their coloration and context. Hohokam rock art does not provide coloration nor do these element forms appear in a context that suggests rainbows. We, therefore, have not included rainbows in our analysis.

We have also not included divided circles and circles with a central dot in our analysis. Based on ethnographic information, both have been interpreted as abstract representations of flowers (Hays-Gilpin and Hill 1999; Hays-Gilpin with Sekaquaptewa 2006; Hays-Gilpin et al. 2010; Sekaquaptewa and Washburn 2006). Both forms are highly abstract and neither resemble flowers, making us entirely dependent on the ethnographic interpretation. In contrast, the other abstract forms (rayed circles, rayed circles with a central dot, and asterisks) are suggestive of flowers without being truly representational. All three are supported by ethnographic information as well and thus have been included in our analysis.

Results

The location of the eight sites studied is shown in Figure 1. The sites are distributed across much of the Hohokam culture area in Southern Arizona. Several sites are in or near Tucson, whereas others are located to the north near Phoenix and to the west near Ajo. As will be described further below, the dating of rock art at these sites ranges from the early portion of the Hohokam Classic Period (i.e., Tanque Verde phase, A.D. 1150–1300) back in time to the Late Archaic/Early Agricultural Period (2100 B.C.–A.D. 50). It should be noted that Archaic rock art motifs are believed to persist in some locations past the end of the Archaic Period and into the Hohokam sequence, until perhaps as late as A.D. 800 (Wallace and Holmlund 1986).

Clear evidence of the Flower World Complex was found at five of the sites studied, but not at the other three. Further, there is some degree of site-to-site variation in the details of how the Flower World is depicted.

Our results from the eight sites are summarized in Figure 2 and Table 1. The graph (Figure 2) plots the number of Flower World petroglyph elements per one thousand glyphs at each of the eight sites. We present the data this way because the sites studied vary substantially in size

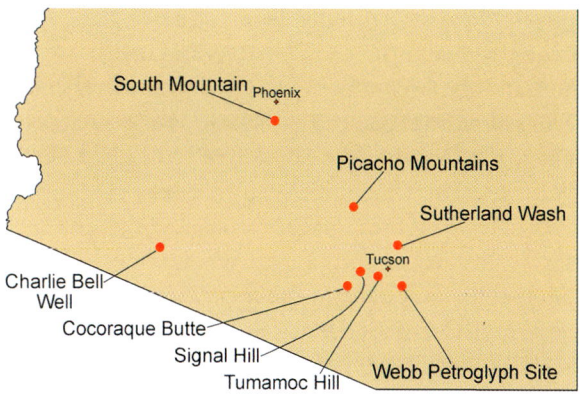

Figure 1. Map showing location of sites discussed in this paper.

with the number of glyphs ranging from 232 to 3,251. The graph, therefore, presents data in a fashion that facilitates cross-site comparisons of the relative frequency of motifs. The table, in contrast, summarizes the data as absolute numbers, i.e., element counts.

Within each bar of Figure 2, there is a breakout of representational flowers in blue; other related imagery (butterflies and birds) in red, and abstract depictions of flowers in green. There is wide variation in the number of Flower World elements, ranging from less than 10 per thousand to nearly 70 per thousand. But, as can

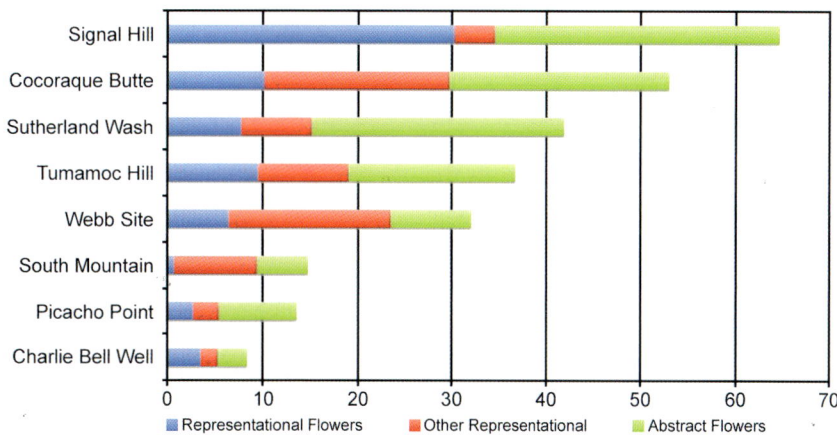

Figure 2. Histogram showing the proportion of core Flower World glyphs expressed as the number of Flower World glyphs per thousand total glyphs. Representational flowers are shown in blue, other representational Flower World imagery in red, and abstract images of flowers in green.

Table 1. Frequency of Core Flower World Imagery at Eight Sites Studied.

	Representational Flowers	Other Representational Imagery	Abstract Flowers	Total Core Flower World Imagery	Total Glyphs at Site
Signal Hill	7	1	7	15	232
Cocoraque	19	37	44	100	1,888
Sutherland	25	24	87	136	3,251
Tumamoc	7	7	13	27	734
Webb Site	3	8	4	15	469
South Mountain	2	26	16	44	3,005
Picacho Point	3	3	9	15	1,115
Charlie Bell Well	8	3	7	18	2,281

be seen, the data naturally divide into two groups; five sites with greater than 30 Flower World images per one thousand glyphs and three sites with considerably fewer. Based on the quantity of Flower World images, we believe the top five sites, should be considered Flower World sites, by which we mean that they contain sufficient Flower World imagery to suggest that the complex is present in addition to whatever other ritual components may exist in the sites. These sites include Signal Hill, Cocoraque Butte, Sutherland Wash, Tumamoc Hill, and Webb Petroglyph Site. We do not have sufficient evidence to suggest that the bottom three sites should be included in this group (Picacho Point, South Mountain, and Charlie Bell Well).

Figure 2 reveals commonalities across sites in terms of the incidence of realistic and abstract flower imagery. The five sites with the largest proportion of Flower World imagery all have a significant number of representational flowers. Of these, four have a fairly similar proportion of representational flower images, ranging from 6 to 10 per thousand glyphs. However, the proportion at Signal Hill is approximately triple the next highest site. The second commonality is that all five of these sites have a substantial concentration of abstract flowers. In all cases, the proportion of abstract flowers equals or exceeds that of representational flowers. Thus, all five sites that we propose as Flower World sites have a significant quantity of both representational and abstract images of flowers.

Inspection of Figure 2 suggests that there may be a difference among the sites in the relative frequency of other representational core imagery, i.e., birds and butterflies. However, this perception may not be correct. Signal Hill has the smallest proportion of other representational imagery at 4.3 glyphs per thousand. However, Signal Hill is a small site with a total of only 232 glyphs; in actual element counts Signal Hill has only one glyph in the other representational category (Table 2). But this needs to be put into perspective. We consider Sutherland Wash as a "type site" for Flower World imagery at Hohokam petroglyph sites. At Sutherland Wash, which is the largest site studied, there are 7.4 other representational images per 1,000 glyphs. If we use this as a standard, we would only expect to see two such images at Signal Hill. Thus, in this case we have a problem with a small sample size and should be cautious about interpreting apparent differences in the distribution of motifs.

Taken together, in our view, the data presented in Figure 2 and Table 1 suggest that five of the eight sites studied have a sufficient quantity of images representing the Flower World to consider those sites as Flower World sites. All five have significant proportions of both representational and abstract images of flowers and at least some other representational Flower World imagery.

South Mountain and 94.4% of the elements at Picacho Point (Wallace and Holmlund 1986) are classified as Hohokam, as are the five sites with a significant amount of Flower World imagery. Representational flower imagery is scant at both sites, as is total core imagery. We do not believe there is sufficient evidence in either case to suggest that the rock art assemblage reflects a belief in the Flower World.

Charlie Bell Well has the lowest incidence of Flower World imagery and relatively few realistic images of flowers. Unlike the other sites studied, Charlie Bell Well is largely an Archaic site, although it has some Hohokam rock art as well (Martynec and Martynec 2008; Schaafsma 1980). Archaic rock art, and specifically the Western Archaic Tradition (Hedges 1982; Wallace and Holmlund 1986), is characterized mostly by abstract and geometric forms and, thus, representational imagery is rather rare. Martynec and Martynec (2008) found that only 2.5% of the imagery at Charlie Bell Well could be called representational, i.e., anthropomorphs and various zoomorphs including insects, snakes, birds, and quadrupeds. Given this, it is not surprising that there are relatively few representational flowers or other representational core images at this site. Using the methodology we have employed in this analysis, it is not appropriate to conclude that Charlie Bell Well is a Flower World site. However, we must leave this possibility open given the preponderance of archaic imagery at this site and seek alternative methods to assess this question at sites that predate the Hohokam. We think this is an important question because the Flower World belief system spans millennia (Hill 1992) and one would expect some degree of continuity over time.

Figures 3 to 5 present examples of the Flower World Imagery enumerated in Figure 2 and Table 1. Other examples can be found in Hernbrode and Boyle (2013; 2016). Here, we present images that have not been published in the literature previously, including images of glyphs from sites for which no published reports are available. Photographs of petroglyphs that we consider to be representational flowers, i.e., circles with zigzag edges, concentric circles with spokes and images with obvious petals are in Figure 3. Interestingly, the flower with petals (Figure 3a) closely resembles

Figure 3. Three types of representational flowers from various sites: (a) two examples in the same panel at Signal Hill; on the left a flower with petals and on the far right a flower formed by concentric circles with spokes—middle rayed circle with a central dot is an abstract form of a flower; (b) a flower with zigzag edges from Tumamoc Hill; (c) an array of interconnected flowers with petals from the Webb Petroglyph Site; (d) a panel with two Flower World elements, both concentric circles with spokes from Sutherland Wash.

Figure 4. Examples of other representational imagery included in the Flower World Complex: (a) an image of a bird from Tumamoc Hill; (b) a panel with several images of butterflies from the Webb Petroglyph Site

Figure 5. Examples of abstract images included in this analysis which most resemble actual flowers: (a) a rayed circle with a central dot located at Tumamoc Hill; (b) a panel with two rayed circles from Signal Hill; (c) an elaborate asterisk from Charlie Bell Well.

the clan symbol used by the Hopi Squash Blossom clan (Russell and Wright 2009). Examples of other representational images depicting chromatic elements of the Flower World Complex, birds and butterflies, are pictured in Figure 4. Figure 5 shows examples of images that are abstract, yet flower-like. Ethnographic information suggests these forms represent flowers (Hays-Gilpin and Hill 1999). Examples of desert flowers that resemble the petroglyphs discussed in this paper are presented in Figure 6.

The map in Figure 7 has a circle enclosing the five sites with clear evidence of the Flower World belief. As can be seen, the five sites cluster in the Tucson area. In our limited sample, we found scant evidence for the Flower World expressed in the sites more distant from Tucson. This pattern suggests the possibility that the importance of the Flower World, or at least its manner of expression, varied geographically among the Hohokam.

Further work is needed to determine if Flower World imagery in rock art is prevalent beyond the Tucson Area. We have personally observed such imagery at one site along the Gila River but have not had the opportunity to quantify the frequency. Ken Hedges (personal communication 2017) has observed a significant incidence of Flower World imagery at sites he has photographed southeast of Phoenix. Clearly there is a cluster of Flower World sites near Tucson. Future quantitative work at additional sites beyond the Tucson area will be needed to determine if the complex of imagery occurs elsewhere.

Discussion

Taken together, the evidence presented in this study suggests to us

Figure 6. Desert flowers resemble images discussed in this paper: (a) Calliandra eriophylla *(fairy duster), strikingly similar to the form in Figure 5c; (b)* Machaeranthera canescens *(tansy aster), similar in form to rayed circles and rayed circles with central dot as in Figures 3a and 5b; (c)* Opuntia sp. *(prickly pear cactus), possibly depicted by rayed concentric circles with central dot as in Figure 5a—note red radiating lines in the outer petals; (d)* Tithonia sp. *(seed-maturing sunflower), resembling glyphs having circles with zigzag edges as in Figure 3b—note that outer "petals" (technically rays in the case of compound flowers) have fallen off; (e)* Cereus giganteus *(saguaro cactus), resembling spoked flower glyphs such as the one shown in the upper portion of Figure 3d.*

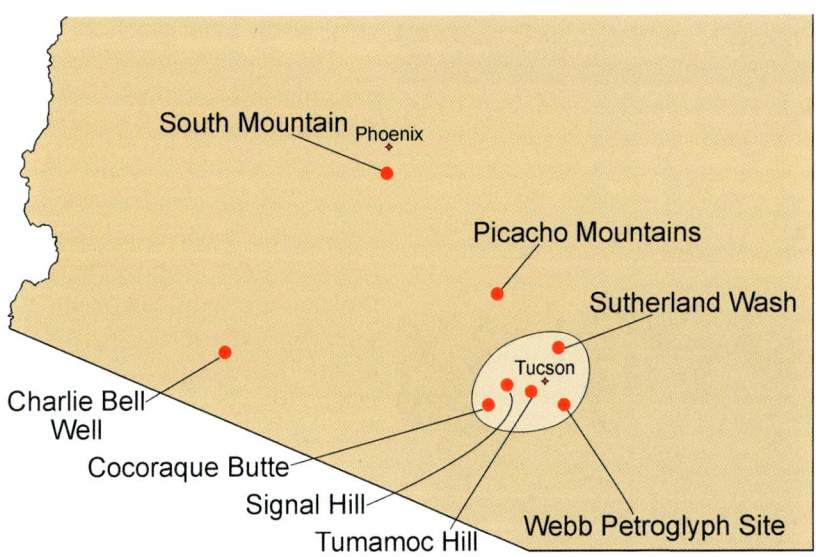

Figure 7. Map showing location of sites discussed in this paper; the circle encloses those sites with a significant amount of Flower World imagery.

that the idea of a Flower World was widespread among the Hohokam. It may not have been universal or at least not universally emphasized in the same way. In addition to possible regional variation, there appears to be at least some local variation in how the Flower World was depicted. Among the five sites that we have classified as Flower World sites, the proportion of total core imagery varies by a factor of about two. Most striking is Signal Hill, which differs from the other four sites in that it has both more total core imagery and three times more representational flowers than any other site.

This suggests that the Hohokam ideology was not a monolithic belief system, replicated across the culture, but an ideology adaptable to the needs and desires of people in each region. This way of thinking is similar to that of Marit Munson who compared Rio Grande rock art among villages. She proposed that the geographic diversity in rock art suggests that different settlements chose the iconography that was most meaningful for their particular location (Munson 2011). Such variation is quite consistent with our understanding of Hohokam social structure prior to A.D. 1150. Based on rock art evidence, Aaron Wright (2011, 2014) has suggested that during Pre-Classic Hohokam times, religious knowledge was inclusive and participatory in nature, rather than the province of an elite group. This assertion is consistent with the landscapes of the sites we have recorded where there appear to be open areas in close proximity to the petroglyphs, areas suitable for large gatherings and social interaction.

Before the beginning of the Classic Period (A.D. 1150) Hohokam lifeways, beliefs, and artistic perception are strongly linked to Mesoamerica (Nelson et al. 2015; McGuire 2011; McGuire and Villalpando 2007). Many artifacts connect the Hohokam to West Mexico, including copper bells, macaws, plaques and mirrors, shell bracelets, and shell trumpets (Nelson et al. 2015) leading some researchers (e.g., McGuire 2011) to suggest that the Hohokam area was the northernmost extension of Mesoamerican influence in the Pre-Classic Period. Hays-Gilpin and Hill (2000), based on linguistic analyses, suggest that the Flower World ideology moved to the Southwest from Mesoamerica with Proto Uto-Aztecan speakers and agriculture.

Six of the sites in this report show evidence of a significant Pre-Classic component. Using surface ceramics as a temporal indicator for Sutherland Wash, we believe it is primarily a Pre-Classic Hohokam site. Other sites in the study that also include Pre-Classic rock art are: Tumamoc Hill (Fish et al. 2013, Hartmann and Boyle 2013), Charlie Bell Well (Schaafsma 1980), Picacho Point (Wallace and Holmlund 1986), and South Mountain (Wright 2014). Signal Hill has similar elements and, based on this, is judged by the authors to date to the Pre-Classic Period as well.

The other two sites have a major early Classic Period component (A.D. 1150–1300). The beginning of the Hohokam Classic period is a time of great change where a transition occurs from inclusive and participatory religious expression to a period where religious elites conducted ceremonies on walled platform mounds (Wright 2014). However, this transition may not have occurred at all sites. Both Cocoraque Butte and Webb Petroglyph Site were used into the Classic period and both have Flower World imagery and a landscape suggesting inclusiveness. Perhaps the community using these sites continued to embrace the traditions of their culture during this time of social upheaval, possibly attracting others who did not want to conform to the emerging ideology evidenced in the platform mound communities. Both of these sites are located away from the Santa Cruz River basin where a number of Hohokam Classic Period mound sites were located (Fish and Fish 2007).

Another landscape consideration concerns the concentration of Flower World imagery within the sites. Although the distribution of Flower World imagery across the site is the same as it is for other petroglyphs, in the three sites we have recorded (Tumamoc Hill, Sutherland Wash, and Cocoraque Butte) there are small areas at each site where the incidence of Flower World imagery is more concentrated. This suggests an area of special use within those sites for a component of the belief system that includes the Flower World. We do not have sufficient data for the sites recorded by others to determine if this is also the case at those sites.

We cannot rule out the possibility that the sites lacking a significant amount of Flower World imagery in petroglyphs did, in fact, include the Flower World as a component of their belief system, but did so in a different way. For example, it is possible that they expressed the Flower World through song, a major and widespread way of evoking the Flower World (Hill 1992; Sekaquaptewa and Washburn 2004). Consistent with this way of thinking, Flower World imagery has been reported on Hohokam ceramics prior to A.D. 1300, especially at Snaketown, which is near South Mountain, one of the sites where there was scant Flower World evidence in petroglyphs (Hays-Gilpin and Hill 1999; Hernbrode and Boyle 2013).

We want to reiterate an important point discussed in Hernbrode and Boyle (2016). The core Flower World imagery at sites we interpret as Flower World sites totals three to seven percent of the elements. This raises the question of the appropriateness of offering an interpretation for this relatively modest number of images. A parallel situation has been reported in other media, such as ceramics and kiva murals, where Flower World imagery also occurs with relatively low frequency (Hays-Gilpin and Hill 2000). This is consistent with the suggestion of Hill (1992) and Hays-Gilpin and Hill (1999, 2000) that the Flower World should be viewed as a "part ideology" that can be combined with other ideas to form a belief system.

Last, we must raise a methodological consideration. Given the wide geographic distribution of the Uto-Aztecan language, one might expect to find Flower World imagery across a broad area and timespan. It is important, therefore, to have clear criteria for determining if the Flower World was a component of the local ideology. Abstract representations of flowers tabulated in this study include rayed circles, rayed circles with a central dot, and asterisks. Additionally, as discussed above, divided circles, and circles with a central dot may represent flowers. However, all of these are fairly common geometric forms in Hohokam rock art and may not always represent flowers. We suggest that these abstract forms should only be considered representations of flowers when realistic images of flowers are also present at the site. Thus, as discussed in the Methods section above, we believe that realistic and abstract flowers as well as other related imagery, such as birds and butterflies, must be present to interpret a particular site as a place where the Flower World was a component of the belief system.

Conclusion

The information presented in this paper substantially expands the evidence for the existence of the Flower World Complex among the Hohokam and, secondly, provides a basis to suggest that the Flower World was not universally expressed in the rock art across the Hohokam culture area. Flower World imagery is clearly evident at five sites in the Tucson area, but is much less evident in our sample of three sites located beyond the Tucson area. Further, the Flower World was depicted somewhat differently in the petroglyphs at the various sites where the idea of the Flower World seems to have been an important component of local ideology. Finally, the presence or absence of Flower World imagery in rock art does not address the existence of the complex in other aspects of Hohokam life such as music, dance, or oral literature.

Present-day peoples with ties to the ancient Hohokam continue to celebrate the Flower World. In southern Arizona, the O'odham do not produce petroglyphs depicting the Flower World, but they continue to evoke the Flower World in their songs (Hill 1992) and their ritual oratory (Barr 1975), thus continuing an ancient belief that extends back many millennia.

Note

1. Site numbers for the eight locations studied are: Charlie Bell Well AZ Y:12:2 (ASM); Cocoraque Butte AZ AA:15:3 (ASM); Picacho Point AZ AA:3:18 (ASM); Signal Hill AZ AA:12:63 (ASM); 108 South Mountain ASM site numbers listed in Wright 2011 Appendix D.1; Sutherland Wash AZ BB:9:66 (ASM), AZ BB:9:59 (ASM), AR-05-05-111, 112, 117, 118, 119, 120, 121, 122, 123, 146, 147, 169, 186, 208, 320, 359, 368, 370, 377, 378, 379, 382, 384, 386, 387, 389 (USFS); Tumamoc Hill AZ AA:16:6 (ASM); Webb Petroglyph Site AZ BB:14:21 (ASM).

Acknowledgments. Several individuals generously provided access to their unpublished data, photographs and other records, notably Henry Wallace, Rick and Sandy Martynec, Robin Rutherfoord, Allen Dart, Mary Kralovec, and the Cabeza Prieta National Wildlife Refuge. We are very grateful for their help.

Our perspective on the Flower World and aspects of the data presented here has benefited from correspondence with Kelley Hays-Gilpin. Henry Wallace, while not accepting some of our conclusions, has provided helpful insights as well. We thank both of them for helping us think through the anthropological implications of our rock art findings. We very much appreciate the comments of Ken Hedges on this paper and his offer to allow us to review his many excellent photos of rock art sites in central Arizona.

We are also grateful for the dedication of Lance K. Trask to enhancing this paper with excellent maps, just as he has done for a number of other papers and presentations.

Photos: Janine Hernbrode, Peter Boyle, Table and Graph: Peter Boyle.

References Cited

Barr, Donald M.
1975 *Pima and Papago Ritual Oratory.* The Indian Historian Press, San Francisco.

Fish, Suzanne K., and Paul R. Fish
2007 *The Hohokam Millennium.* School for Advanced Research Press, Santa Fe.

Fish, Suzanne K., Paul R. Fish, Todd Pitezel, Gary Christopherson, James T. Watson, and Phillip O. Leckman
2013 Emerging Settlement Differentiation in Preceramic and Early Hohokam Villages on Tumamoc Hill. In *New Perspectives on the Rock Art and Prehistoric Settlement Organization of Tumamoc Hill, Tucson, Arizona*, edited by Gayle Harrison Hartmann and Peter C. Boyle, pp. 1–22. Arizona State Museum Archaeological Series 208. Arizona State Museum, University of Arizona, Tucson.

Hartmann, Gayle Harrison, and Peter C. Boyle
2013 Tumamoc Hill Rock Art Revisited: With a focus on Temporal Affiliation and Management. In *New Perspectives on the Rock Art and Prehistoric Settlement Organization of Tumamoc Hill, Tucson, Arizona*, edited by Gayle Harrison Hartmann and Peter C. Boyle, pp. 23–111. Arizona State Museum Archaeological Series 208. Arizona State Museum, University of Arizona, Tucson.

Hays-Gilpin, Kelley, and Jane H. Hill
1999 The Flower World in Material Culture: An Iconographic Complex in the Southwest and Mesoamerica. *Journal of Anthropological Research* 55(1):1–37.

Hays-Gilpin, Kelley, and Jane H. Hill
2000 The Flower World in Prehistoric Southwest Material Culture. In *The Archaeology of Regional Interaction*, edited by Michelle Hegmon, pp. 411–428. University Press of Colorado, Boulder.

Hays-Gilpin, Kelley, with Emory Sekaquaptewa
2006 Siitalpuva: "Through the Land Brightened with Flowers." *Plateau* 3(1):12–25

Hays-Gilpin, Kelley, Elizabeth A. Newsome, and Emory Sekaquaptewa
2010 Siitalpuva, "Through the Land Brightened with Flowers": Ecology and Cosmology in Mural and Pottery Painting, Hopi and Beyond. In *Painting the Cosmos: Metaphor and Worldview in Images from the Southwest Pueblos and Mexico*, edited by Kelley Hays-Gilpin and Polly Schaafsma, pp. 121–138. Museum of Northern Arizona Bulletin 67. Museum of Northern Arizona, Flagstaff.

Hedges, Ken
1982 Great Basin Rock Art Styles: A Revisionist View. In *American Indian Rock Art, Volumes 7–8*, edited by Frank G. Bock, pp. 205–211. American Rock Art Research Association, El Toro, California.

Hernbrode, Janine, and Peter Boyle
2013 Flower World Imagery in Petroglyphs: Hints of Hohokam Cosmology on the Landscape. In *American Indian Rock Art, Volume 40*, edited by Peggy Whitehead, pp. 1077–1092. International Rock Art Congress (IRAC) 2013 Proceedings. American Rock Art Research Association, Glendale, Arizona.

Hernbrode, Janine, and Peter Boyle
2016 Petroglyphs and Bell Rocks at Cocoraque Butte: Further Evidence of the Flower World Belief Among the Hohokam. In *American Indian Rock Art, Volume 42*, edited by Ken

Hedges, pp. 91–105. American Rock Art Research Association, San Jose, California.

Hill, Jane H.
1992 The Flower World of Old Uto-Aztecan. *Journal of Anthropological Research* 48(2):117–144.

McGuire, Randall H.
2011 Pueblo Religion and the Mesoamerican Connection. In *Religious Transformations in the Late Pre-Hispanic Pueblo World*, edited by Donna M. Glowacki and Scott Van Keuren, pp.23–49. University of Arizona Press, Tucson.

McGuire, Randall H., and Elisa Villalpando C.
2007 The Hohokam and Mesoamerica. In *The Hohokam Millennium*, edited by Suzanne K. Fish and Paul R. Fish, pp. 56–63. School for Advanced Research Press, Santa Fe, New Mexico.

Martynec, Rick, and Sandy Martynec
2008 Charlie Bell Canyon: Petroglyphs and the Archaic Presence. In *Fragile Patterns: The Archaeology of the Western Papagueria*, edited by Jeffrey H. Altschul and Adrianne G. Rankin, pp.329–346. SRI Press, Tucson.

Munson, Marit K.
2011 Iconography, Space, and Practice: Rio Grande Rock Art, AD 1150–1600. In *Religious Transformations in the Late Pre-Hispanic Pueblo World*, edited by Donna M. Glowacki and Scott Van Keuren, pp. 109–129. University of Arizona Press, Tucson.

Nelson, Ben A., Elisa Villalpando Canchola, Jose Luis Diaz, and Paul E. Minnis
2015 Prehispanic Northwest and Adjacent West Mexico, 1200 B.C.–A.D. 1400: An Inter-Regional Perspective. *Kiva* 81(1–2):31–61.

Russell, Will G., and Aaron M. Wright
2009 Footprints to the South: The Search for Proto-Hopi Clan Symbols in the South Mountains of Phoenix, Arizona. In *American Indian Rock Art, Volume 35*, edited by James D. Keyser, David A. Kaiser, George Poetschat, and Michael W. Taylor, pp. 43–60. American Rock Art Research Association, Phoenix, Arizona.

Schaafsma, Polly
1980 *Indian Rock Art of the Southwest*. School of American Research, Santa Fe, and University of New Mexico Press, Albuquerque.

Sekaquaptewa, Emory, and Dorothy Washburn
2004 They Go Along Singing: Reconstructing the Hopi Past from Ritual Metaphors in Song and Image. *American Antiquity* 69(3):457–486.

Sekaquaptewa, Emory, and Dorothy Washburn
2006 Metaphors of Meaning in Mural Paintings, Pottery, and Ritual Song. *Plateau* 3(1):26–47.

2010 Living in Metaphor: Hopi Traditions in Song and Image. In *Painting the Cosmos: Metaphor and World View in Images from the Southwest Pueblos and Mexico*, edited by Kelley Hays-Gilpin and Polly Schaafsma, pp. 139–177. Museum of Northern Arizona Bulletin 67.

Wallace, Henry D., and James P. Holmlund
1986 *Petroglyphs of the Picacho Mountains, South Central Arizona*. Anthropological Papers No. 6. Institute for American Research, Tucson, Arizona.

Wright, Aaron M.
2011 *Hohokam Rock Art, Ritual Practice, and Social Transformation in the Phoenix Basin*. Ph.D. Dissertation, Washington State University.

2014 *Religion on the Rocks: Hohokam Rock Art, Ritual Practice, and Social Transformation*. University of Utah Press, Salt Lake City.

Finding the Dog in Arizona Rock Art

Barbara J. Gronemann

This research begins with the arrival of the domesticated dog (Canis familiaris) *with people into North America about 14,000 years ago. Ethnographic information refers to early dogs and historic illustrations show some characteristics of these canines. To identify the dog among the many quadrupeds in rock art, diagnostic characteristics of the domesticated dog, the wolf* (Canis lupus), *and the coyote* (Canis latrans) *are presented along with photographs as aids to distinguish between these three canines in Arizona petroglyphs. Ethnographic research on early dogs in the Southwest and the ever-growing body of scientific research on dogs in the archaeological record help to round out the understanding of this early canine. Results of this research have brought about not only the recognition of dogs in rock art panels but also insights into previously unrecognized roles that they might have played for indigenous peoples.*

It is said that domesticated dogs were brought by the first Paleoindian people that migrated to North America (Allen 1920:439–440). Among the earliest migrating groups were people from the Altai region of southern Siberia. They crossed the Bering land/ice bridge nearly 14,000 years ago during the last glacial episode (Dulik et al. 2012:237). Whether these first people brought dogs cannot be demonstrated, but certainly some groups of early immigrants did, because "when Columbus touched shore, there were dogs over much of the two Americas and in many varieties" (Underhill 1953:11). The Early Europeans that came into America reported that most indigenous groups had dogs (Schwartz 1997).

Figures 1–3, from the mid-1800s, show indigenous peoples from California and Arizona with their dogs. Note how the dogs exhibit several of the listed characteristics in the canine identification chart (Table 1), as discussed further below.

In a chromolithograph published by Major William H. Emory in his 1857 *Report on the United States and Mexican Boundary Survey*, a Diegueño (Kumeyaay) family in southern California travels with a donkey and a dog (Figure 1). The dog in the lithograph is shown with a natural bobtail, a short upright tail that is caused by a mutated gene. Sometimes the tail is missing completely. The petroglyph dogs in Arizona rock art are frequently seen with the bobtail.

In his article "On the Indian Reservations," published in *The Century Magazine* in 1889, Frederic Remington illustrates the distribution of beef rations to Apaches at the San Carlos Agency. In the foreground is a dog, shown with a long drooping tail with a white tip (Figure 2).

In 1864, self-styled adventurer and explorer J. Ross Browne embarked on an extensive journey from the California coast through Arizona and Sonora, and ultimately to the silver fields of Nevada (Browne 1869). In southern Arizona he recorded his impression of a Pima village (Figure 3). In the fore-

Barbara J. Gronemann
Southwest Learning Sources, Inc.

Table 1. Canid Identification Chart (based on WDNR 2017 and Caninet 2009).

	Wolf – *Canis lupis*	Coyote – *Canis latrans*	Dog – *Canis familiaris*
Head	Large, long, blocky snout, low forehead	Long pointed snout and low forehead	Short, blocky snout, high forehead
Ears	Erect, rounded, and furry	Erect, pointed, and furry Large for his head size	Floppy or erect
Shoulder Height	27–33" from shoulder	20–22" from shoulder	10–32" from shoulder, few over 25"
Body Length	5–6 feet including tail 41–63 inches body only	3½–4½ feet including tail 30–34 inches body only	Highly variable
Chest and Legs	Narrow chest, legs close together	Narrow chest, legs close together	Often broad or barrel chest, legs spread apart
Tail when neutral	Held flaccid or out straight, no curve	Held flaccid or out straight, no curve	Tightly curled, corkscrew, bobtail, saber, sickle, wheel
Weight (adult)	50–100 lbs.	25–45 lbs.	5–105 lbs.

Canine Characteristics

Before the dog (*Canis familiaris*) can be recognized in Arizona rock art, a good knowledge of the physical characteristic of dogs and the other two canids, the wolf (*Canis lupis*) and the coyote (*Canis latrans*), is needed. The chart in Table 1 summarizes the physical characteristics of these three canids.

Most quadrupeds in the rock art are created in profile. Profile comparison of the three canids is especially important. The most significant differences between the three canids is the head and body size.

The wolf is usually larger than most dogs and the coyote. Notice how large the wolf's head is in Figure 4, and that the wolf's ears are short and rounded. The tail

Figure 2. Beef ration distribution, San Carlos Agency, drawing by Frederic Remington (1889:397).

Figure 1. A Diegueño family, chromolithograph by Arthur Schott (Emory 1857:facing p. 106).

Figure 3. A Pima village, drawing by J. Ross Browne (1864:108).

ground Browne includes two canines: one with a characteristic sickle-shaped dog's tail confronts another which, due to the carriage of its tail, we might wonder if it is not a coyote.

is held straight out from just below the back line (Figure 5). When the wolf's tail is neutral it hangs loosely down and has no true curl.

The coyote has a long narrow muzzle, broad pointed ears which are very large compared to its skull size, and long legs (Figure 6). The very definite claws are typically visible (Figure 6 inset) and the tail is carried out behind when running, hanging down when neutral.

Dogs have many variations of their body parts. Their ears are pointed or droopy and vary in size. A dog's tail has many shapes. It could be tightly curled, short and twisted like a corkscrew, bobtail, or no tail at all. Others may go up in a slight saber-like curve, or up in a semicircle in the shape of a sickle, or carried up and over the back and around resembling a wheel (Caninest

Figure 6. Coyote on the move, photo by Marty Murphy, Fermilab Today.[3] Inset: Coyote stretching (detail), photo by Eric Kilby (CC BY-SA 2.0 license).[4]

2009). These tail shapes are very diagnostic in finding the dog in Arizona rock art.

Ritual Significance of Dogs

White Dog Cave, a Basketmaker II Site in Northern Arizona, is well known for its two mummified dogs. One looks to be like a black-and-white terrier and the other resembles a small-size collie. What is important to note is that the smaller dog was buried with a woman and a baby, while the larger collie-like dog was buried with a man. The burial context suggests that the dogs were killed to accompany the man and woman after death, possibly to guide them to another world (Amsden 1949:62-65).

Early archaeologists did not pay much attention to dog remains unless it looked like they had been eaten. Today they are more concerned with dog burials. Dody Fugat, Assistant Curator at the Museum of Indian Arts and Culture/Laboratory of Anthropology in Santa Fe, has been keeping an ongoing record of dog burials, mostly concentrated in northwestern New Mexico and along the Arizona/New Mexico Border. She has almost 700 burials listed in which dogs have been buried alongside children and adults. She states that these animals were more than just pets, suggesting "that the dogs in the New World in the Southwest were used to escort people into the next world" (Casselman 2008:1).

Figure 4. Wilderness wolf. Photo by Pixel.la (CC0 1.0 license).[1]

Figure 5. Gray wolf. Photo by Idaho Department of Fish and Game.[2]

Dogs appear as shamanic spirit helpers in many traditions. Siberian and Eskimo shamans counted dogs among their spirit helpers (Balzer 1996:309; Eliade 1964:90; Zhukova 2014:99), as did Etchemin shamans in Maine (Haviland 2012:71–72). The Iroquois regarded dogs as important animal helpers with supernatural powers to assist not only shamans but also ordinary humans in times of difficulty (Martinelli 2012:29).

Canines in Arizona Rock Art

The petroglyph photo in Figure 7, was sent to me with the comment, "I would hesitate to call this a dog. Dogs do not usually have long claws". It is forgotten that canines do not retract their claws. They just wear down or, with pet dogs, they may be clipped. This petroglyph shows definite characteristics of a coyote. The claws are quite predominant. The claws of the wolf and coyote are very important for the capture of their prey. The tail is straight out. The body size is smaller than a wolf. The head shows ears that are large and pointed with a narrow pointed snout.

This drawing of a coyote in Figure 8 was replicated by Mariah Fox Housman from a very old Diné (Navajo) dry-painting or sandpainting of the Featherway ceremony. When comparing this drawing with the petroglyph in Figure 7, it is easy to see that their characteristics look very similar. The rock art coyote could be said to have most of the characteristics of the coyote drawn from a Navajo sandpainting. Notice that the tail of the rock art coyote and the sandpainting coyote goes straight out (Housman 1993:87).

Figure 9 shows part of a rock art panel found in the City of Phoenix South Mountain Park. The Hohokam have long been assumed to be the creators of the rock art in the South Mountains since these mountains are located in their cultural core area. Archaic hunter-gatherers came before the Hohokam but are not known to have made small representational figures like these. Comparable designs on Hohokam pottery date from the 7th to the 12th century. Native people who came after the Hohokam and lived in the same areas could have possibly made these dog petroglyphs, but this notion is not supported by stylistic evidence (Bostwick 2002:30, 38–39). Reflecting the many possible shapes of a dog's tail, we see in Figure 9, at top left, a dog with a saber tail, at top right a wheel tail, and at the bottom a sickle tail. Archaeological data from a number of Hohokam village sites have shown that the Hohokam people did have the domesticated dog (Bostwick 2002:18).

Figure 7. Petroglyph, McDowell Mountain Regional Park, Fountain Hills, Arizona. Photo courtesy of Sandy Haddock/ Bill Nightwine.

Figure 8. Navajo Coyote drawing, courtesy of Mariah Fox Housman.

Figure 9. Detail from a rock art panel in South Mountain Park.

Animals on Hohokam Santa Cruz red-on-buff pottery sherds from Snaketown (Gladwin et al. 1937:Plate 164) include examples that appear to portray dogs. Tails of animals on sherds b, d, f, and h in Figure 10 are very similar to dog tail styles found on the rock art panel in South Mountain Park (Figure 9). These could be the domesticated dog breeds found in Hohokam villages.

The rock art boulder in Figure 11 is on a terrace in the Lake Pleasant Regional Park, Arizona, facing the Agua Fria River. When the rock art in the Park was recorded, it was noted that 70% of the panels were found to face south or southeast toward the watercourse nearest the boulder (Moreno 2003:215). The chevron lines on this panel may represent the terraces where this boulder sits or the water below, which in this case is the Agua Fria River.

The figure in horizontal position is thought to represent death, according to a widespread convention by which the deceased may be shown in inverted or horizontal position, sometimes headless as well (Patterson 1992:81). For example, in the 1960s Hopi con-

Figure 10. Hohokam Santa Cruz red-on-buff pottery sherds from Snaketown (Gladwin et al. 1965:Plate 164). © 1965 The Arizona Board of Regents. Reprinted by permission of the University of Arizona Press.

helper bringing this dead person across the water to the underworld? It is thought by the recorders that the rock art in the Lake Pleasant Park may represent sacred activities (Moreno 2003:209).

The Little Black Mountain petroglyph site is at the northern edge of Arizona, just over the border from Utah on land managed by the BLM. Watercourses nearby are Dutchman Wash and, about 15 miles away, the Virgin River. A prominent boulder here (Figure 14) has its upper surface covered with an extensive array of repatinated Western Archaic petroglyphs with superimposed later rock art. A potential age of 6,000 years has been suggested for the older petroglyphs (BLM 2016), but later components of the site exhibit Western Virgin Kayenta Pueblo and Fremont style characteristics (Bock and Bock 1994). A detail from the main panel

Figure 11. Petroglyph panel at Lake Pleasant Regional Park. Photo by Bryan M. Lausten, courtesy of the Bureau of Reclamation, U.S. Department of the Interior.

Figure 12. Panel detail from Petroglyph Point, Mesa Verde National Park. Photo by Ken Hedges.

sultant John Lansas identified a detail of a horizontal figure from the Petroglyph Point panel (Figure 12) at Mesa Verde as a representation of Salavi, the deceased ancient leader of the Badger clan (Waters 1963:51). In addition to representing physical death, figures in inverted or horizontal position are classic metaphors of shamanic flight and shamanic trance, supernatural "death" in which the shaman travels to supernatural realms (Turpin 1994:84–85; Whitley 2000:109–111), often in the company of a spirit helper.

Figure 13 is a detail of the panel shown in Figure 11. A small dog with pointed ears and a sickle tail appears to be pulling a dead person by the hand/arm possibly to cross the water. Could this dog be an animal spirit

Figure 13. Detail of the Lake Pleasant panel shown in Figure 11. Photo by Bryan M. Lausten, courtesy of the Bureau of Reclamation, U.S. Department of the Interior.

(Figure 15) shows a possible dog with a sickle-shaped tail as spirit helper, pulling the hand/arm of a dead person to escort it into the underworld, or assisting a shaman in the journey to the spirit world.

Figure 14. Boulder in the Little Black Mountain Petroglyph Site in northwestern Arizona.

Figure 15. Detail enlargement from the top of the boulder in Figure 14.

The rock art panel in Figure 16 is on a boulder outcrop in a very secluded wash outside Prescott, Arizona. Here are seen two anthropomorphs and an animal. Hedges (1985:85) writes that frequently an animal can be shown in attendance to an anthropomorph and may represent a shaman's animal spirit. The physical location of this rock art site could be perceived as a supernatural power spot. Rock outcrops are one of the three main categories of power spots—along with permanent water sources and caves—for shamanic vision quests (Whitley 1996:9).

Several studies have shown that shamans around the world created rock art to depict their dreams or trance experiences. Among universal depictions by shamans are therianthropes—figures with combined human and animal attributes (Bostwick 2002:218). The Figure 16 panel shows a human with a subtly animal-like head, possibly an image of the shaman in transformation. In noting the cracks on this rock art panel, it appears that both anthropomorphs and the animal appear to be going in or out of the cracks. Moreno (2003:209–210) pointed out that, according to Eliade (1964), shamanistic art concerns the journey through the spirit world levels of sky or underworld. The passageway to the spirit world is transposed onto the rock surface by the illustration of human and animal figures "emanating from or terminating in natural rock crevices and holes" (Turpin 1994:75), so this second anthropomorph could possibly be another shaman.

Figure 16. Petroglyph panel on an outcrop in a secluded wash outside Prescott, Arizona.

The dogs in the early Hohokam villages served as companions, assisting with hunting and guarding the villages (Bostwick 2002:18). This last petroglyph panel (Figure 17) illustrates another way that the dog may have helped early people. This panel is interpreted as a dog barking furiously at a snake that may have just shed its skin. Why would the early people take the time to create this petroglyph? If you are new to living on the Sonoran Desert and own a dog, you would not want it to meet up with a rattlesnake. There is a class called "Rattlesnake Avoidance" just for those dogs new to the desert. Some dogs know the smell of the rattlesnakes and their danger from their experiences. In the spring, the snakes come out of hibernation and they shed their skins. I was told by a dog-owner friend that this skin has

Figure 17. One of many rock art panels at the Lime Creek Rock Art Site.

a very strong odor and that her dog has a very different bark when it detects the snake odor. This knowledge brought about the hypothesis that this panel shows a bobtailed dog barking at a snake that has just shed its skin. The image below the snake is interpreted as its skin, which is almost a mirrored image of the snake's body, pecked lighter to show the translucence of the skin. It is proposed that it was important for dogs to accompany people on excursions into the hills to protect them from snakes when they were out gathering plant foods. The dogs would warn the people of the presence of snakes with their significant bark.

Conclusion

For too long the dog has barely been noticed in Southwestern rock art. The dog has usually been categorized as a quadruped, coyote/dog, or simply ignored. Could the dog one day be just as visibly recognized as deer or bighorn sheep? This brief paper is presented as a foundation for future work, and it is hoped that additional researchers will take up the task of finding the dog in the rock art.

Acknowledgments. I extend my gratitude to all who shared their photos of dog petroglyphs they found in Arizona rock art. Thanks to Dr. Christy Turner who shared his knowledge and research advice. And last, I would like to thank my dear granddaughter, Chrystine Bohman, for all of her computer help.

Notes

1. Wilderness wolf, photo by www.Pixel.la Free Stock Photos–nature-animal-wolf-wilderness, Creative Commons CC0 1.0 Public Domain Dedication, https://commons.wikimedia.org/w/index.php? curid=51439565

2. Gray wolf, photo from Wolves in Idaho, Idaho Department of Fish and Game, https://idfg.idaho.gov/public/wildlife/wolves

3. Coyote on the move, photo by Marty Murphy, Fermilab Today, Fermi National Accelerator Laboratory, U.S. Department of Energy, http://www.fnal.gov/pub/today/images/images12/coyote-3.jpg

4. Coyote Stretching, photo by Eric Kilby from Somerville, MA, USA, Creative Commons Attribution-Share Alike 2.0 Generic license, https://commons.wikimedia.org/wiki/File:Coyote_Stretching_6811853436).jpg

References Cited

Allen, Glover M.
  1920 Dogs of the American Aborigines. *Bulletin of the Museum of Comparative Zoology at Harvard College* 63(9):431–517.

Amsden, Charles Avery
  1949 *Prehistoric Southwesterners from Basketmaker to Pueblo.* Southwest Museum, Los Angeles.

Balzer, Marjorie M.
  1996 Flights of the Sacred: Symbolism and Theory in Siberian Shamanism. *American Anthropologist* 98(2):305–318.

Bock, Frank G., and A. J. Bock
  1994 Rock Art of the Arizona Strip. In *American Indian Rock Art, Volumes 13–14,* edited by A. J. Bock, pp. 27–46. American Rock Art Research Association, San Miguel, California.

Bostwick, Todd W.
  2002 *Landscape of the Spirits: Hohokam Rock Art at South Mountain Park.* University of Arizona Press, Tucson.

Browne, J. Ross
  1869 *Adventures in the Apache Country: A Tour through Arizona and Sonora, with Notes on the Silver Regions of Nevada.* Harper & Brothers, New York.

Bureau of Land Management (BLM)
  2016 Little Black Mountain Petroglyph Site. Electronic document, http://www.blm.gov/az/st/en/prog/cultural/lil-blk-mtn.html, accessed March, 2017.

Caninest
  2009 Dog Tail Types. Blog post by Paige. Caninest.com, November 2, 2009. Electronic document, http://www.caninest.com/dog-tail-types/, accessed April 10, 2017.

Casselman, Anne
  2008 Buried Dogs were Divine "Escorts" for Ancient Americans. *National Geographic News,* April 23, 2008. Electronic document, http://news.nationalgeographic.com/news/2008/04/080423-dog-burials.html, accessed April 9, 2017.

Dulik, Matthew C., Sergey I. Zhadanov, Ludmila P. Osipova, Ayken Askapuli, Lydia Gau, Omer Gokcumen, Samara Rubinstein, and Theodore G. Schurr
  2012 Mitochondrial DNA and Y Chromosome Variation Provides Evidence for a Recent Common Ancestry Between Native Americans and Indigenous Altaians. *The American Journal of Human Genetics* 90:229–246.

Eliade, Mircea
  1964 *Shamanism: Archaic Techniques of Ecstasy.* Translated by Willard R. Trask. Bollingen Series 76. Princeton University

Press, Princeton, New Jersey. Reprint edition 1972, Princeton University Press. Originally published as *Le Chamanisme et les techniques archaïques de l'extase*, Librairie Payot, Paris, 1951.

Emory, William H.
1857 *Report on the United States and Mexican Boundary Survey, Volume 1*, made under the direction of the Secretary of the Interior. A. O. P. Nicholson, Printer, Washington, D.C.

Gladwin, Harold S., Emil W. Haury, E. B. Sayles, and Nora Gladwin
1937 *Excavations at Snaketown: Material Culture*. Medallion Papers 25. Gila Pueblo, Globe, Arizona. Facsimile reprint 1965, University of Arizona Press, Tucson.

Haviland, William A.
2012 *Canoe Indians of Down East Maine*. The History Press, Charleston, South Carolina.

Hedges, Ken
1985 Rock Art Portrayals of Shamanic Transformation and Magical Flight. In *Rock Art Papers, Volume 2*, edited by Ken Hedges, pp. 83–94. San Diego Museum Papers 18. San Diego Museum of Man, San Diego.

Housman, Gerald
1993 *The Gift of the Gila Monster: Navajo Ceremonial Tales*. Simon & Schuster, New York.

Martinelli, Melissa J.
2012 *The Sacred Role of Animal Beings in Iroquois Lore*. Master's Thesis, State University of New York College at Buffalo.

Moreno, Jerryll
2003 Petroglyphs of Lake Pleasant Regional Park. *Kiva* 68(3):185–219.

Patterson, Alex
1992 *A Field Guide to Rock Art Symbols of the Greater Southwest*. Johnson Books, Boulder, Colorado.

Remington, Frederic
1889 On the Indian Reservations. *The Century Magazine* 38(3):394–405.

Schwartz, Marion
1997 *A History of Dogs in the Early Americas*. Yale University, New Haven, Connecticut.

Turpin, Solveig A.
1994 On a Wing and a Prayer: Flight Metaphors in Pecos River Art. In *Shamanism and Rock Art in North America*, edited by Solveig A. Turpin, pp. 73–102. Special Publication 1. Rock Art Foundation, San Antonio, Texas.

Underhill, Ruth Murray
1953 *Red Man's America: A History of Indians in the United States*. University of Chicago Press, Chicago.

Waters, Frank
1963 *Book of the Hopi*. Recorded by Oswald White Bear Fredericks. Viking Press, New York.

Whitley, David S.
1996 *A Guide to Rock Art Sites: Southern California and Southern Nevada*. Mountain Press Publishing Company, Missoula, Montana.

2000 *The Art of the Shaman: Rock Art of California*. University of Utah Press, Salt Lake City.

Wisconsin Department of Natural Resources (WDNR)
2017 Canid Identification: Wolves, Coyotes and Dogs. Wisconsin Department of Natural Resources, Madison. Electronic document, http://dnr.wi.gov/topic/wildlifehabitat/wolf/identify.html, accessed April 10, 2017.

Zhukova, Lyudmila
2014 The Odul Folklore: On the Functional Significance of Shamans. *Sibirica* 13(2):93–104.

The Rock Paintings of Divisadero

César A. Quijada

In Memory of William Breen Murray
Pioneer in the study of rock art in Northeast Mexico

This archaeological site is located in the municipality of La Colorada in the Sonora River basin. This is one of the regions in my proposed regionalization of the rock art in the State of Sonora. In this cave there is only one concentration of rock paintings, which consists of anthropomorphic forms. The main character is black. At his sides are two human figures in red. They draw our attention because they look like paintings observed in the region of the La Pintada site in the Sierra Libre, located south of the city of Hermosillo. These two paintings can be considered as part of the style of La Pintada.

This archeological site is located in the municipality of La Colorada in the Sonora River basin, one of the regions into which the State of Sonora has been divided according to my proposed regionalization of the rock art manifestations (Quijada López 1998). Most of these types of cultural manifestations have been interpreted by several researchers as the product of initiates, priests, or shamans, giving them a magical religious overtone. We personally think that the rock art is not only that, but also the expressions of the ancient inhabitants of this territory that we know today as the State of Sonora, where they left embodied in rocks and in caves what they saw, knew, and felt—what was important to them.

The intention is to present this place in a simple way, considering its location and its relation to other pictorial sets near Hermosillo (Quijada Hernandez 1976), or to the archaeological site of La Pintada, located in the Sierra Libre, 60 km to the south of Hermosillo (Messmacher 1981).

Site Description

This site is very close to the junction of two streams. The soil on the hill is stony and the rock is of volcanic origin. Currently, the area is being used by livestock. The site is located within the land of Ejido La Colorada, belonging to the same municipality, and access to the cave is on the western side of El Divisadero hill (Figure 1). The entrance to the cave is 1.80 m high (Figure 2). In the middle, the height decreases to 1.20 m. Inside the cave, the major axis has a length of 3.20 m from north to south, and the minor axis is 3.00 m from east to west.

The cave exhibits natural deterioration, with two window-like openings on its east side—one in the middle and the other almost at floor level—from which it is possible to see part of the desert plateau toward the town La Colorada as well as the surrounding hills, hence the name El Divisadero or Cerrito del Divisadero. There is also a collapse or detachment of the floor, which communicates with a rockshelter whose access is by the eastern slope of the hill;

César A. Quijada
Centro INAH Sonora

Figure 1. Access to the cave is on the West side of the hill.
Figura 1. Acceso a la cueva es por la ladera oeste del cerro.

Figure 2. Overview of the cave on the hill El Divisadero.
Figura 2 Vista general de la cueva en el cerro El Divisadero.

Figure 3. Use of DStretch confirmed that there is no overlapping of paintings. DStretch YUV enhancement.
Figura 3. Utilizando DStretch se confirmó que no hay sobre posición de pinturas.

Figure 4. The anthropomorphic figure in black is the largest in Panel 1.
Figura 4. La figura antropomorfa en color negro, es la de mayor tamaño del panel 1.

in this second shelter no cave paintings were found, but it is occasionally visited, as shown by modern surface trash such as plastic containers.

In the cave are two small areas where paintings can be observed. The first concentration (Panel 1) is around 1 meter from the entrance of the cave, on the northeast side. It is composed of 26 elements (Figure 3). Three of these are anthropomorphic, and the most outstanding is a figure 22 cm high and 12 cm wide in black with the upper body outline and the feet in red (Figure 4). On each side, at the level of the hips, are two other anthropomorphic figures in red in a horizontal position, giving the impression of lying down. These figures are oriented toward the west.

The one on the west side is a little larger and the position of arms and legs is different in relation to the figure on the east side, but the shape of the head and body, as well as the pigment color, are similar (Figure 5). The rest of the paintings around the black anthropomorphic figure are geometric shapes, such as straight lines, angles, triangles, isolated points, and curved lines, all of them in red, whereby we consider that they were painted at the same time and by the same person.

On the left shoulder of the larger figure our attention is caught by two small triangles joined by a straight line that starts at the apex of the lower triangle and extends up to the base of the second triangle at the top (Figure 6).

Below the arms of the larger figure are sets of geometrically shaped figures, a set of five horizontal parallel lines is on the figure's left side and a square with two crossed lines on the other side. Between the legs are two

Figure 5. Anthropomorphs at the sides of the larger figure.
Figura 5. Antropomorfos de los lados de la figura mayor.

Figure 6. Triangles joined over the left shoulder.
Figura 6. Triángulos unidos sobre el hombro izquierdo

semicircles joined by a horizontal line. On the side of the figure's right leg there is a set of three angles and two broken lines. At the bottom, there are two sloping lines. All of these paintings are in red color. Below them are two broad lines in black coming together at the bottom.

For this set of geometric designs, without knowledge of the code or meaning by which they were made, interpretation is difficult. I personally consider that some of the painted elements, such as the parallel and broken lines, can be related to the presence of watercourses, due to the proximity of the site to them. Knowing the importance of this vital liquid for human beings leads me to consider this possible interpretation.

To the upper right (viewer's left) of the figure in black are other geometric paintings in red, in particular two triangles whose bases are parallel, giving the impression, at a distance, of a rhombus, but in fact they are two figures. On the other side of the panel, and separated from the set by a fracture in the rock, there is a curved line, also in red, whose upper part is wider than the bottom.

Panel 2 is located on the back of the cave (Figure 7a), south of the natural window that is located near the floor level. This panel includes two anthropomorphic figures and approximately ten geometric elements in red (Figure 7b), and several lines in black. The size of the figures varies from one to eight centimeters high and they are not easily seen because the wall in this part of the cave has been covered with a dark layer, the origin of which, so far, is unknown. In order to observe and photograph them, it is necessary to be seated at a very short distance, but if you wish to appreciate some details, you need to lie down.

In a small depression of the south wall are two very schematic anthropomorphic figures in red that are difficult to appreciate. From the front view, the one on the viewer's left, approximately 9 cm high, is not very clear from its central part to the east side, but it is possible to see that it has open legs, one arm up, and the other arm down, giving the impression of moving. The other painting, located a little higher and to the right of the first one, is 6 cm high and has its arms turned down at the elbow. This painting calls attention to its neck and head, shaped as if it were a bird (Figure 8).

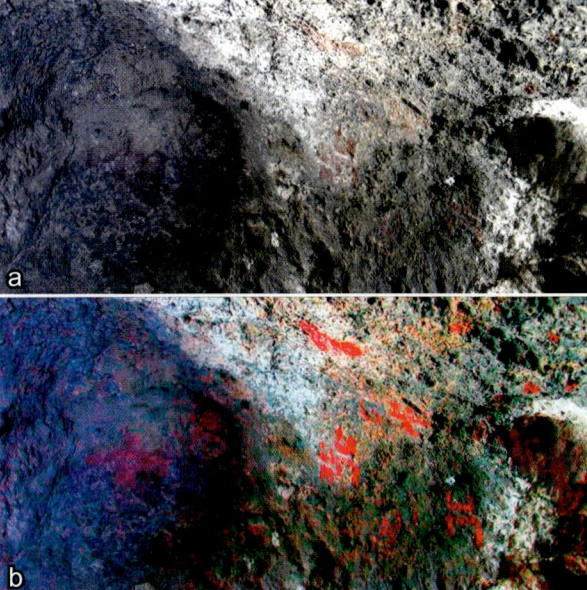

Figure 7. (a) Overview of the second panel of the paintings; (b) DStretch (LAB) enables better appreciation of the paintings.
Figura 7. (a) Vista general del segundo panel de las pinturas; (b) Utilizando DStrech (LAB) se aprecian mejor las pinturas.

Figure 8. Schematic anthropomorph (left) and anthropomorphic figure with head of bird (right).
Figura 8. Antropomorfo esquimatico (a la izquierda) y figura antropomorfa como con cabeza de ave (a la derecha).

Outside this depression on the south wall and a little farther to the west are very schematic geometric (Figure 9) and anthropomorphic figures in red. One figure, 9 cm high, gives the impression of being an anthropomorphic figure with its legs opened and its arms up.

Above the paintings mentioned here is a geometric figure in the shape of a triangle in red (Figure 10), and on the right side, farther down, is another painting, also in red, but it is not possible to visualize its original shape.

Final Considerations

To summarize, in the cave are two concentrations of paintings. The first concentration has anthropomorphic motifs, the figure in black being the largest. However, the two red anthropomorphic figures situated on their sides, giving the impression of lying down, are the ones that catch our attention due to their similarity to cave paintings observed in our several visits to the archeological site of La Pintada in the Sierra Libre, located in the southern part of the municipality of Hermosillo. We consider that these two anthropomorphic paintings can be compared to the Sierra Libre painting style.

In the municipality of Hermosillo, the first site with cave paintings that most of its inhabitants know or have some reference to is La Pintada, located 60 kilometers south of Hermosillo, the study of which began in 1963 (Messmacher 1981). In the landscape of the city of Hermosillo, to the northwest, are the hills Largo y Colorado; a site with cave paintings in the Cerro Largo was reported for the first time in the 1970s (Quijada Hernandez 1976).

Another site near Hermosillo is the Cueva del Vaquero, given this name because there we see an anthropomorphic figure over a zoomorphic one. One more site is located southwest of the city, the Cueva Cañada de la Matanza, situated on the north side. The paintings are anthropomorphic and geometric, including such forms as straight and curved lines, spirals, and squares in black (Quijada López 2005).

El Tijerito is located north of Hermosillo, in the Ejido La Victoria on the hills of El Bachoco. This place is distinguished by having stylized anthropomorphic figures, geometric figures, and one zoomorphic figure that gives the impression of being a turtle. In 1992, we discovered Las Pinturas del Jito, located on the West side of one of the hills of the old cement plant of Hermosillo, in the area known as El Tiro al Blanco, next to the neighborhood of El Jito. Various pictographs are located there, almost within the city, with anthropomorphic and geometric paintings (Quijada López 2005) in a 5

Figure 9. Geometric figures outside the small depression.
Figura 9. Figuras geométricas fuera de la depresión.

Figure 10. Geometric figure in the shape of a triangle.
Figura 10. Figura geométrica en forma de triángulo.

m long shelter and varying in depth from 1 to 4 m. Las Pinturas del Divisadero is the seventh place with rock paintings reported near Hermosillo (Figure 11).

The site of Las Pinturas del Divisadero presents a high degree of erosion, suffering the loss of fragments of the eastern wall with windows opened by the action of the wind. Light coming through in the afternoons affects most of the paintings, so they are in delicate condition.

References Cited.

Messmacher, Miguel.
　1981 *Pinturas rupestres de La Pintada, Sonora: Un enfoque metodológico.* Departamento de Prehistoria, Instituto Nacional de Antropología e Historia, México.

Quijada Hernández, Armando.
　1976 Arte rupestre en Sonora. In *Primer Simposio de Historia de Sonora*, pp. 433–455. Instituto de Investigaciones Históricas, Universidad de Sonora. Hermosillo, Sonora.

Quijada López, César Armando.
　1998 Propuesta de regionalización de los sitios en Sonora con manifestaciones gráfico-rupestre. In *Antropología e Historia del Occidente de México, XXIV Mesa Redonda de la Sociedad Mexicana de Antropología*, Tomo II, pp. 1039–1061. Sociedad Mexicana de Antropología y Universidad Nacional Autónoma de México. México.

　2005 Pintura Rupestre y Petroglifos en Sonora. In *Arte rupestre en México: Ensayos 1990-2004*, María del Pilar Casado López, Compiladora, Lorena Mirambell Silva, Coordinadora, pp. 189–218. Instituto Nacional de Antropología e Historia. México.

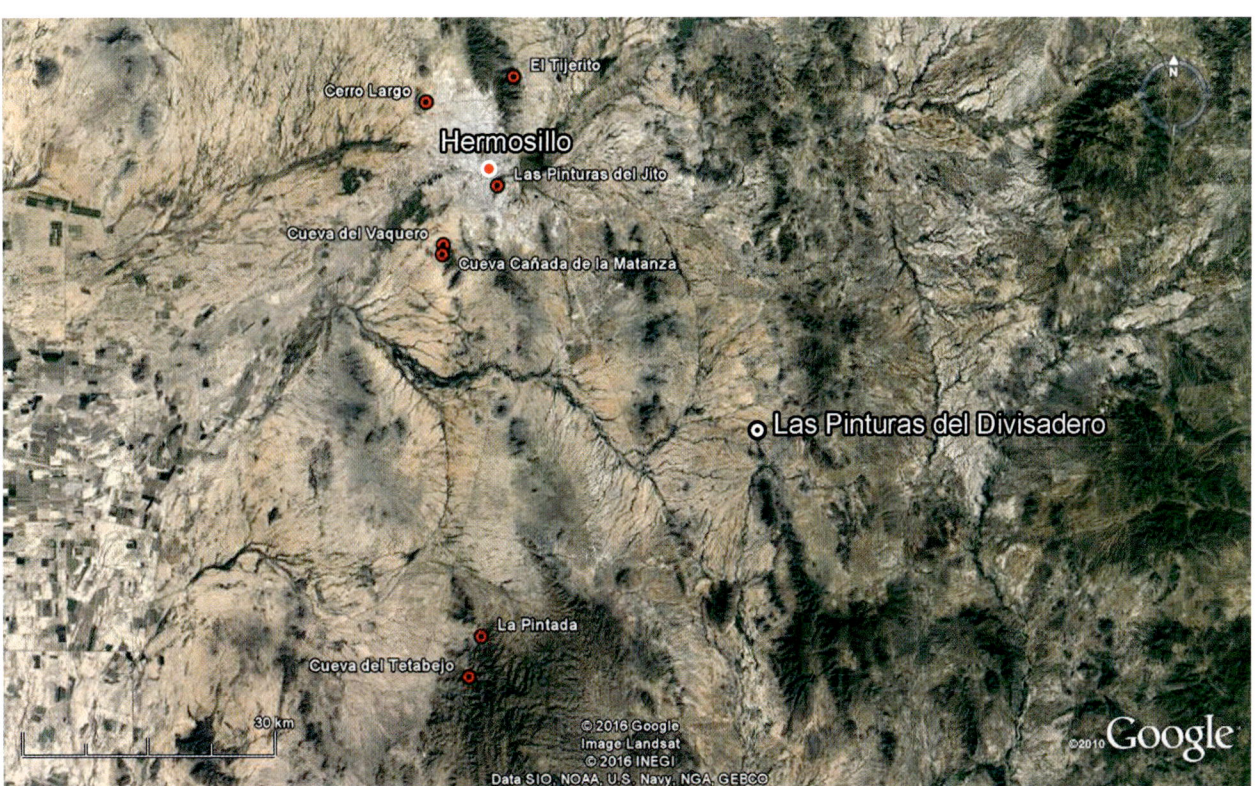

Figure 11. Location of the sites with engravings and cave paintings near the city of Hermosillo.
Figura 11. Ubicación de los sitios con grabados y pinturas rupestres cercanos a la ciudad de Hermosillo.

The Spanish version of this paper begins on the next page.

La versión en Español de este artículo comienza en la página siguiente.

Las Pinturas Rupestres del Divisadero

César Armando Quijada López

En memoria a William Breen Murray
Pionero en el estudio del Arte Rupestre del Noreste de México

Este sitio arqueológico está ubicado en el municipio de La Colorada, en la cuenca del río Sonora. Esta es una de las regiones en mi propuesta de regionalización del arte rupestre en el Estado de Sonora. En esta cueva sólo hay una concentración de pinturas rupestres, que consiste en formas antropomórficas. El personaje principal es negro. A sus costados hay dos figuras humanas en rojo. Ellos llaman nuestra atención porque se parecen a pinturas observadas en la región del sitio La Pintada en la Sierra Libre, ubicada al sur de la ciudad de Hermosillo. Estas dos pinturas pueden ser consideradas como parte del estilo de La Pintada.

Este sitio arqueológico actualmente se encuentra en el municipio de La Colorada, pertenece a la cuenca del río Sonora, una de las regiones en que se ha dividido el estado de Sonora, en la propuesta de regionalización de las manifestaciones gráfico rupestres (Quijada López 1998). La mayoría de este tipo de manifestaciones culturales, se han interpretado por parte de varios investigadores, como el producto de iniciados, sacerdotes o chamanes, dándole un matiz mágico religioso. En lo personal pensamos que la gráfica rupestre no es solamente lo anteriormente expuesto, sino que también estas son expresiones de los antiguos habitantes de este territorio, que hoy conocemos como el estado de Sonora, donde dejaron plasmado en rocas y cuevas, lo que ellos vieron, conocieron y sintieron, en fin, lo que les era importante.

Se desea presentar de una forma sencilla este lugar, con algunas consideraciones sobre su ubicación y la relación con otros conjuntos pictóricos cercanos a Hermosillo (Quijada Hernández 1976), o del sitio de La Pintada, ubicado en la Sierra Libre unos 60 kilómetros al sur de Hermosillo (Messmacher 1981).

Descripción del Sitio.

Este sitio está muy cercano a la unión de dos arroyos. El suelo en el cerro es pedregoso y la roca es de origen volcánico. El terreno actualmente tiene un uso ganadero. El sitio se encuentra dentro de los terrenos del Ejido La Colorada, perteneciente al mismo municipio. El acceso a la cueva es por la ladera del lado occidental del cerro El Divisadero (Figura 1), la entrada a la cueva tiene una altura de 1.80 metros (Figura 2), en la parte media la altura ha disminuido a los 1.20 metros. En el interior de la cueva el eje mayor tiene una longitud de 3.20 metros en dirección de norte a sur y su eje menor es de 3.00 metros de este a oeste.

La cueva presenta deterioro natural, tiene dos especies de ventanas en su parte oriental, una de las oquedades está en la parte media y la otra casi a nivel del piso, desde las cuales se puede observar parte de la planicie desértica en dirección a la población de La Colorada, así como los cerros aledaños, de ahí el nombre El Divisadero o Cerrito del Divisadero. También existe un derrumbe o desprendimiento del piso, que comunica hacia un abrigo rocoso cuyo acceso es por la falda oriental del cerro, en este segundo abrigo no se encontraron pinturas rupestres, pero si es visitado ocasionalmente, observándose en superficie basura moderna, como envases de plástico.

En la cueva existen dos pequeñas áreas en donde se observan las pinturas rupestres. A la primera concentración se le denominó panel 1, ésta se encuentra a un metro aproximadamente de la entrada de la cueva, del lado noreste, cuenta con unos 26 motivos (Figura 3), tres de ellos son antropomorfos, el que más destaca es un personaje de 22 centímetros de alto y 12 centímetros de ancho en color negro, su contorno y pies son de color rojo (Figura 4), a cada uno de sus lado a la altura de la cadera se encuentras las otras dos figuras antropomorfas en color rojo en posición horizontal, dando la impresión de estar acostadas, estas figuras se encuentran viendo al oeste. La del lado oeste (Figura 5) es un poco más grande y la posición de los brazos y piernas es diferente, en relación a la figura del lado este, pero la forma de la cabeza y el cuerpo es similar, así como el color del pigmento. El resto de las pinturas alrededor de la figura antropomorfa de color negro, son de forma geométrica, como líneas rectas, ángulos, triángulos, puntos aislados y líneas curvas todas en color rojo, por lo cual consideramos que fueron elaboradas en el mismo momento y por la misma persona.

Sobre el hombro izquierdo de la figura mayor, llama la atención dos pequeños triángulos unidos por una línea recta, la cual se inicia en el ángulo superior del triángulo que está más abajo y que llega hasta la base del segundo triángulo que se ubica un poco más arriba (Figura 6).

Por debajo de los brazos de la figura mayor existe una serie de figuras geométricas, del lado izquierdo se observa una serie de cinco líneas horizontales de forma paralela, del otro lado de la figura hay un cuadro con dos líneas cruzadas y entre las piernas hay dos semicírculos unidos por una línea horizontal. Del lado de la pierna derecha del personaje, hay una serie de tres ángulos y dos líneas quebradas. En la parte inferior dos líneas inclinadas, todas estas pinturas son en color rojo, más abajo hay dos líneas en color negro, que se unen en su parte inferior.

En este conjunto de diseños geométricos, al desconocer el código o significado con el cual fueron realizados, resulta difícil su interpretación. En lo personal considero que algunos de los elementos pintados como las líneas paralelas y quebradas pueden estar relacionados con la presencia de cursos de agua, debido a la cercanía del sitio con ellos y sabiendo la importancia del vital líquido para el ser humano, es que consideramos esta posible interpretación.

En la parte superior derecha de la figura de color negro, se encuentran otras pinturas de forma geométrica y en color rojo, sobresalen dos triángulos cuyas bases están paralelas, dando la impresión a la distancia de un rombo, pero se trata de dos figuras. En el otro lado del conjunto y separado del conjunto por una fractura de la roca, se encuentra una línea curva, también en color rojo, cuya parte superior es más gruesa que la inferior.

El panel 2 se encuentra en el fondo de la cueva (Figura 7a), al sur de la ventana natural que se encuentra cercana al nivel del piso. Este segundo panel cuenta con dos figuras antropomorfas, unas diez figuras geométricas de color rojo (Figura 7b) y varias líneas en color negro. Las figuras en su tamaño varían entre uno y ocho centímetros de alto y son poco visibles, ya que la pared de esta parte de la cueva se ha ido cubriendo con una capa obscura, cuyo origen hasta el momento desconocemos. Para poderlas observar y fotografiar hay que estar sentado y a corta distancia, pero si se desea apreciar algunos detalles para su descripción, es necesario tener que acostarse.

En una pequeña depresión de la pared sur encontramos las dos figuras antropomorfas muy esquemáticas en color rojo y difícil de apreciar. Viéndolas de frente la del lado izquierdo de unos nueve centímetros de altura, no se ve muy clara desde su parte central hacia el lado este, pero si se aprecia con sus piernas abiertas y un brazo hacia arriba y el otro hacia abajo, dando la impresión de estar en movimiento. La otra pintura ubicada un poco más arriba y a la derecha de la primera, tiene seis centímetros de alto y se le aprecian los brazos hacia abajo a partir del codo, de esta pintura llama la atención su cuello y la cabeza, como si fueran de un ave (Figura 8).

Fuera de esta depresión de la pared sur y un poco más al oeste, se ven figuras geométricas y antropomorfas muy esquemáticas en color rojo (Figura 9). Observando de frente, la pintura del lado izquierdo tiene 9 centímetros de altura y da la impresión de ser una figura antropomorfa con sus piernas abiertas y los brazos hacia arriba.

Arriba de las pinturas anteriormente mencionadas, se ve una figura geométrica en forma de un triángulo en color rojo (Figura 10) y a mano derecha un poco más abajo existe otra pintura también en color rojo, pero ya no se aprecia bien la forma que tuvo originalmente.

Consideraciones finales

Como mencionamos anteriormente en la cueva existen dos concentraciones de pinturas rupestres. La primera concentración cuenta con motivos antropomorfos, siendo el personaje en color negro el de mayor tamaño, pero son las dos figuras antropomorfas en color rojo que se encuentran a sus costados y que dan la impresión de estar acostadas, las que llaman nuestra atención, por su parecido con pinturas rupestres observadas en varias de nuestras visitas al sitio de La Pintada en la Sierra Libre, en la parte sur del municipio de Hermosillo, considerando que estas dos pinturas antropomorfas en color rojo se les puede considerar como del estilo de la Sierra Libre.

En el municipio de Hermosillo, el primer sitio con pinturas rupestres que la mayoría de sus habitantes conoce o tiene alguna referencia, es el de La Pintada, ubicado en la Sierra Libre unos 60 kilómetros al sur de Hermosillo y que en 1963, se empezó su estudio (Messmacher 1981). En el paisaje de la ciudad de Hermosillo, hacia el noroeste están los cerros Largo y Colorado, un sitio con pinturas rupestres en el Cerro Largo fue reportado por primera vez en la década de los setenta del siglo XX (Quijada Hernández 1976).

Otro sitio cercano a Hermosillo es la Cueva del Vaquero, que recibe este nombre debido a que ahí se ve una figura antropomorfa sobre una zoomorfa. Un sitio más se encuentra al suroeste, es la Cueva Cañada de la Matanza, sobre la ladera norte, las pinturas son antropomorfas y geométricas como líneas rectas, curvas, espirales y cuadros en color negro. (Quijada López 2005).

El sitio de El Tijerito se encuentra al norte de Hermosillo, en el ejido La Victoria en los cerro de El Bachoco, este lugar se distingue por ser figuras antropomorfas estilizadas, hay figuras geométricas y una figura zoomorfas que da la idea de una tortuga. En 1996 conocimos Las Pinturas del Jito se localizan en la ladera oeste de uno de los ceros de la antigua cementera de Hermosillo, en el paraje conocido como el Tiro al Blanco, junto al barrio del Jito. Diversas pictografías se encuentran ahí, prácticamente dentro de la ciudad, este pequeño abrigo de 5 metros de largo y una profundidad variable de 1 a 4 metros se encuentran pinturas antropomorfas y geométricas (Quijada López 2005). Siendo Las Pinturas del Divisadero el séptimo lugar del que se tiene noticia cercano a la ciudad de Hermosillo (Figura 11).

El sitio Las Pinturas del Divisadero, en cuanto a su estado de conservación, presenta un grado de erosión alto, sufriendo la perdida de fragmentos de la pared oriental, quedando como "ventanas", por la acción del viento. La luz que entra por la tarde, afecta a las pinturas en su mayoría, por lo cual se encuentran en un delicado estado de conservación.

Rhythms in the Landscape: The Archaic Pictorial Tradition of Durango, Mexico

In Memory of William Breen Murray

Daniel Herrera Maldonado

The archaeological study I have undertaken in Cañón de Molino, located in the Guatimapé valley, has led me to recognize the presence of several sites belonging to the so-called Archaic Pictorial Tradition, the distribution of which includes a significant part of the Sierra Madre Occidental of Durango state. This work aims to explore the main features and variations that define this abstract tradition in terms of the organization of its images and the symbolic construction of landscapes.

For more than 10 years I have studied rock art in the Mexican state of Durango, which has made me familiar with the so-called "Archaic Pictorial Tradition." This tradition has a strong compositional unity across a wide distribution of space in the highlands and eastern valleys of the Sierra Madre Occidental of Durango (Figure 1), the home of hunter-gatherer communities before the well-known and well-studied colonization of Mesoamerican peoples around A.D. 600 (Berrojalbiz and Hers 2012:96; Berrojalbiz et al. 2014:155, 157; Forcano 2000:490–491, 504–507; Hers 2001; Punzo 2008).

Since this is a markedly abstract and geometric form of art, my proposed analysis focuses on the crucial component of rhythm in these kinds of languages about the depicted subject (Leroi-Gourhan 1971:369, 384). Rhythm is best understood as regular movements and recurring constructions of space and time. Rhythms become manifested in forms and figures, and are thus considered an essential feature of all art (Leroi-Gourhan 1971:301, 307, 353). In this regard, although the precise meaning of each representation may not be fully understood, this study will focus on the search for an ideological framework present in the organization of the particular forms, values, and rhythms, that is, the meaning and harmony of the motifs at the site (Forcano 2000:501–502; Leroi-Gourhan 1971:274, 282, 316, 373).

To accomplish this, I have decided to focus on the study of various sites that belong to this tradition located in Cañón de Molino (Figure 2) in the region of the Guatimapé plains that makes up the central portion of Durango state. The unusual concentration of these sites in Cañón de Molino is likely due to its location at the mouth of an enormous drainage basin that, even today, in spite of continuous droughts in the region, contains the impressive Laguna de Santiaguillo lake (Figure 1). The hunter-gatherers who inhabited the area not only benefitted from the abundance of fish and fowl that the lake itself provided, but also from the diversity of ecosystems arising from the marked differences in altitude of the mountain ranges surrounding the basin,

Daniel Herrera Maldonado
Universidad Nacional Autónoma de México

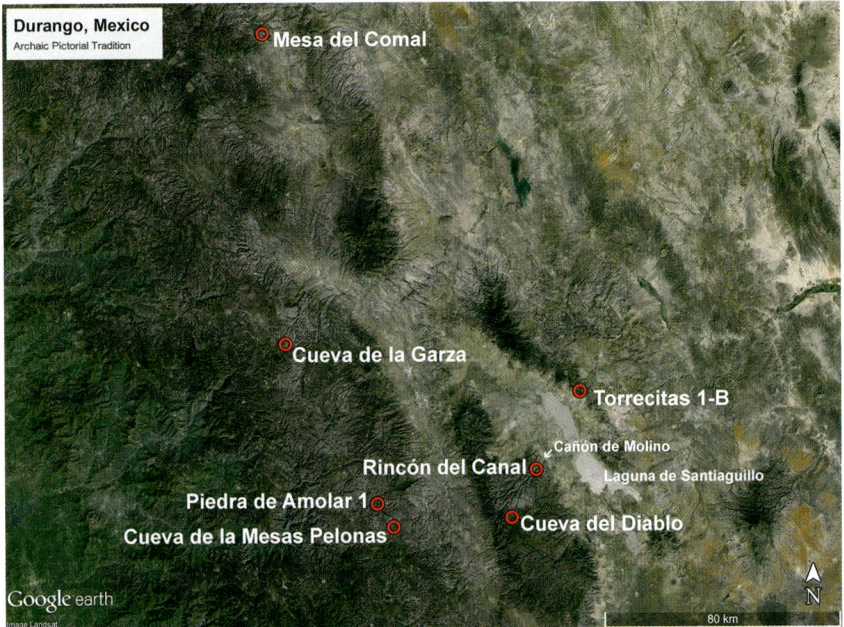

Figure 1. Map showing the general location of Archaic Pictorial Tradition sites in the Sierra Madre Occidental of the state of Durango, Mexico.
Figura 1. Mapa con la ubicación general de los sitios de la Tradición Pictórica del Arcaico en la Sierra Madre Occidental de Durango.

the way in which, because of the natural formation of this space as an inside corner, a more private space of seclusion and reflection is created. This sensation is enhanced by the abundant humidity concentrated there, facilitating the growth of a dense vegetation, such as pine and red oak trees, blocking the surroundings from view.

The sense of isolation in Rincón del Canal is perceived upon entering the site, as if you were passing over some kind of threshold. There is a significant sonorous effect due to the shape and orientation of the wall, as though it were a large rocky earphone, and the volume of surrounding sounds is notably increased as they bounce off this great nook in the canyon. These features make it possible to hear voices and sounds generated by people located more than a kilometer away while seated in front of the paintings.

Figure 2. Panoramic view of Cañón de Molino, Durango, Mexico.
Figura 2. Vista panorámica, Cañón de Molino, Durango, México.

Figure 3. Inside corner of the Mesa de los Jabalíes where the paintings of Rincón del Canal are located, Cañón de Molino.
Figura 3. Rinconada de la Mesa de los Jabalíes, espacio en donde se ubican las pinturas de Rincón del Canal, Cañón de Molino.

making it possible to obtain a wide variety of resources without having to travel more than a few kilometers (Tsukada 2006:46). Thus, it is no coincidence that several important Archaic rock art sites are found in this area, specifically in the Promontorio and Epazote ranges to the east and west, respectively, of this great basin. Cañón de Molino is located in the Epazote range (Berrojalbiz et al. 2014:160–161).

Approximately 4.5 kilometers upstream inside Cañón de Molino it is possible to observe the large rocky face of Mesa de los Jabalíes (Figure 3), which appears to tuck in and form an inside corner where the paintings of Rincón del Canal are located (Figure 4). One of the most remarkable characteristics of this place is

Once you climb the large slope that leads to the base of the painted vertical walls your eyes are immediately directed towards one of the most emblematic compositions of the site, located in the upper portion of Panel 11 (Figure 5). I will begin my analysis with this panel so that it serves as an introduction to the general characteristics of the Archaic Pictorial Tradition, and at the same time allows me to define the particularities of the Rincón del Canal.

Figure 4. Panels 9, 10, and 11, Rincón del Canal site, Cañón de Molino.
Figura 4. Páneles 9, 10, y 11, Rincón del Canal, Cañón de Molino.

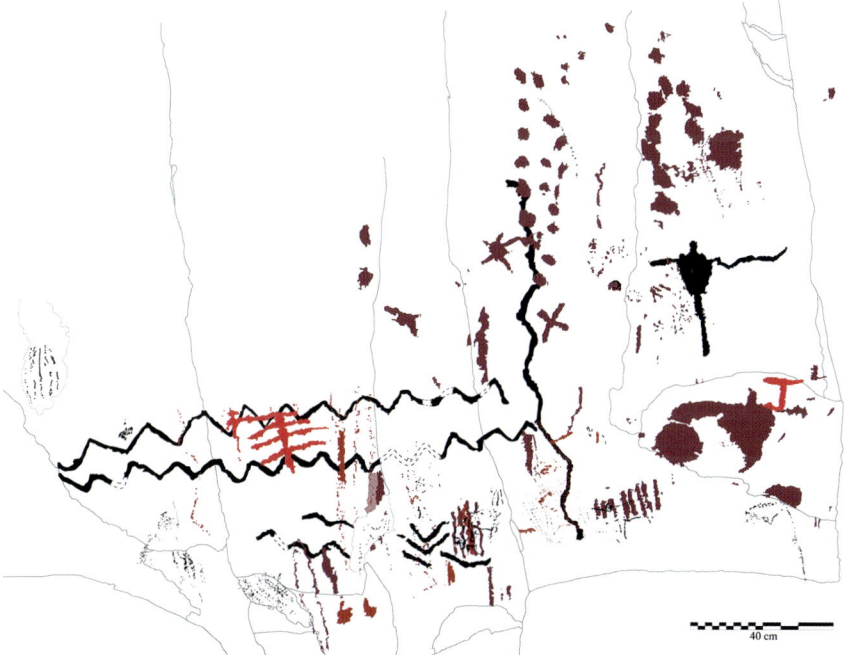

Figure 5. The upper portion of Panel 11, Rincón del Canal site, Cañón de Molino.
Figura 5. Parte superior del panel 11, Rincón del Canal, Cañón de Molino.

Rhythms of the Archaic Pictorial Tradition

The repeated use of this space for numerous repaintings, new renditions, and superimpositions has allowed me to establish the exact sequence of the various phases of execution that are involved in the final constitution of the present composition (Figure 5). This feature is closely related to the particular way in which this tradition utilizes polychromatic painting techniques. In the majority of cases, the polychrome consists of a combination of colors added during several stages of execution, each one in a different tone, rather than a synthesis of different colors of a single motif. The most frequently used colors are black, yellow, orange, white and various tones of red, among which is found a distinctive Maroon, #800000 according to HTML nomenclature (Berrojalbiz et al. 2014:158; Herrera 2016:17–22, 24–28).

One attribute that clearly distinguishes the Archaic Pictorial Tradition is the way the figures are organized, as exemplified by a panel at the site of Cueva de la Garza in the upper basin of the Humaya River, 96 km northwest of Rincón del Canal (Figure 6). We can see that an essentially horizontal axis dominates the structure of the painting, formed by a large band consisting of at least one line that runs horizontally across the entire wall and establishes a division of space into upper and lower regions (Berrojalbiz et al. 2014:157–161). These lines may be straight, wavy, or zigzag. In our example from Rincón del Canal there are two black parallel zigzag lines that constitute the first phase of motifs defining the horizontal axis (Figure 5). These two lines are about 1.36 m long.

It is very important to consider that the compositional function of the horizontal band at Rincón del Canal is very distinct from that found in other ex-

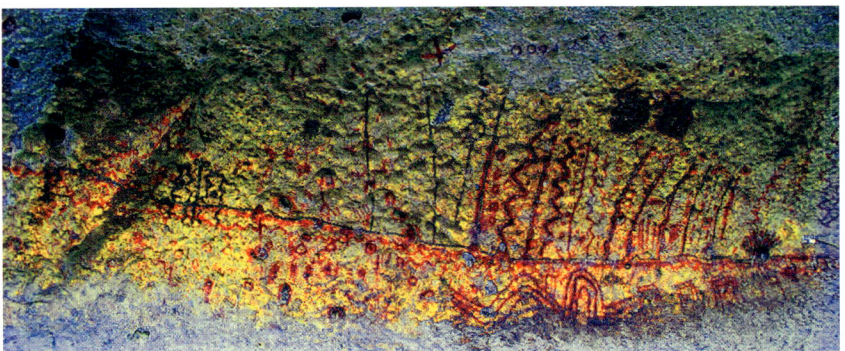

Figure 6. Cueva de la Garza site, Sierra Madre Occidental, Durango, Mexico. DStretch LDS enhancement.

Figura 6. Cueva de la Garza, Sierra Madre Occidental, Durango, México. Modificación DStretch LDS.

amples of the Archaic Pictorial Tradition. We can see that the band has a prominent purpose, as in the uninterrupted drawing that runs across the whole site of Cueva de la Garza, giving meaning and structure to the entire pictorial group (Figure 6). In the case of Rincón del Canal, the extent of the horizontal band appears to be limited to Panel 11, indicating a much more restricted function, in spite of the fact that most images in this section are spread out beneath this horizontal band in a long strip of the lower portion of the rock face (Figure 7). This, then, leaves the band in a position that is much more elevated in relation to the rest of the panels that surround it.

Within the Archaic Pictorial Tradition, a number of distinct vertical elements are positioned perpendicularly along the entire length of the large horizontal band. One of the best examples of this compositional unity is the Cueva de la Garza site (Figures 6, 8) (Berrojalbiz et al. 2014:159; Forcano 2000). These elements may include straight lines, wavy lines, zigzag lines, groups of dots, spots, fingerprints, and rows of circles. When these appear in alternating or repetitive patterns and include variations in shape, color, height, and line thickness, they provide a deliberate rhythmic structure to the composition (Berrojalbiz et al. 2014:158–162). It is here that we can appreciate the function of the large horizontal band as a central axis that gives structure and meaning to the whole pictorial group. For this reason, I think the much more limited role of the horizontal band in Rincón del Canal indicates a significant difference in rhythmic and compositional meaning compared to other sites belonging to the same tradition.

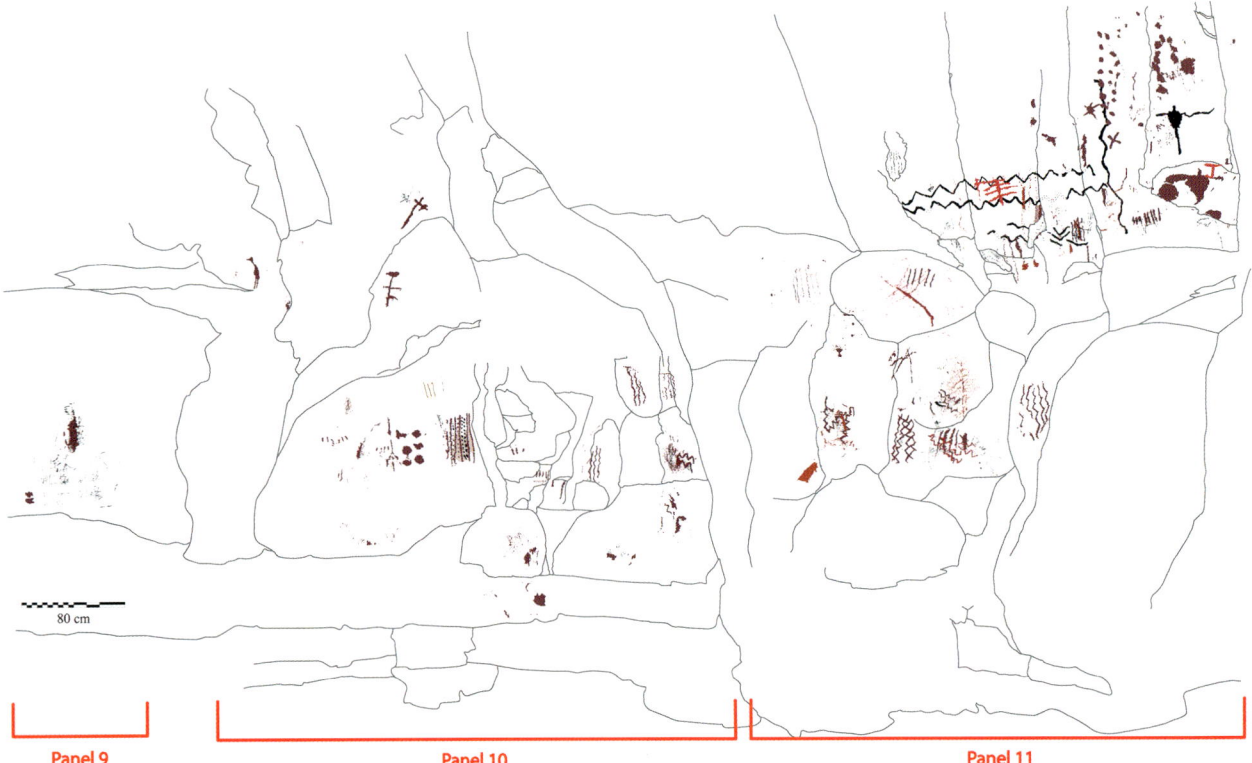

Figure 7. Panels 9, 10, and 11, Rincón del Canal site, Cañón de Molino.

Figura 7. Páneles 9, 10, y 11, Rincón del Canal, Cañón de Molino.

Figure 8. Detail, Cueva de la Garza site, Sierra Madre Occidental, Durango, Mexico. DStretch YDT enhancement.

Figura 8. Detalle, Cueva de la Garza, Sierra Madre Occidental, Durango, México. Modificación DStretch YDT.

Unlike other spaces, the frequent ritual use at Rincón del Canal, with its diverse executions and superimpositions, leads to less homogeneity in the general organization of the composition (Figure 5). This second phase of painting is composed of red figures, the majority of which consist of circular dots. The specific relationship between a color and a particular shape appears to be important in this tradition.

Significantly, accompanying the sequences of dots is a sunburst motif and a cross design that looks like a star (Figure 5). The inclusion of astral elements is a constant in certain compositions from the Archaic Pictorial Tradition and is one of the few figurative themes included in this predominantly geometric tradition (Berrojalbiz et al. 2014:159; Forcano 2000:495, 500). Another type of figurative element is represented by projectile points at the Mesa del Comal site in the basin of the Zape-Sextín River, which are associated with the site's large horizontal band (Berrojalbiz et al. 2014:159–160).

Series of Parallel Vertical Lines

Another form of composition closely related to those discussed above is constituted by long sequences of parallel vertical lines with lengths from a few centimeters to nearly half a meter. Once again, there is a visible alternating or repeating rhythmic expression in color, form, height, and line thickness (Berrojalbiz et al. 2014:158, 162–164; Forcano 2000:506). Four of these sequences are directly associated with the composition of the large horizontal band, all significantly located beneath it (Figure 5).

At Rincón del Canal, this type of compositional unit has a particular importance as a central theme of the panels, replacing the centrality of the horizontal band. These units tend to be distributed below the main arrangement of Panel 11 and occupy a large strip of the lower zone of the rock face encompassing Panels 9, 10, 11, 12, and 13 (Figure 7) (Herrera 2016:25–26, 32–34, 42–44, 49).

Each of these series of parallel vertical lines, whether straight, wavy, or zigzag, is clearly and expressly separated from the others by distinct natural planes that divide the rock face (Figure 7). At the same time, because of their shape and size, these lines tend to be located on flat surfaces and are usually rectangular in form, with a dominant vertical axis around which the depicted designs are also oriented (Herrera 2016:32–33, 42–43, 49).

The particular concentration of these lines on Panel 10 as well as on Panel 11 indicates, on the one hand, the particular specialization and autonomy of this kind of symbol, and on the other hand identifies this grouping as one of the more convincing pieces of evidence of image organization at Rincón del Canal, in which similar symbols are found within the same space (Herrera 2016:34, 49).

The Numeric Properties of Certain Symbols

One hypothesis about the likely function of these symbols is related to their probable numeric properties, which may be the case with some of the compositions found at the Rincón del Canal site (Herrera 2016:35–38). The numerical properties of these signs appear to be more plausible in the following series of parallel vertical lines in Panel 10 (Figure 9). Their sequential order and graphic symmetry (especially note the identical sums in several rows of fingerprints) immediately suggest some kind of numerical property. The total sum of 41 dots appears to correspond with a recording of the observable periods of the lunar cycle equivalent to a month and a half, and is very similar to the counting system and reading order of other ex-

Figure 9. Composition from Panel 10, Rincón del Canal site, Cañón de Molino.

Figura 9. Composición del panel 10, Rincón del Canal, Cañón de Molino.

amples of rock art found among the hunter-gatherer groups of Northeastern Mexico. William Breen Murray (1990, 1996, 2007) has documented for several decades a number of these configurations of engraved or painted dots and tally marks that illustrate an "archaic" tradition of numbering and counting of time in relation to the observation of lunar cycles. The importance of astronomical knowledge for the subsistence of these peoples originates, as Murray has noted, in the advantage gained by anticipating the seasonal changes in the environment and by scheduling the necessary actions for the exploitation of certain seasonal and dispersed food resources (Murray 1990:470, 1996:20, 23).

An example of the complexity of these temporal markers is found in the recording of lunar cycles in the petroglyph at the Presa de la Mula site in the state of Nuevo León. The petroglyph in question contains 207 tallies signifying seven synodic months organized in an intricate grid of 24 cells formed by six horizontal and four vertical lines (Murray 1990:455–456, 2007:76–78). This grid includes three distinct methods of recording the lunar month that make use of all the observable points of the synodic cycle (Murray 1990:458–459, 2007:79). Two of these methods appear to be used at the Rincón del Canal site (Figure 9). In the first, the month is divided into two unequal parts, which in this case refers to the 21 dots or days that are the sum of the two contiguous black columns to the right containing 10 and 11 fingerprints, respectively, corresponding to the observation from the new moon phase to the waning quarter moon phase. The second part adds the six black dots of the third column of fingerprints to record the last quarter of the lunar cycle, for a total of 27 days in the synodic cycle.

This format is similar to the lunar cycle registry in the first line of the Presa de la Mula petroglyph (Murray 1990:456–459, 2007:79). The remaining half month of 14 days that divides the lunar cycle into two parts around the full moon includes the five (4 + 1) red dots of the third and fourth lines plus the remaining nine black dots of the fourth line (Murray 1990:457–459, 2007:79). The remaining 15 days of this first line in the Presa de la Mula lunar registry combine to give a total of a lunar month and a half (Murray 1990:457–458, 2007:79). At this site and at Boca de Potrerillos, also in Nuevo León, there are petroglyphs with lunar registries of 42 and 43 days, or a lunar month and a half. The fact that there is such a petroglyph at Presa de la Mula is significant because it has the same reading order—right to left—and counting sequence divided in three large sections: 20+9+14 = 43 (Murray 1990:465, 2007:81).

A First Approximation of the Circle-Sequence Vertical Lines Convention

As I have been able to show in my analysis of the rock art at Rincón del Canal, the repeated grouping and association in various compositions of vertical lines sequences with circular shapes is a common practice or convention (Herrera 2016:31–32, 38–39, 42–44). Yet, despite the fact that in each one of the analyzed compositions there is a persistent close relationship between these expressions, there is also great variability in the way they are associated due to, among other factors, their specific ordering, the inclusion of additional symbols, and the formal diversity of the two groups of principal symbols (Herrera 2016:31–32, 39–40). The following example from Panel 13 illustrates this convention (Figure 10). This is without a doubt one of the most striking examples because of its remarkable polychromy and evident rhythmic harmony. It consists of three stages of execution—the first in black, the second in yellow, and the third in red. The explicitly structured order of the composition's stages of production has led me to consider the significance of its specific chromatic sequence. Based on its documentation with the use of a digital microscope, I have identified two main patterns for the Archaic Pictorial Tradition (Herrera 2016:45). The first consists of a black-red-orange chromatic sequence, as is the case of the upper part of Panel 11; the second pattern reveals a sequence of black-yellow-red, as is the case with the composition seen in Panel 13 (see Figure 11 for examples of specific color superimpositions) (Herrera 2016:24–28, 43–45).

Figure 10. Polychrome composition from Panel 13, Rincón del Canal site, Cañón de Molino.
Figura 10. Composición policromada del panel 13, Rincón del Canal, Cañón de Molino.

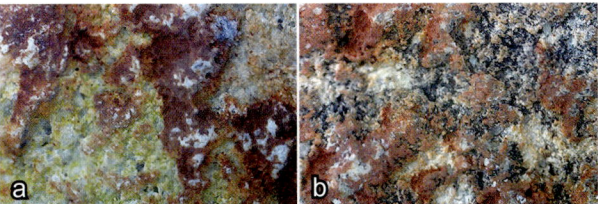

Figure 11. Images taken with Dino-Lite digital microscope: (a) superimposition of red painting over yellow painting; (b) superimposition of red painting over black painting.
Figura 11. Imágenes con microscopio digital Dino-Lite: (a) sobreposición rojo sobre amarillo; (b) sobreposición rojo sobre negro.

These chromatic sequences appear to be present in other sites of the Archaic Pictorial Tradition (Herrera 2016:43); however, they must continue to be verified during the documentation of these spaces. For example, in the case of the Cueva de la Garza site, in which the use of the color yellow had not been documented until now (Forcano 2000), a new study is required using the best available technology. I was able to detect the constant superimposition of red motifs over yellow ones thanks to the use of digital microscopes, which are of great utility for the observation and confirmation of the order of the superimpositions (Herrera 2016:24–28; Herrera and Chacón 2016:100).

Regarding Some Variants of this Tradition

In reference to the distinctive polychromatic aspects of this tradition, I have initially documented a variant based on the new sites that I have located in Cañón de Molino (Herrera 2016:46–48). We have yet to complete a deeper analysis and documentation of this variant and its relevant sites. One of these is Charco Azul, well known for its extraordinary setting that combines the beauty of the deep wells that feed the El Molino river and the enormous formations of volcanic rock that surround it (Figure 12). Four small concentrations of rock art are found in this space. The images are geometric-abstract in style, typical of Archaic sites. A key difference, however, is that these images are monochromatic in the Maroon color (HTML #800000). Regarding their composition, we can see examples of vertical straight or zigzag line sequences, although the emphasis of the images is focused on highlighting certain characteristics of the rocky surface—typically small cavities at the base of the wall—with markings a few centimeters in length (Herrera 2016:47).

Another of these sites is Rinconada de Flores. As in Charco Azul, the images are monochromatic in the distinctive Maroon. Once again, here the similarity to Charco Azul is that marking the rocky surface appears more important than the designs themselves. The features of the supporting rock structure may have strongly attracted the attention of the artists, such that the nodules of black rock that make up the structure

Figure 12. Charco Azul site, Cañón de Molino.
Figura 12. Charco Azul, Cañón de Molino.

are covered with tiny points or marks using a dotting technique, or used as surfaces for linear designs with these same marks (Figure 13) (Herrera 2016:47–48).

Figure 13. Paintings on black nodules, Rinconada de Flores site, Cañón de Molino.
Figura 13. Pinturas sobre nódulos negros, Rinconada de Flores, Cañón de Molino.

The Construction of Symbolic Landscapes

The likely ritual function of some of these sites seems intimately related to the selection of certain physical and environmental conditions of the spaces that the artists chose for painting, which reflect their vision of a symbolic construction of Cañón de Molino landscapes. For example, the Charco Azul and Cueva de Galindo sites portray reflective and secluded canyon environments similar to those found at Rincón del Canal, with its high vegetation that tends to block the view of surrounding areas (Herrera 2016:12–13, 22–23, 46–47).

Another important condition of these spaces is their constant relationship with water and humidity (Figure 12). This can be presented as a straightforward association of the paintings with natural springs, as occurs in Cueva de Galindo, where the large horizontal band terminates in one of several springs that are there (Herrera 2016:23–24). The site's association with water is also presented in relation to the existence of small seasonal creeks, as in the case of Rincón del Canal during the months of July and August when the heaviest rains fall and a small creek forms with the water that descends from the ravine of Rincón del Canal (Herrera 2016:14). Finally, if this association was not clear enough, the authors of the rock art left another kind of evidence directly related to the paintings in Rincón del Canal. Just before the end of Sector C, between Panels 14 and 15, there is a large area without any paintings because of the existence of an important runoff of water that has noticeably blackened the rock surface (Figure 14). During the rainy months, you can also see various seeps that run along the wall and fall into a series of small basins that have been carefully carved there with the clear purpose of collecting water (Herrera 2016:24). The same situation appears to be present in Cueva de la Garza, where small basins currently fill with water from the considerable runoff that has completely blackened the rock just to the side of the large group of Archaic paintings (Forcano 2000:504).

Figure 14. Note the group of small basins that have been carefully carved there with the clear purpose of collecting water. Rincón del Canal site, Cañón de Molino.
Figura 14. Note el conjunto de pequeñas pozas que han sido labradas precisamente ahí con el claro propósito de contener el agua. Rincón del Canal, Cañón de Molino.

The strong symbolic properties that appear to characterize these spaces immediately recall the methods pertaining to rites of passage or initiation (Campbell 2014:45). In these rites the participants must fulfill a "separation" or withdrawal from the everyday world, accessing a new realm of experience; once the threshold is crossed, participants confront, through various tests, the dangerous forces concentrated there. Their successful completion of these tests (that is, their "initiation") signifies their transformation or rebirth, and therefore their eventual "return" to bestow their received gifts upon other members of the community (Campbell 2014:45, 73–74, 94–99). In this sense, the particular gesture of leaving print marks of the middle fingers as evidence of the visitor's presence (Figure 15), or the repeated use of the fingers to paint, as is characteristic of this tradition (Figure 16), express the profound interest in connecting with these symbolically relevant spaces, in which the artists find themselves constantly drawn to associate themselves not only with the rock to touch it and feel it, but also with the precious, life-giving liquid that emerges from it in natural springs or runs down its walls in a serpentine fashion, like the zigzag lines painted on the rock faces of Rincón del Canal (Figure 17) (Herrera 2016:26, 35, 39–40, 44, 50).

Much remains to be investigated regarding the Archaic Pictorial Tradition; however, one of the most important conclusions throughout these years of research has been the power to recognize the diversity and complexity of this language beyond that which we were initially able to understand.

Figure 15. We see the gesture of leaving print marks of the middle fingers as evidence of the visitor's presence on at least two occasions, Panel 13, Rincón del Canal site, Cañón de Molino.

Figura 15. Es posible apreciar en dos ocasiones el gesto de imprimir tres dedos mayores con pintura de arriba hacia abajo como constancia del visitante en el lugar, panel 13, Rincón del Canal, Cañón de Molino.

Figure 16. Detail of the finger tracing, Panel 13, Rincón del Canal site, Cañón de Molino.

Figura 16. Detalle del trazo elaborado con los dedos, panel 13, Rincón del Canal, Cañón de Molino.

Figure 17. Composition from Panel 11, Rincón del Canal site, Cañón de Molino.

Figura 17. Composición del panel 11, Rincón del Canal, Cañón de Molino.

Acknowledgments. This fieldwork would have been impossible without the unconditional support of the members of the Cañón de Molino community. Among these, I would like to express my enormous gratitude to Eulalio Rivera Aguilar, Esperanza Solís Chávez, Luis Rocha Solís, Miguel Rocha Solís, Faustina Rodríguez Vargas, Andrés Rocha Solís, Natividad Samaniego, and José Miguel Rocha Rodríguez. Three pillars of support have been fundamental to this research: Fernando Berrojalbiz, Marie-Areti Hers, and William Breen Murray, teachers who have shared with me their extensive knowledge of Durango and rock art. To Ana Laura Chacón Rosas, my lifelong companion.

References Cited

Berrojalbiz, Fernando, and Marie-Areti Hers
 2012 Memoria y paisaje cultural: diversas estrategias de la apropiación del arte en la Sierra Madre Occidental de Durango. In *Apropiarse del arte: impulsos y pasiones, XXXII Coloquio Internacional de Historia del Arte*, edited by Olga Sáenz, pp. 93–115. Instituto de Investigaciones Estéticas, Universidad Nacional Autónoma de México.

Berrojalbiz, Fernando, Marie-Areti Hers, and José Luis Punzo Díaz
2014 Arte rupestre arcaico. In *Historia de Durango, Tomo I, Época Antigua*, edited by José Luis Punzo Díaz and Marie-Areti Hers, pp. 154–167. Instituto de Investigaciones Históricas, Universidad Juárez del Estado de Durango.

Campbell, Joseph
2014 *El héroe de las mil caras*. Psicoanálisis del mito. Fondo de Cultura Económica, Mexico.

Forcano, Marta
2000 Las pinturas rupestres de Potrero de Cháidez, Durango. In *Nómadas y sedentarios en el Norte de México. Homenaje a Beatriz Braniff*, edited by Marie-Areti Hers, José Luis Mirafuentes, María de los Dolores Soto, and Miguel Vallebueno, pp. 489–509. Instituto de Investigaciones Antropológicas, Instituto de Investigaciones Estéticas, Instituto de Investigaciones Históricas, Universidad Nacional Autónoma de México.

Herrera Maldonado, Daniel
2016 *Formas, valores y ritmos en la tradición pictórica del Arcaico en Durango*. Master's thesis, Universidad Nacional Autónoma de México.

Herrera Maldonado, Daniel, and Ana Laura Chacón Rosas
2016 Análisis de las técnicas pictóricas rupestres a partir de su registro con el microscopio digital Celestron. El caso del sitio el Rincón del Canal, Cañón de Molino, Durango. In *Arte rupestre de México para el mundo. Avances y nuevos enfoques de la investigación, conservación y difusión de la herencia rupestre mexicana*, edited by Gustavo A. Ramírez Castilla, Francisco Mendiola Galván, William Breen Murray, and Carlos Viramontes Anzures, pp. 87–103. Instituto Tamaulipeco para la Cultura y las Artes, Consejo Nacional para la Cultura y las Artes, Tamaulipas.

Hers, Marie-Areti
2001 La sombra de los desconocidos: los no mesoamericanos en los confines tolteca-chichimecas. In *La gran chichimeca. El lugar de las rocas secas*, edited by Beatriz Braniff, pp. 65–70. Consejo Nacional para la Cultura y las Artes, Editoriale Jaca Book Spa, Mexico.

Leroi-Gourhan, André
1971 *El gesto y la palabra*. Ediciones de la Biblioteca de la Universidad Central de Venezuela, Caracas.

Murray, William Breen
1990 Arte rupestre en Nuevo León. In *El Arte Rupestre en México*, edited by María del Pilar Casado and Lorena Mirambell, pp. 453–485. Instituto Nacional de Antropología e Historia, Mexico.

1996 The Northeast Mexican Petroglyphic Counting Tradition: A Methodological Summary. In *Astronomical Traditions in Past Cultures*, edited by Vesselina Koleva and Dimiter Kolev, pp. 14–24. Institute of Astronomy, Bulgarian Academy of Sciences, National Astronomical Observatory Rozhen, Sofia.

2007 Petroglifos calendáricos del norte de México. In *Arte rupestre del noreste*, edited by William Breen Murray, pp. 75–85. Fondo Editorial de Nuevo León, Monterrey.

Punzo, José Luis
2008 La ruta de las praderas en época prehispánica. El caso del abrigo de piedra de amolar 1, Durango. In *Las vías del noroeste II: propuesta para una perspectiva sistémica e interdisciplinaria*, edited by Carlo Bonfiglioli, Arturo Gutiérrez, Marie-Areti Hers, and María Eugenia Olavarría, pp. 103–129. Instituto de Investigaciones Antropológicas, Universidad Nacional Autónoma de México.

Tsukada, Yoshiyuki
2006 Grandes asentamientos chalchihuiteños de la Sierra Madre durangueña: estudio comparativo entre Cañón de Molino y Hervideros. In *La sierra tepehuana. Asentamientos y movimientos de población*, edited by Chantal Cramaussel and Sara Ortelli, pp. 45–55. El Colegio de Michoacán, Universidad Juárez del Estado de Durango.

Ritmos en el paisaje: la Tradición Pictórica del Arcaico de Durango, México

En memoria de William Breen Murray

Daniel Herrera Maldonado

El estudio arqueológico que he emprendido en el Cañón de Molino, ubicado en el valle de Guatimapé, me ha llevado a reconocer la presencia de varios sitios pertenecientes a la denominada Tradición Pictórica del Arcaico cuyo campo de distribución abarca buena parte de la Sierra Madre Occidental de Durango. En ese sentido este trabajo tendrá como objetivo explorar las principales características y variantes que definen a esta tradición de carácter abstracto, en términos de la organización de sus imágenes y de la construcción simbólica de los paisajes.

El estudio de más de diez años que he realizado acerca del arte rupestre del estado de Durango me ha llevado a conocer la denominada "Tradición Pictórica del Arcaico". Se trata de una tradición de fuerte unidad compositiva con una amplia distribución a lo largo de las tierras altas y los valles orientales de la Sierra Madre Occidental de Durango (Figura 1), perteneciente a las comunidades de cazadores-recolectores que antecedieron la bien conocida y muy bien estudiada colonización mesoamericana en el 600 d.C (Berrojalbiz y Hers 2012:96; Berrojalbiz et al. 2014:155, 157; Forcano 2000:490–491, 504–507; Hers 2001; Punzo 2008).

Al tratarse de un arte con un carácter marcadamente abstracto y geometrizante mi propuesta de análisis va dirigida a la mayor importancia que se le da al ritmo en este tipo de lenguajes sobre el sujeto figurado (Leroi-Gourhan 1971:369, 384). Es importante entender a los ritmos como aquellos movimientos regulares y recurrentes creadores del espacio y del tiempo. Éstos llegan a materializarse en las formas, por ello se les considera como un rasgo esencial de todas las artes (Leroi-Gourhan 1971:301, 307, 353). De esta manera si bien el significado preciso de cada figuración puede escapar de nuestra comprensión, mi estudio se enfocará en la búsqueda del "esqueleto ideológico" presente en la estructuración de las formas, valores y ritmos particulares, es decir en el sentido y equilibrio de los motivos en el espacio (Forcano 2000:501–502; Leroi-Gourhan 1971:274, 282, 316, 373).

Para ello he decidido enfocarme en el estudio de los varios sitios pertenecientes a esta tradición localizados en el Cañón de Molino, en la región de los llanos de Guatimapé, que conforman la porción central del estado de Durango (Figura 2). Su particular concentración en este cañón se debe probablemente a la importancia de su ubicación en la desembocadura de una enorme cuenca lacustre que aún hoy a pesar de las continuas sequías que azotan a la región es posible apreciar a la imponente Laguna de Santiaguillo (Figura 1). Los antiguos cazadores-recolectores disfrutaban aquí no sólo de la permanencia de recursos que les proveía la laguna misma, con la abundancia de peces y aves como alimento, sino también de la diversidad de ecosistemas que origina las diferencias de altura tan marcadas de las serranías que delimitan alrededor a la cuenca, poniendo a disposición en unos cuantos kilómetros de recursos muy variados sin la necesidad de realizar grandes traslados (Tsukada 2006:46). No es casual en ese sentido que en esta área se concentren varios santuarios de arte rupestre del Arcaico, específicamente en las serranías del Promontorio y del Epazote que rodean por el oriente y poniente respectivamente esta gran cuenca, siendo esta última cordillera donde se localiza precisamente el Cañón de Molino (Berrojalbiz et al. 2014:160-161).

Río arriba, aproximadamente a 4.5 km al interior del Cañón de Molino es posible observar como el gran frente rocoso de la Mesa de los Jabalíes (Figura 3) parece remeterse formando una rinconada precisamente en donde se ubican las pinturas de Rincón del Canal (Figura 4). Una de las características más llamativas del lugar es la manera en la que por la forma natural de este espacio, en una rinconada, éste expresa un carácter más bien privado, de recogimiento y reflexión. Condición que se incrementa por la abundante humedad que se concentra aquí y que favorece el crecimiento de un espesa vegetación, con bellos ejemplos de pinos y encinos, imposibilitado el disfrutar de una buena visibilidad de los alrededores.

En contraste con el estado de aislamiento respecto al resto del cañón que se percibe al ingresar al sitio, como si se traspasara algún tipo de umbral, existe un significativo efecto sonoro que fue determinante también para escoger este espacio para pintar. Por su orientación y forma de la pared, como si se tratara de un gran audífono rocoso, los sonidos de los alrededores se incrementan notablemente rebotando en este gran recoveco del cañón. De manera que es posible escuchar situado frente a las pinturas las voces y ruidos generadas por personas ubicadas a más de un kilómetro de distancia.

Una vez que se ha subido por el extenso talud de deposición hasta la base de las paredes verticales que fueron pintadas, nuestros ojos se dirigirán inmediatamente hacia una de las composiciones más emblemáticas del sitio: en la parte superior del panel 11 (Figura 5). Para fines de una mejor explicación he decidido iniciar mi análisis en este panel con el doble propósito de que sirva como introducción a las características generales de esta tradición y al mismo tiempo me permita definir sus particularidades en Rincón del Canal.

Ritmos de la Tradición Pictórica del Arcaico

El uso reiterado de este espacio con numerosos repintes, nuevas ejecuciones y sobreposiciones me ha permitido establecer la secuencia exacta de las varias fases de plasmación que están implicadas en la constitución final de la presente composición (Figura 5). Este rasgo está estrechamente vinculado a la forma particular en la que en esta tradición se emplea la policromía. En la mayoría de los casos más que la conjugación de varios colores en un mismo motivo, la policromía se conforma por la combinación de varias etapas de plasmación, cada una de ellas de tonalidad distinta. Entre los colores más frecuentemente usados estan el negro, amarillo, naranja, blanco y varios tonos de rojo entre los cuales se encuentra el característico rojo Maroon:#800000 de acuerdo a la nomenclatura html (Berrojalbiz et al. 2014:158; Herrera 2016:17–22, 24–28).

Uno de los atributos que más claramente distinguen a la Tradición Pictórica del Arcaico es la manera en la que se organizan sus figuras, como se ejemplifica por un panel en el sitio Cueva de la Garza, ubicado en la cuenca superior del río Humaya, 96 km al noroeste de Rincón del Canal (Figura 6). En su estructura vemos como domina un eje esencialmente horizontal, formado por una larga banda de una o varias líneas que recorren toda la pared horizontalmente lo que establece en principio una división del espacio en un arriba y abajo (Berrojalbiz et al. 2014:157–161). Estas líneas pueden ser de forma recta, ondulada o en zigzag. En el caso de Rincón del Canal se trata de dos líneas zigzagueantes paralelas en color negro que constituyen la primera fase de plasmación (Figura 5). Estas dos líneas son de cerca de 1.36 m de largo.

Es muy importante considerar que la función compositiva de la banda horizontal en Rincón del Canal es muy distinta al de otros emplazamientos de la Tradición Pictórica del Arcaico en donde vemos como esta lleva un patente protagonismo en razón de su ininterrumpido trazado a lo largo de todo el sitio, dando sentido y estructura a todo el conjunto pictórico (Figura 6). En el caso de Rincón del Canal su extensión parece limitarse a panel 11, denotando su función mucho más restringida, a pesar de que como se aprecia, el grueso de imágenes del sector se despliegan bajo ésta ocupando una larga franja de la zona inferior del frente rocoso (Figura 7). Esto la deja entonces en una posición mucho más elevada, si bien también central, respecto al resto de paneles que la rodean.

Como es propio de la Tradición Pictórica del Arcaico a partir de la gran banda horizontal y a todo su largo, sobre todo en su parte superior, se disponen perpendicularmente distintos elementos verticales. Uno de lo espacios que expresan mejor por su homogeneidad esta particular unidad compositiva es Cueva de la Garza (Figuras 6, 8) (Berrojalbiz et al. 2014:159; Forcano 2000). Estos elementos pueden incluir líneas rectas, ondulantes y en zigzag, conjuntos de puntos, manchas y digitaciones, o hileras de círculos, que por su alternancia o repetición en forma, color, altura y grosor de trazo le otorgan una estructura expresamente rítmica a la composición (Berrojalbiz et al. 2014:158–162). Es realmente aquí donde podemos apreciar la función de la gran banda horizontal como eje central que da estructura y sentido a todo el conjunto pictórico. Por ello me parece sumamente significativo, su carácter mucho más circunscrito en Rincón del Canal, lo cual perfila desde ahora una diferencia muy notable en su sentido rítmico y compositivo con los otros sitios pertenecientes a la misma tradición.

A diferencia de otros espacios, el uso ritual reiterado de Rincón del Canal con sus varias ejecuciones y sobreposiciones promovió una menor homogeneidad en la organización general de la composición (Figura 5). Esta segunda etapa de plasmación está integrada por figuras de color rojo en su mayoría de forma circular. La relación especifica entre un color y una forma determinada parece ser importante en esta tradición.

Es significativo que acompañando a las secuencias de círculos se encuentre la figura de un soliforme y un diseño de cruz que recuerda a un esteliforme (Figura 5). La inclusión de elementos astrales suele ser constante en ciertas composiciones de la Tradición Pictórica del Arcaico siendo una de las pocas temáticas figurativas que son incluidas en esta tradición predominantemente geométrica (Berrojalbiz et al. 2014:159; Forcano 2000:495, 500). Otro tipo de elementos figurativos que también es posible reconocer son las puntas de proyectil como las del sitio de Mesa del Comal en la cuenca del río Zape-Sextín asociadas a la gran banda horizontal (Berrojalbiz et al. 2014:159–160).

Series de líneas verticales paralelas

Otra forma de composición en estrecha cercanía con la que venimos analizando la constituyen las largas secuencias de trazos verticales paralelos de un largo que va de apenas unos cuantos centímetros hasta casi medio metro. Nuevamente aquí observamos una alternancia o repetición expresamente rítmica en color, forma, altura y grosor de trazo (Berrojalbiz et al. 2014:158, 162–164; Forcano 2000:506). Cuatro de éstas es posible apreciarlas directamente asociadas a la composición de la gran banda horizontal, todas significativamente ubicadas debajo de ésta (Figura 5).

En Rincón del Canal este tipo de unidad compositiva tiene una particular importancia como tema central de los paneles, sustituyendo el protagonismo de la banda horizontal. Estas unidades tienden a distribuirse bajo la composición principal del panel 11, ocupando una extensa franja de la zona inferior del frente rocoso correspondiente a los paneles 9, 10, 11, 12 y 13 (Figura 7) (Herrera 2016:25–26, 32–34, 42–44, 49).

Cada una de estas series de líneas verticales paralelas, ya sea rectas, onduladas o en zigzag, se encuentra claramente y expresamente separada de la otra por los distintos planos naturales en los que el frente rocoso se divide (Figura 7). Al mismo tiempo de que por su forma y tamaño éstas tienden a ubicarse en superficies en la medida de lo posible planas y de una forma tendiente a la rectangularidad, es decir con un eje vertical dominante al cual también se orientan los diseños plasmados (Herrera 2016:32–33, 42–43, 49).

Su concentración en el panel 10 y 11, me permite considerar, por un lado, la particular especialización y autonomía de este tipo de signo, y por el otro reconocer a esta agrupación como una de las evidencias más contundentes de organización de las imágenes en Rincón del Canal en la que signos de la misma naturaleza se sitúan bajo un mismo espacio (Herrera 2016:34, 49).

Las propiedades numéricas de ciertos signos

Una de las hipótesis en torno a la función de este tipo de signos, la cual es necesario seguir contrastando a medida que se continúe con el registro de estos sitios, está relacionada con sus probables propiedades numéricas, como así parece registrarse en el caso de algunos de éstos en Rincón del Canal (Herrera 2016:35–38). La propiedad numérica de estos signos se hace más fehaciente en la siguiente serie de líneas verticales paralelas del panel 10 (Figura 9). Su orden secuencial y simetría gráfica (nótese sobre todo las sumas idénticas en varias de las hileras de digitaciones) nos hacen sospechar inmediatamente sobre sus propiedades numéricas. La suma total de 41 puntos parece corresponder a un registro relacionado con los periodos observables del ciclo lunar equivalente a un mes y medio, muy parecido tanto en el sistema de conteo y orden de lectura a otros ejemplos que se encuentran en el arte rupestre de los cazadores-recolectores del Noreste de México. William Breen Murray (1990, 1996, 2007) ha documentado a lo largo de varias décadas numerosos de estas configuraciones de puntos y líneas grabadas o pintadas que registran una "arcaica" tradición de numeración y de computo del tiempo en relación a la observación de los ciclos lunares. La importancia acerca del conocimiento astronómico para la subsistencia de estos pueblos deriva como ha denotado este mismo autor en la ventaja que les proporciona el anticipar los cambios ambientales estacionales y programar los movimientos necesarios para la explotación de ciertos recursos alimenticios dispersos y temporales (Murray 1990:470; 1996:20, 23).

Un ejemplo ilustrador de la complejidad que llegan a alcanzar estos registros temporales se encuentra en la llamada cuenta lunar del petroglifo de Presa de la Mula, Nuevo León. El petrograbado en cuestión cuenta con 207 rayas equivalentes a 7 meses sinódicos lunares, organizadas en una compleja cuadrícula de 24 celdas formada por seis líneas horizontales y cuatro verticales (Murray 1990:455–456; 2007:76–78). En éste se reconocen tres modos distintos para registrar el mes lunar que hacen uso de todos los puntos observables del ciclo sinódico, de los cuales dos parecen utilizarse en el conteo de Rincón del Canal (Murray 1990:458–459; 2007:79). En el primero de éstos se divide el mes en dos partes desiguales que en el caso de Rincón del Canal (Figura 9) se refiere a los 21 puntos o días que suman las dos columnas contiguas negras de la derecha de 10 y 11 digitaciones, correspondientes al periodo de observación de la luna nueva al cuarto menguante. La segunda parte suma los 6 puntos negros de la tercera columna de digitaciones para alcanzar el último cuarto del ciclo lunar hasta su desaparición, teniendo en total un mes sinódico de 27 días a semejanza de lo que se registra en la primera línea del petrograbado de Presa de la Mula (Murray 1990:456–459; 2007:79). El restante medio mes de 14 días que divide el ciclo lunar en dos mitades alrededor de la luna llena, suma los 5 (4 + 1) puntos rojos de la tercera y cuarta línea más los 9 puntos negros restantes de la cuarta (Murray 1990:457–459; 2007:79). Los días restantes de esta primera línea en la cuenta de Presa de la Mula corresponden a 15 días para dar un total también de un mes y medio lunar (Murray 1990:457–458; 2007:79). En este mismo sitio y en Boca de Potrerillos también en Nuevo León se presentan petrograbados con registros de 42 y 43 puntos o días que concuerdan también con el mes y medio lunar, el caso de un petroglifo en Presa de la Mula es sumamente interesante pues su orden de lectura se realiza también de derecha a izquierda y con una secuencia de conteo dividida también en tres grandes secciones: 20+9+14 = 43 (Murray 1990:465; 2007:81).

Un primer acercamiento a la convención círculo-secuencia de líneas verticales

Como lo he podido atestiguar a medida que he avanzado en el registro de Rincón del Canal, la reiterada agrupación y asociación en varias de sus composiciones de las secuencias de líneas verticales con las formas circulares evidencia una convención en la asociación entre estos dos tipos de signos (Herrera 2016:31–32, 38–39, 42–44). No obstante que en cada una de las composiciones analizadas persiste esa relación de proximidad entre ambos temas, también se registra una enorme variabilidad en cada una de sus conjunciones en razón, entre otros factores, de su ordenación especifica, la inclusión de lo que llamaré como signos o temáticas "auxiliares", y en la diversidad formal de los dos grupos de signos principales (Herrera 2016:31–32, 39–40). El siguiente ejemplo del panel 13 ilustra esta convención (Figura 10). Por su llamativa policromía y marcado equilibrio rítmico la hacen sin duda una de las versiones más bellas de ésta. Tres son las etapas de ejecución que la componen—la primera en color negro, la segunda en color amarillo y la tercera en color rojo. El orden tan explícitamente estructurado de las fases que integran la presente composición me ha llevado a reflexionar sobre la importancia de su secuencia cromática específica. A partir de su documentación he identificado dos patrones principales para la Tradición Pictórica del Arcaico (Herrera 2016:45). El primero de éstos se ordena siguiendo la secuencia cromática negro-rojo-naranja, como en el caso de la parte superior del panel 11; el segundo patrón dispone los colores en el orden negro-amarillo-rojo, como en la composición del panel 13 (ver Figura 11 para ejemplos de superposiciones de color específicas) (Herrera 2016:24–28, 43–45).

Estas mismas secuencias cromáticas parecen tentativamente observarse en otros sitios de la Tradición Pictórica del Arcaico (Herrera 2016:43); sin embargo, es necesario seguir constatándolas a medida que se continúe con el registro sistemático de estos espacios. Por ejemplo en el sitio Cueva de la Garza, santuario en el que hasta ahora no se había documentado una etapa de plasmación en color amarillo (Forcano 2000), lo cual plantea la necesidad de realizar un nuevo registro de este importante lugar con lo último en cuanto a tecnología que disponemos, pude apreciar la sobreposición constante de los motivos rojos sobre los de amarillo gracias a la ayuda de los microscopios digitales, de gran utilidad para la observación y confirmación del orden de las sobreposiciones (Herrera 2016:24–28; Herrera y Chacón 2016:100).

De algunas otras variantes en esta tradición

En referencia precisamente a la distintiva policromía de esta tradición, he registrado inicialmente una variante a partir de los nuevos sitios que he podido localizar en el Cañón de Molino (Herrera 2016:46–48). De esta variante así como de sus sitios, queda pendiente realizar un análisis y registro más profundo. Uno de estos espacios es el de Charco Azul bien conocido por tratarse de un extraordinario escenario que conjunta la belleza de las profundas pozas que alimenta el río El Molino y las enormes formaciones de cantera que rodean las aguas de este afluente (Figura 12). Como parte de este espacio se plasmaron cuatro pequeñas concentraciones de arte rupestre. En sus imágenes permea el carácter geométrico-abstracto como es propio de los sitios del Arcaico, sin embargo una característica que lo diferencia es su manifiesta monocromía en color rojo Maroon (HTML #800000). En cuanto a composición vemos también presentes algunos ejemplos de las secuencias de líneas verticales rectas o en zigzag, si bien es cierto es que el énfasis en la disposición de sus imágenes está enfocado a marcar con pequeños trazos de unos pocos centímetros ciertas características del soporte como pueden ser pequeñas cavidades al pie de la pared rocosa (Herrera 2016:47).

Otro de estos sitios es el de Rinconada de Flores. Como en Charco Azul permea la monocromía de sus imágenes con el distintivo rojo Maroon. Nuevamente aquí a semejanza de Charco Azul parece más importante el gesto de pintar sobre la roca que los diseños representados. Las características del soporte parece haber llamado poderosamente la atención de los artistas, de manera que los nódulos de roca negra que lo integran son rellenados de pequeñas puntuaciones a través de la técnica del tamponado o son aprovechados para plasmar algunos diseños lineales conformados también por estas diminutas manchas (Figura 13) (Herrera 2016:47–48).

Una misma construcción de los paisajes simbólicos

La probable función ritual de algunos de estos sitios parece íntimamente relacionada con la selección de ciertas condiciones físicas y ambientales de los espacios que fueron escogidos para pintar, lo cual conjunta una visión de sus autores de la construcción simbólica de los paisajes del Cañón de Molino. Por ejemplo, a semejanza de Rincón del Canal, en sitios como Charco Azul o Cueva de Galindo vemos como también permea un ambiente más bien privado, de recogimiento y reflexión. Estas condiciones son favorecidas tanto por la forma que presenta el cañón en esos sitios, como por la alta vegetación que crece allí, lo cual no permite disfrutar de una buena visibilidad de los alrededores (Herrera 2016:12–13, 22–23, 46–47).

Otra condición importante es su relación constante con el agua y la humedad (Figura 12). Está puede presentarse a partir de la asociación directa de las pinturas con manantiales como sucede en Cueva de Galindo donde se aprecia como la gran banda horizontal llega a concluir en uno de los varios manantiales presentes en este sitio (Herrera 2016:23–24). Su asociación con el agua suele presentarse también a partir de la existencia de pequeños arroyos temporales, como en el caso de Rincón del Canal en el que durante los meses de julio y agosto cuando se concentran las lluvias más intensas, se favorece a la formación de un pequeño arroyo con el agua que desciende intensamente de la cañada de Rincón (Herrera 2016:14). Finalmente, si esta asociación no fuera suficientemente clara, los autores del arte rupestre han dejado otro tipo de evidencia con relación directa a las pinturas de Rincón del Canal. Un poco antes de la finalización del sector C, entre los paneles 14 y 15, existe una amplia área con ausencia de pinturas debido a la existencia de un importante escurrimiento de agua que ha ennegrecido notablemente el reliz (Figura 14). Es precisamente también en estos meses de mayor lluvia donde es posible apreciar las varias goteras que escurren de la pared justamente para caer en un conjunto de pequeñas pozas que han sido labradas precisamente ahí con el claro propósito de contener el vital líquido (Herrera 2016:24). Esta misma situación parece repetirse en Cueva de la Garza donde pequeñas pozas se llenan actualmente de agua por el amplio escurrimiento que ha ennegrecido completamente la roca, justo a lado del cual se ubica la gran composición del Arcaico (Figura 15) (Forcano 2000:504).

Las fuertes propiedades simbólicas que parecen denotar estos espacios, me refieren inmediatamente a las formulas que son propias de los ritos de paso o iniciación (Campbell 2014:45). En ellos los participantes debían cumplir con una "separación" del mundo de todos los días accediendo a una nueva zona de experiencia; una vez cruzado el umbral los participantes enfrentarían a través de varias pruebas con las fuerzas exacerbadas y peligrosas que se concentran ahí; su paso exitoso por éstas (es decir su "iniciación"), implicaría su transformación o nuevo renacer, y por lo tanto su eventual "retorno" para otorgar los nuevos dones recibidos a los otros miembros de la comunidad (Campbell 2014:45, 73–74, 94–99). En ese sentido el particular gesto de imprimir los tres dedos mayores con pintura de arriba hacia abajo como constancia del visitante en el lugar (Figura 15), o la recurrencia de emplear los dedos de las manos para pintar como es característico de esta tradición (Figura 16), expresan el profundo interés de vincularse con estos espacios de clara relevancia simbólica, en el que sus autores se ven constantemente urgidos a asociarse a la roca, tocándola, sintiéndola, y en consecuencia también a ese líquido precioso de vida que surge a través de ella en los manantiales, o que escurre a lo largo de sus paredes a semejanza del serpentear de las líneas zigzagueantes pintadas en Rincón del Canal (Figura 17) (Herrera 2016:26, 35, 39–40, 44, 50).

Resta mucho por hacer respecto a la Tradición Pictórica del Arcaico sin embargo una de las conclusiones más importantes a lo largo de estos años de investigación ha sido el poder reconocer la diversidad y complejidad de este lenguaje más allá de lo que en un primer momento se había podido comprender.

Agradecimientos. Sin el apoyo incondicional de la comunidad del Molino el trabajo de campo hubiera sido imposible, entre ellos me gustaría agradecer enormemente a: Eulalio Rivera Aguilar, Esperanza Solís Chávez, Luis Rocha Solís, Miguel Rocha Solís, Faustina Rodríguez Vargas, Andrés Rocha Solís, Natividad Samaniego y José Miguel Rocha Rodríguez. Tres pilares han sido fundamentales en esta investigación: Fernando Berrojalbiz, Marie-Areti Hers y William Breen Murray, maestros que me han compartido su amplio conocimiento de la historia de Durango y del arte rupestre. A Ana Laura Chacón Rosas compañera permanente en la vida.

The Woman with Butterfly Hair Whorls in Chalchihuites Rock Art of Durango, Mexico

Daniel Herrera Maldonado and Ana Laura Chacón Rosas

In this paper we analyze various representations of women with butterfly hair whorls that have been documented in rock art sites in northwestern Durango. This image, which first appeared in Durango around A.D. 600, has its origin in the ancestral Pueblo cultures of the southwestern United States, as a result of the strong links they had established with the Chalchihuites culture. With this in mind, we conduct an iconographic study of the image and its relationship to the other motifs in the same grouping, in addition to considering the importance of the landscape features associated with the spaces where the image is found. This will allow us to establish the likely function of the image in comparison to its original role, with the understanding that its assimilation by the Chalchihuites culture implies an adaption to the new cultural context.

The rock art which we will now introduce belongs to the so-called "Chalchihuites" culture. The presence of this culture in the state of Durango, Mexico, originated with a large migratory movement in A.D. 600 when its members populated the interior and the eastern valleys of the Sierra Madre Occidental. This important migration, which represented a northward expansion of the Mesoamerican frontier, began in the states of Zacatecas and Jalisco, where the Chalchihuites people had lived for five centuries. The migration extended as far north as Malpaís de la Breña, a large volcanic area that includes part of southern Durango (Hers 2014a:179–181).

In this first period of occupation in Durango, which lasted from A.D. 600 to 900, the Chalchihuites people established an important communication bridge with the ancestral Puebloan peoples of the southwestern United States (Carot and Hers 2011; Hers 2014b). The results of this contact can be seen in rock art images—and thus in the exchange of ideas and beliefs—as well as in other spheres of expression.

This connection led to the introduction in Durango of rock art images with a long history in the American Southwest. Among these images are those of the well-known flute players (Carot and Hers 2011:Figures 2 and 3), commonly confused with the Kokopelli kachina, and, as in the case that interests us, the image of a female character with butterfly hair whorls (Carot and Hers 2011:39; Hers 2001; 2014b:415–420; Punzo 2008).

Daniel Herrera Maldonado
Universidad Nacional Autónoma de México

Ana Laura Chacón Rosas
Escuela Nacional de Antropología e Historia

The Woman with Butterfly Hair Whorls in the American Southwest

The Pueblo communities (such as Hopi, Zuni, and Taos) devised this hairstyle, which is characterized by fixing the hair in such a way as to create two circular extensions on each side of the head (Figure 1). Women wear

Figure 1. Hopi woman with butterfly hair whorls. Oil on albanene (vellum), painting by Araceli Maldonado González.
Figura 1. Mujer Hopi con peinado de mariposa. Oleo sobre albanene. Autor: Araceli Maldonado González.

this hairstyle during certain ceremonies starting with their first menstruation and continuing until marriage (Hays-Gilpin 2004:133).

This hairstyle appears in the traditional iconography of the kivas, ceramics, and rock art of the Southwest in three important periods. The oldest recording is seen in rock art dating to A.D. 200. Later, several examples were identified in ceramics from the Basketmaker III Era and in rock art of the period from A.D. 600 to 900. The most recent examples, corresponding to a third stage, are found in kiva mural paintings, pottery, and rock art dating from 1350 to 1700 (Hays-Gilpin 2004:128–137).

For Puebloan communities, the woman with this hairstyle represents the growth of corn and other aspects of fertility, abundance, and creation itself (Hays-Gilpin 2004:139–141). The motif sometimes includes related elements such as those representing vulvas and flute players (Hays-Gilpin 2004:137).

Cueva del Diablo

In Durango we have documented five sites with the presence of this character. With the exception of the La Cantera site, which is located much farther north in the Tepehuanes river valley, a majority of these sites are concentrated in the central portion of the state along an east-west axis that runs from the Sierra Madre Occidental to the Santiago Papasquiaro river valley and the Sierra del Epazote mountains (Figure 2). It is important to mention that the image of the flute player is also present at these sites and in others nearby (Figure 3) (Punzo 2008:116–117). The presence of both characters is also a recurring pattern in the rock art of the Southwest (Hays-Gilpin 2004:138).

One site in particular that has captured our attention is the so-called Cueva del Diablo. To gain access to this site one must cross the heart of the Sierra del Epazote, which is predominately forested and higher in altitude than the valleys that surround the mountain range. From the bottom of a small mountain valley near a small creek called Arroyo el Piojo, which runs east to west, it is possible to see, from a distance of several kilometers, the caves containing the rock art. This is because of their location in the highest part of the mountain range that surrounds the valley to the north (Figure 4).

While climbing the steep hill leading to the site, one can appreciate the striking panoramic view of the Sierra del Epazote mountains to the south (Figure 5). The paintings pertaining to the Chalchihuites culture are

Figure 2. Map showing the location of the sites with images of the woman with butterfly hair whorls. Durango, Mexico.
Figura 2. Mapa con la localización de los sitios con presencia de la mujer con peinado de mariposa. Durango, México.

distributed in two of the three caves that make up the site. The middle cave is the one where the female images are concentrated (Figure 6). All of the motifs of this space are anthropomorphic in nature, painted with the color orange, and always arranged in pairs (Figure 7). These figures are approximately 20 cm in height with a frontal view of the body. A single stroke delineates the form of the body, with slightly elevated arms and open legs. The fingers of the hands and feet are almost always drawn in groups of three. The motif on the left in Figure 8 is represented with the characteristic butterfly whorl hairstyle. If this figure's female identity was not evident enough, there is a clear representation of a vulva between her legs. The same is true for the three surrounding figures (Figure 7).

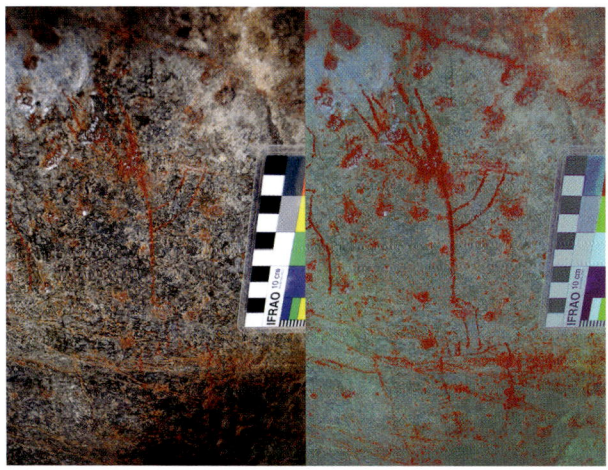

Figure 3. Fluteplayer. Cueva de Molino site, Cañón de Molino, Durango. DStretch LRE enhancement.

Figura 3. Flautista. Cueva de Molino, Cañón de Molino, Durango. Modificación DStretch LRE.

Figure 4. Caves with rock art. Cueva del Diablo site, Sierra del Epazote, Durango.

Figura 4. Cuevas con arte rupestre. Cueva del Diablo, Sierra del Epazote, Durango.

Figure 5. The view from Cueva del Diablo site, Sierra del Epazote, Durango.

Figura 5. Vista desde la Cueva del Diablo, Sierra del Epazote, Durango.

Figure 6. Cave with the female figures. Cueva del Diablo site, Sierra del Epazote, Durango.

Figura 6. Cueva con las figuras femeninas. Cueva del Diablo, Sierra del Epazote, Durango.

Figure 7. The female images are concentrated in the middle cave. Cueva del Diablo site, Sierra del Epazote, Durango. DStretch LRE enhancement.

Figura 7. La cavidad del centro es en donde se concentran las imágenes femeninas. Cueva del Diablo, Sierra del Epazote, Durango. Modificación DStretch LRE.

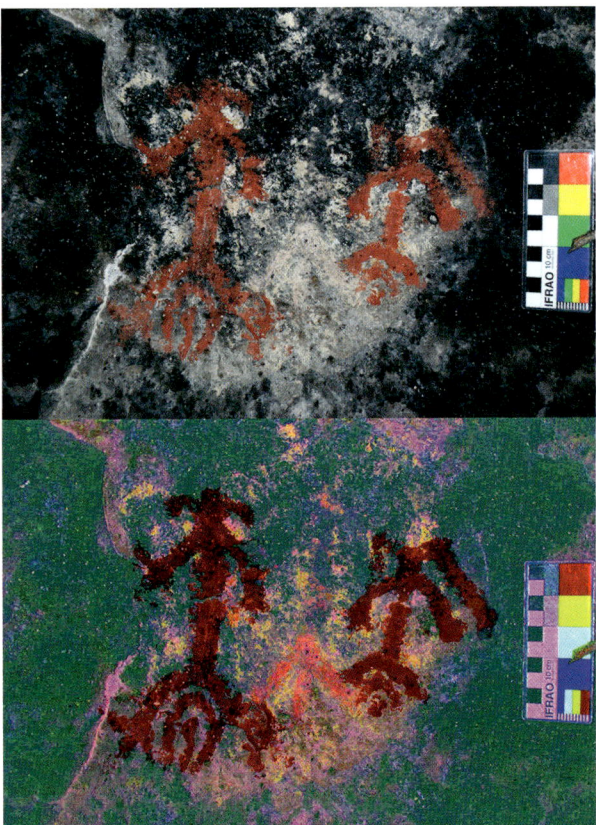

Figure 8. Pair of women with butterfly hair whorls. Cueva del Diablo site, Sierra del Epazote, Durango. DStretch CRGB enhancement.
Figura 8. Par de mujeres con peinado de mariposa. Cueva del Diablo, Sierra del Epazote, Durango. Modificación DStretch CRGB.

Several occurrences of natural springs around these female figures reaffirm their association with fertility and water. One significant feature is that water emerges from and drips along the walls at the same height where the women are located. Some of the crevices from which the water emerges even appear to have the form of a large rocky vulvas.

These properties with which the images in this cave appear to be linked include a sensation of dampness, seclusion, and darkness that can be perceived upon entering. The completely blackened surface, which contrasts markedly with the color of the paintings, increases this perception (Figure 6). Another interesting feature is that entering the cave requires one to crouch down due to the low height of the entrance, which obligates the visitor to "bow" to the images and revere their "spiritual power."

The second group of images is located in the adjacent cave to the east, where we again see a predominance of human figures over other themes (Figure 9).

Figure 9. Images in the third cave. Cueva del Diablo site, Sierra del Epazote, Durango. DStretch YBK enhancement.
Figura 9. Tercera cueva. Cueva del Diablo, Sierra del Epazote, Durango. Modificación DStretch YBK.

All of the anthropomorphic figures are painted black and are accompanied by a pair of red hands painted in positive. Among the seven characters represented, one stands out from the rest because of very clearly depicted vulva (Figure 10). Another attribute that distinguishes this character is the presence of a variant of the butterfly hair whorls. As drawn, this hairstyle consists of two long strokes that begin at the head and extend downward to the level of the chest. In comparing this image with the iconography seen in Chalchihuites pottery, we note a similarity to a female Mesoamerican deity painted on a plate from the La Atalaya site in Durango (Figure 11) (Hers 2014a:180–182). References to the sex of this figure are seen in the way her nipples are drawn, in her skirt decorated with a pair of serpents, and in small lines that allude to her relationship with water. Like the female characters of Chalchihuites rock art, her hairstyle is depicted by two long strokes that extend from each side of her head which, in the case of the plate image, are easier to recognize as the representations of two snakes.

Salto del Perro

The reaffirmation of the link to fertility and sexuality of these figures is once again present at the Salto del Perro site, located in the Cañón de Potrerillos, one of several canyons that provide access from the east to the Sierra del Epazote mountains. The environment of this site has the same conditions of abundant water and vegetation that appear to be associated with the sites where women with butterfly whorl hairstyles are depicted. The canyon is narrow, with several natural

Figure 10. Female figure, third cave. Cueva del Diablo site, Sierra del Epazote, Durango. DStretch LDS enhancement.
Figura 10. Figura femenina, tercera cueva. Cueva del Diablo, Sierra del Epazote, Durango. Modificación DStretch LDS.

Figure 12. Salto del Perro site, Cañón de Potrerillos, Durango.
Figura 12. Salto del Perro, Cañón de Potrerillos, Durango.

terrupted by a shift in elevation and a waterfall, below which water from the creek accumulates in several small pools distributed around a large semicircular wall that forms the waterfall (Figure 12). To one side of the waterfall, on the wall of a small, natural semicircle are paintings of human figures of notable importance (Figure 13). Even though the motifs are painted in black, yellow, red, and white, the female figures with butterfly hair whorls are painted in orange and appear in pairs, like those at the Cueva del Diablo site. These figures are also the ones with clearly marked sexual features (Figure 14). An important difference in the versions found in this space is the way in which some of these women are depicted with enlarged bellies (Figure 15). Furthermore, instead of genital organs between their legs, they are drawn as though a semicircle with a pair of parallel lines is emerging from their abdomens. These images may be depicting a birth scene, thereby associating these figures with the important domain of creation (Berrojalbiz and Hers 2012:99–101; 2014a:261–265).

springs and a small creek that appear to provide water for the vegetation, once again creating a dark and secluded environment (Berrojalbiz and Hers 2012:99–101; 2014a:261–265).

Following the small creek upstream, the path is in-

Las Latas and Piedra de Amolar

Las Latas is a site located near the waters of the Santiago Papasquiaro river in the valley that separates the Sierra del Epazote from the Sierra Madre Occidental. In this area petroglyphs are the predominant form of rock art, as is usually the case in rock art sites associated with this river as well as with other rivers and creeks that make up the upper Nazas river basin (Berrojalbiz and Hers 2014b:308–314; Herrera

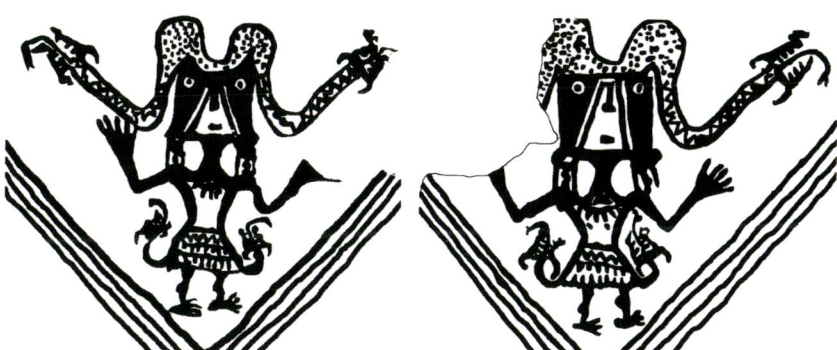

Figure 11. Female Chalchihuites deity painted on a plate from the La Atalaya site in Durango. Drawing by Marie-Areti Hers (Flores et al. 2008:Figure 4).
Figura 11. Deidad femenina chalchihuiteña pintada en un plato procedente del sitio La Atalaya en Durango. Dibujo: Marie-Areti Hers (Flores et al. 2008:Figure 4).

Figure 13. Women with butterfly hair whorls. Salto del Perro site, Cañón de Potrerillos, Durango. DStretch LRD enhancement.
Figura 13. Mujeres con peinado de mariposa. Salto del Perro, Cañón de Potrerillos, Durango. Modificación DStretch LRD.

Figure 14. Pair of women with butterfly hair whorls. Salto del Perro site, Cañón de Potrerillos, Durango. DStretch LDS enhancement.
Figura 14. Par de mujeres con peinado de mariposa. Salto del Perro, Cañón de Potrerillos, Durango. Modificación DStretch LDS.

2012:170–192). Its link with water, fertility, and sexuality is reaffirmed not only by its proximity to the waters of this river, but also in the iconographic repertoire of this site. Large engraved vulvas, which serve to identify examples of the Chalchihuites rock art tradition in other sites farther north, are associated here with the figures with butterfly hair whorls.

Figure 15. Woman depicted with an enlarged belly. Salto del Perro site, Cañón de Potrerillos, Durango. DStretch RGB0 enhancement.
Figura 15. Mujeres representadas con un vientre abultado. Salto del Perro, Cañón de Potrerillos, Durango. Modificación DStretch RGB0.

An important element of these female images is their particular arrangement (Figure 16). Just as with ceramics of the Basketmaker III period found near Durango, Colorado, the figures with butterfly hair whorls are arranged in a row and holding hands, as if they were doing some kind of dance (Figure 17) (Hays-Gilpin 2004:Figure 7.3). A similar representation is seen at the Piedra de Amolar site in the Sierra Madre Occidental (Figure 18), where the female images are accompanied, in an adjacent panel, by the flute player (not shown here) (Punzo 2008:116).

La Cantera

The last space we will discuss is the La Cantera site. As in the case of Las Latas, its location is related to its proximity to the waters of an important river, in this case the Tepehuanes. The recording and systematic analysis of the organization of the images at La Cantera has highlighted the structure that guides a majority of its compositions (Herrera 2012). This

Figure 16. Figures with butterfly hair whorls arranged in a row and holding hands. Las Latas site, Santiago Papasquiaro river valley, Durango. Photo by Cindy Sandoval Mora.

Figura 16. Figuras femeninas con peinado de mariposa dispuestas en fila y tomadas de la mano. Las Latas, valle del río Santiago Papasquiaro, Durango. Foto: Cindy Sandoval Mora.

Figure 17. Ceramic bowl of the Basketmaker III period found near Durango, Colorado. Drawing by Kelley Hays-Gilpin (2004:Figure 7.3).

Figura 17. Cerámica del periodo Basketmaker III de Durango, Colorado. Dibujo: Kelley Hays-Gilpin (2004:Figura 7.3).

structure consists of complimentary oppositions between, on the one hand, the sacrificial, transformative, masculine, and solar forces represented by the deer and a fluteplayer in the upper register and, on the other hand, the forces related to sexuality, fertility, femininity, and the domain of earth and water, which are represented by the wolf and the woman with butterfly hair whorls in the lower half of the panel (Figure 19) (Herrera 2012:231–250, 2017). The struggle between these forces recreates the moment of original creation as well as the constant opposition that allows the birth of worldly beings and the passing of time (López-Austin 1994:20–21, 77, 160).

Figure 18. Women with butterfly hair whorls arranged in a row holding hands. Piedra de Amolar site, Sierra Madre Occidental, Durango. DStretch LRE enhancement. Photo: Marie-Areti Hers.

Figura 18. Mujeres con peinado de mariposa dispuestas en fila y tomadas de la mano. Piedra de Amolar, Sierra Madre Occidental, Durango. Modificación DStretch LRE. Foto: Marie-Areti Hers.

In addition to occupying the lower section of the panel associated with this earthly component of the cosmos (Figure 19), where the forces of growth and reproduction predominate, the iconographic features of the female figure at La Cantera reaffirm its inclusion in this domain (Figure 20). Even though the motif

Figure 19. Panel F, La Cantera site. Tepehuanes river valley, Durango.
Figura 19. Panel F, La Cantera. Valle del río Tepehuanes, Durango.

is fragmented, her earthly position is expressed in the quadripartite arrangement of her body, with her two arms elevated in a horizontal plane extending from the vertical axis of her body, thus alluding to the four directions and the center, symbolizing the structure of the surface of the earth. Her hands were created in detail with the palms open towards the front and with each finger carefully outlined, a feature that is somewhat unusual for anthropomorphic rock art figures, and which makes it stand out even more. If we add to this the exaggerated size of her hands with respect to the rest of her body, it is clear that the intention was to exalt certain qualities of the figure, possibly in relationship to her power to act and create, as occurs in other Mesoamerican contexts (Herrera 2012:245–246, 2017; López-Austin 1994:200).

Finally, we observe how her right hand is superimposed on the head of what could be a deer, since it is possible to see the outline of antlers despite the position of the hand (Figure 20). It is important to note that the composition of these two images shares a similar structure (Figure 19). In the group of images just above, there are two canids on either side of a third quadruped with its head disappearing into the jaws of the larger canid hunter. To its left (viewer's right) two cervids observe the fatal destiny of what was likely one of their own kind. The natural confrontation between these species suggests that the quadruped with the devoured head is indeed a deer.

The most relevant observation here is that the antagonism between the two species, which is also present in Huichol myths (Gutiérrez 2010:71–72, 90, 94–95, 58–59, 62–63), probably represents the conflict between two opposing yet complementary forces embodied by these two figures, thus structuring the order of the cosmos. The role of the beings associated with the female and sexual realms in these adjacent scenes is that of protagonists involved in the final outcome of the struggle between opposing forces—the sacrifice of the deer (Herrera 2012:248–250, 2017). The importance of sacrificing the deer lies, as explained by the Huichol, in the profound sense of creation and transformation implied by this sacred act, thereby contributing to the continued existence of the world (Gutiérrez 2010:72; Neurath 2013:51).

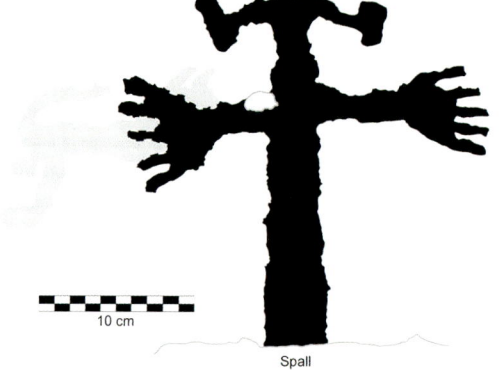

Figure 20. Woman with butterfly hair whorls. La Cantera site, Tepehuanes river valley, Durango.
Figura 20. Mujer con peinado de mariposa. La Cantera, valle del río Tepeuhanes, Durango.

Conclusion

As we have been able to see in the rock art sites discussed above, the image of the woman with butterfly hair whorls not only reproduces the same iconographic elements that identify her in the Southwestern United States, but is frequently combined with other symbols and themes, such as the vulvas and flute players, that play similar roles in the rock art of that region. The case of the Las Latas and Piedra de Amolar sites illustrates very well how the arrangement and ordering of these women is inspired by a model that has its origin in Basketmaker III ceramics of Durango, Colorado.

The images confirm that the links between both regions were sufficiently close so that characters such as the flute player and the woman with butterfly hair whorls were adopted not only in the sense of their formal aspects as attractive figures, but also in the sense of their original symbolic function. This idea seems clearly expressed in the association of the images with other motifs and in the natural conditions and landscapes of the spaces that were chosen for painting or engraving. Of course, much work remains to be done to fully document and analyze each one of these sites, with the purpose of deepening the knowledge and understanding of how each one of these images relates to the cosmovision of the Chalchihuites culture.

Acknowledgments. We are grateful to Dr. William Breen Murray for his support and inspiration. Many thanks to the National Autonomous University of Mexico (UNAM) and to the Molino community: Esperanza Solís, Luis Rocha Solís, Miguel Rocha Solís, Faustina Rodríguez, Natividad Samaniego, and Eulalio Rivera. Thanks also to Marie Areti Hers and Fernando Berrojalbiz.

References Cited

Berrojalbiz, Fernando, and Marie-Areti Hers
 2012 Memoria y paisaje cultural: diversas estrategias de la apropiación del arte en la Sierra Madre Occidental de Durango. In *Apropiarse del arte: impulsos y pasiones, XXXII Coloquio Internacional de Historia del Arte*, edited by Olga Sáenz, pp. 93–115. Instituto de Investigaciones Estéticas, Universidad Nacional Autónoma de México.
 2014a La ocupación chalchihuiteña en el Valle de Guatimapé. In *Historia de Durango, Tomo I, Época Antigua*, edited by José Luis Punzo Díaz and Marie-Areti Hers, pp. 246–270. Instituto de Investigaciones Históricas, Universidad Juárez del Estado de Durango.
 2014b El alto Nazas. La Comarca del Venado. In *Historia de Durango, Tomo I, Época Antigua*, edited by José Luis Punzo Díaz and Marie-Areti Hers, pp. 272–317. Instituto de Investigaciones Históricas, Universidad Juárez del Estado de Durango.

Carot, Patricia, and Marie-Areti Hers
 2011 De Teotihuacan al cañón de Chaco: nueva perspectiva sobre las relaciones entre Mesoamérica y el suroeste de los Estados Unidos. *Anales del Instituto de Investigaciones Estéticas* 33(98):5–53.

Flores, Daniel, Marie-Areti Hers, and Antonio Porcayo
 2008 Sobre el trópico en un mar de lava: análisis astronómico, arqueológico e iconográfico en el septentrión mesoamericano. In *Las vías del noroeste II: propuestas para una perspectiva sistémica e interdisciplinaria*, edited by Carlo Bonfiglioli, Arturo Gutiérrez, Marie-Areti Hers, and María Eugenia Olavarría, pp. 241–286. Instituto de Investigaciones Antropológicas, Universidad Nacional Autónoma de México.

Gutiérrez del Ángel, Arturo
 2010 *Las danzas del padre sol: ritualidad y procesos narrativos en un pueblo del occidente mexicano*. Universidad Autónoma Metropolitana, El Colegio de San Luis, Universidad Nacional Autónoma de México, Miguel Ángel Porrúa, Mexico.

Hays-Gilpin, Kelley
 2004 *Ambiguous Images: Gender and Rock Art*. Alta Mira Press, Walnut Creek, California.

Herrera Maldonado, Daniel
 2012 *Estudio del sitio de arte rupestre "La Cantera", valle del río Tepehuanes, Durango: Una aproximación a la representación del cosmos chalchihuiteño*. Thesis, Escuela Nacional de Antropología e Historia, Mexico.
 2017 Arte rupestre y cosmovisión de las poblaciones chalchihuiteñas del valle del río Tepehuanes, Durango. In *Estudios de iconografía en la cultura chalchihuites (Zacatecas y Durango) y regiones afines*, edited by Nora Rodríguez Zariñán. In press, El Colegio de Michoacán, Zamora, Mexico.

Hers, Marie-Areti
 2001 La música amorosa de Kokopelli y el erotismo sagrado en los confines mesoamericanos. In *Amor y Desamor en las Artes*, edited by Arnulfo Herrera Curiel, pp. 293–335. Instituto de Investigaciones Estéticas, Universidad Nacional Autónoma de México.
 2014a El occidente durangueño: los chalchihuiteños. La presencia mesoamericana en Durango: origen y desarrollo. In *Historia de Durango, Tomo I, Época Antigua*, edited by José Luis Punzo Díaz and Marie-Areti Hers, pp. 168–191. Instituto de Investigaciones Históricas, Universidad Juárez del Estado de Durango.
 2014b Durango y el antiguo camino de tierra adentro. In *Historia de Durango, Tomo I, Época Antigua*, edited by José Luis Punzo Díaz and Marie-Areti Hers, pp. 400–426. Instituto de Investigaciones Históricas, Universidad Juárez del Estado de Durango.

López-Austin, Alfredo
 1994 *Tamoanchan y Tlalocan*. Fondo de Cultura Económica, Mexico City.

Neurath, Johannes
 2013 *La vida de las imágenes: Arte huichol*. Artes de México, Consejo Nacional para la Cultura y las Artes, Mexico.

Punzo, José Luis
 2008 La ruta de las praderas en época prehispánica: El caso del abrigo de piedra de amolar 1, Durango. In *Las vías del noroeste II: propuesta para una perspectiva sistémica e interdisciplinaria*, edited by Carlo Bonfiglioli, Arturo Gutiérrez, Marie-Areti Hers, and María Eugenia Olavarría, pp. 103–129. Instituto de Investigaciones Antropológicas, Universidad Nacional Autónoma de México.

La mujer con peinado de mariposa en el arte rupestre chalchihuiteño de Durango, México

Daniel Herrera Maldonado y Ana Laura Chacón Rosas

En este escrito analizaremos las varias representaciones de mujeres con peinado de mariposa que se han documentado en el arte rupestre del noroccidente de Durango. Esta imagen tiene su origen entre las culturas ancestrales del Suroeste de los Estados Unidos a través de las cuales arriba a Durango en el 600 d.C., producto de los fuertes contactos que establecieron con la cultura chalchihuites. Teniendo en cuenta ésto, realizaremos un estudio iconográfico de la imagen y de las relaciones que guarda con el resto de motivos que la acompañan, además de considerar la importancia de los rasgos del paisaje a los cuales se asocian los espacios en que se le encuentra. Ésto nos permitirá establecer la probable función de este personaje en comparación con lo que sucede en su lugar de origen, en el entendido de que su asimilación implicaría una adaptación al contexto de esta nueva cultura.

El arte rupestre en el cual ahora nos introduciremos pertenece a la denominada cultura "Chalchihuites". Su presencia en el estado de Durango, México, se origina a partir de un gran movimiento migratorio en el 600 d.C. llevándoles a poblar el interior de la Sierra Madre Occidental y sus valles orientales. El punto de origen de esta importante migración, y de la consecuente expansión de la frontera mesoamericana, se ubica en los estados de Zacatecas y Jalisco en donde los "chalchihuiteños" habitaron por cerca de cinco siglos teniendo como límite septentrional el gran malpaís de La Breña que se extiende al sur del estado de Durango (Hers 2014a:179–181).

Producto de esta expansión hacia el norte, se establece en este primer periodo de ocupación chalchihuiteña en Durango que va del 600 al 900 d.C., un importante puente de comunicación con los pueblos ancestrales del Suroeste de los Estados Unidos (Carot y Hers 2011; Hers 2014b). Lo cual se expresa, en entre otros muchos ámbitos, en el de las imágenes. Y por consiguiente en el de los posibles intercambios a nivel de sus ideas y creencias.

Esta conexión trae la introducción al arte rupestre de esta región de imágenes de largo historial en el Suroeste de los Estados Unidos. Entre éstas se encuentra la del conocido flautista, comúnmente confundido con la kachina Kokopelli, o también, como en el caso que nos interesa, del personaje femenino con peinado de mariposa (Carot y Hers 2011:39; Hers 2001; 2014b:415–420; Punzo 2008).

La mujer con peinado de mariposa en el Suroeste

Las comunidades Pueblo (Hopi, Zuni y Taos) han acuñado este peinado, el cual se caracteriza por acomodar el cabello generando dos extensiones circulares de cada lado de la cabeza (Figura 1). Las mujeres lucen este peinado durante ciertas ceremonias a partir de su primera menstruación hasta el matrimonio (Hays-Gilpin 2004:133).

Este peinado aparece en la iconografía tradicional de las kivas, la cerámica y el arte rupestre del Suroeste en tres grandes periodos. El registro más antiguo pertenece al arte rupestre fechado en el 200 d.C. Posteriormente existen varios ejemplos en la cerámica Basketmaker III y en el arte rupestre durante el periodo del 600 al 900 d.C. Finalmente se le encuentra en la pintura mural de las kivas, la cerámica y el arte rupestre en una tercera etapa que abarca del 1350 al 1700 (Hays-Gilpin 2004:128–137).

Para las comunidades Pueblo, la mujer con este peinado representa el crecimiento del maíz y otros aspectos de la fertilidad, la abundancia y la creación en sí misma (Hays-Gilpin 2004:139–141). El motivo llega a tener otros elementos asociados como el de las vulvas y los flautistas (Hays-Gilpin 2004:137).

Cueva del Diablo

En Durango hemos registrado hasta ahora cinco sitios con presencia de este personaje. A excepción del espacio de La Cantera que se localiza mucho más al norte en el valle del río Tepehuanes, buena parte estos sitios se concentran en la porción central del estado, a lo largo de un eje con dirección este-oeste que atraviesa la Sierra Madre Occidental, el valle del río Santiago Papasquiaro y la Sierra del Epazote (Figura 2). Es importante mencionar que tanto al interior de los mismos sitios, así como de otros que se encuentran en sus cercanías se constata la presencia también del flautista (Figura 3) (Punzo 2008:116–117). La conjunción de ambos personajes es un patrón recurrente también en el arte rupestre del Suroeste (Hays-Gilpin 2004:138).

Entre estos sitios uno que ha llamado poderosamente nuestra atención es la llamada Cueva del Diablo. Para acceder a ella es necesario introducirse al corazón de la Sierra del Epazote en dónde prevalece un ambiente boscoso y de mayor altitud en comparación a los valles que rodean esta serranía. Situados al fondo de un pequeño valle intermontano, junto al Arroyo el Piojo que sigue en este punto una dirección este-oeste, es posible apreciar a una distancia de varios kilómetros las cuevas que concentran el arte rupestre, dada su ubicación en las partes más altas de la serranía que nos rodea hacia el norte (Figura 4).

A medida que subimos la fuerte pendiente hacia el sitio damos cuenta que una de sus características se encuentra en la posibilidad de disfrutar de un amplio panorama de la Sierra del Epazote hacia el sur (Figura 5). Las pinturas pertenecientes a la cultura chalchihuiteña se distribuyen en dos de las tres cavidades que lo conforman. Siendo justo la de en medio la que concentra las imágenes femeninas (Figura 6). Todos los motivos de éste último espacio son de carácter antropomorfo y de color naranja, además de que siempre se ordenan en pares (Figura 7). Se trata de figuras de alrededor de 20 cm y con el cuerpo diseñado visto de frente. Un sólo trazo delinea de manera esquemática el cuerpo, los bazos ligeramente levantados y las piernas abiertas. Los dedos de las manos y pies son trazados casi siempre en conjuntos de tres. Del personaje de la izquierda en la figura 8 reconocemos el característico peinado de mariposa. Si su identificación femenina no nos fuera suficientemente clara entre sus piernas se reconoce la presencia de su vulva. Lo mismo sucede con los tres personajes restantes que le rodean (Figura 7).

Reafirmando su asociación hacia el ámbito de la humedad y la fertilidad, se aprecian varios manantiales que parecen rodear a los personajes femeninos. Un aspecto muy significativo es que esta agua "nace" y escurre sobre las paredes a las misma altura en donde se ubican las mujeres. Algunas de las grietas de donde procede recuerda inclusive la forma de una gran vulva rocosa.

Estas propiedades a las cuales las imágenes de esta cavidad parecen vincularse es coincidente con la sensación de mayor humedad, recogimiento y oscuridad que se percibe al ingresar a esta cavidad rocosa. Su superficie fuertemente ennegrecida que contrasta con el color de las pinturas incrementa esa percepción (Figura 6). Otro rasgo interesante es que el ingreso a este espacio debe realizarse en cuclillas, por la poca altura del mismo, lo cual obliga al visitante a "inclinarse" ante las imágenes y reverenciar su "fuerza espiritual".

La segunda concentración de imágenes se localiza en la concavidad contigua al oriente. Ahí apreciamos nuevamente el predominio de la figura humana con respecto a otras temáticas (Figura 9). Todos los antropomorfos son en color negro y se ven acompañados por un par de manos en positivo de color rojo. De entre los siete personajes representados, uno se diferencia del resto por tener muy bien marcado el sexo femenino (Figura 10). Otro rasgo que lo distingue es la presencia de una variante del peinado de mariposa. Se trata de un tocado conformado por dos largos trazos que salen de su cabeza y se extienden hasta la altura de su pecho. Al compararlo con la iconografía presente en la cerámica chalchihuiteña, existe cierta analogía con los elementos presentes en esta deidad femenina y telúrica mesoamericana representada en un plato procedente del sitio La Atalaya en Durango (Figura 11) (Hers 2014a:180–182). Las referencias a su sexo se reconocen en el diseño de sus pezones y su falda decorada por un par de serpientes y pequeñas líneas que hacen alusión a su aspecto acuático. Como en los personajes femeninos rupestres, su tocado se conforma por dos largos trazos que salen de su cabeza dividiéndola, y que en el caso de la cerámica es más fácil de reconocer como la representación de dos ofidios.

Salto del Perro

La reiteración hacia el aspecto de la fertilidad y de la sexualidad de estos personajes se ve presente nuevamente en el sitio Salto del Perro, ubicado en el Cañón de Potrerillos, uno de los varios que da acceso desde el oriente a la Sierra del Epazote. El entorno de este sitio reproduce nuevamente las condiciones de mayor humedad y abundante vegetación que parece asociarse a los sitios donde vemos presente a las mujeres con peinado de mariposa. El cañón es estrecho, con varios manantiales y un pequeño arroyo que parecen nutrir a la vegetación que conforma nuevamente ese ambiente de oscuridad y retraimiento (Berrojalbiz y Hers 2012:99-101; 2014a:261–265).

Siguiendo el pequeño arroyo hacia el interior del cañón, el camino se ve interrumpido por un pequeño salto elevado, del cual cae el agua de este arroyo acumulándose en varias pozas distribuidas alrededor de la gran pared semicircular que conforma este salto (Figura 12). A un costado de la caída de agua, empleando la pared de este pequeño hemiciclo natural, se plasmaron las pinturas con un marcado protagonismo nuevamente de la figura humana (Figura 13). Aunque los motivos son de color negro, amarillo, rojo y blanco, las figuras femeninas con peinado de mariposa coinciden como en Cueva del Diablo en ser de color naranja y ordenadas en pares. Los personajes con este peinado son también aquellos con el sexo bien marcado (Figura 14). Una diferencia notable con las versiones de este último espacio, es la manera en la que algunas de estas mujeres tienden a presentar un vientre marcadamente ensanchado (Figura 15). Además, en lugar del órgano genital entre sus piernas, se diseña como si saliera de su vientre una semicircunferencia con un par de líneas paralelas. Estaríamos pues ante una posible escena de alumbramiento, asociando a estos personajes al importante dominio de la creación que significa el momento del parto (Berrojalbiz y Hers 2012:99–101; 2014a:261–265).

Las Latas y Piedra de Amolar

Las Latas es un sitio localizado junto a las aguas del río Santiago Papasquiaro, en el valle que separa la Sierra del Epazote de la Sierra Madre Occidental. Se trata de un espacio en donde predominan los petrograbados, como suele suceder con los sitios de arte rupestre asociados a este afluente, y a los varios que conforman la parte alta de la cuenca del Nazas, al noroeste del estado de Durango (Berrojalbiz y Hers 2014b:308–314; Herrera 2012:170–192). Su vínculo con lo acuático, la fertilidad y la sexualidad aparece reiterado no sólo por su cercanía con las aguas de este río, sino en el propio repertorio iconográfico de este sitio. Grandes vulvas grabadas, que apreciamos como un elemento de identificación del arte rupestre de tradición chalchihuiteña en otros sitios más al norte, se ven asociadas a los personajes con peinado de mariposa.

Una condición importante de estas mujeres se reconoce en su particular ordenación (Figura 16). Como sucede en la cerámica del periodo Basketmaker III, procedente de Durango, Colorado, las figuras femeninas con peinado de mariposa se disponen en hilera, tomadas de las manos, como si realizaran algún tipo danza (Figura 17) (Hays-Gilpin 2004:Figura 7.3). Algo semejante sucede en la disposición de este personaje femenino en el sitio Piedra de Amolar, en el interior de la Sierra Madre Occidental (Figura 18), donde además también se les ve acompañadas, en un panel contiguo, por el flautista (Punzo 2008:116).

La Cantera

El último espacio al que nos referiremos es el sitio La Cantera. Como en el caso de Las Latas su ubicación concreta está relacionada con su cercanía a las aguas de un importante afluente, en este caso el río Tepehuanes. El registro y análisis sistemático de la organización y disposición de las imágenes de La Cantera ha permitido reconocer la estructura que rige buena parte de sus composiciones (Herrera 2012). Se trata de un esquema de oposiciones complementarias entre las fuerzas sacrificiales, transformativas, masculinas y solares protagonizadas por el venado, y las fuerzas relacionadas con la sexualidad, la fertilidad y con el dominio húmedo, femenino y terrestre del cosmos, entre cuyos representantes se encuentra el lobo y la mujer con peinado de mariposa (Figura 19) (Herrera 2012:231–250, 2017). La lucha de estas fuerzas recrea el momento de creación original así como la oposición constate que permite el nacimiento de los seres mundanos y el transcurrir del tiempo (López-Austin 1994:20–21, 77, 160).

Además de ocupar la parte inferior del panel asociada a ese ámbito terrestre del cosmos (Figura 19), donde gobiernan las fuerzas del crecimiento y la reproducción, los propios rasgos iconográficos del personaje femenino de La Cantera nos reiteran su pertenencia a este dominio (Figura 20). Por un lado su carácter telúrico se expresa en la disposición cuadripartita de su cuerpo, no obstante que el motivo se encuentra fragmentado, con sus dos brazos levantados en plano horizontal y el eje vertical de su cuerpo, en alusión a los cuatro rumbos y el centro, a partir de los cuales se estructuraba la superficie de la tierra. Sus manos fueron detalladamente elaboradas con las palmas abiertas hacia enfrente trazando con cuidado cada uno de sus dedos, un rasgo que suele ser poco usual en los antropomorfos rupestres y que lo convierte en uno de sus elementos más sobresalientes. Si a ello agregamos el tamaño exagerado de sus manos con respecto al resto del cuerpo, parece clara la intención de exaltar cierta cualidad del personaje, tal vez en relación a su poder de obrar y crear como sucede en otros contextos en Mesoamérica (Herrera 2012:245–246, 2017; López-Austin 1994:200).

Por último notemos cómo su mano derecha se sobrepone a la cabeza de lo que podría ser un venado, pues a pesar de la sobreposición aún es posible apreciar los trazos de su cornamenta (Figura 20). Es significativo que la composición de estas dos imágenes se estructura de manera análoga a la de arriba (Figura 19). En esta última los dos cánidos rodean a un tercer cuadrúpedo cuya cabeza desaparece entre las fauces del cazador mayor. A su izquierda dos cérvidos observan el destino fatal del que fue seguramente uno de sus congéneres. La confrontación natural entre estas especies permite sugerir que el cuadrúpedo con la cabeza devorada se trate también de un cérvido.

Lo más relevante aquí es que el antagonismo entre estas especies, como lo vemos en los mitos huicholes (Gutiérrez 2010:71-72, 90, 94-95, 58-59, 62-63), es probablemente una representación del conflicto de las dos fuerzas opuestas y complementarias que sintetizan estos dos personajes y que estructuran la disposición del cosmos. El papel de los seres asociados al ámbito de lo femenino y de la sexualidad en estas escenas contiguas, es el de ejecutores del desenlace final de tal oposición de fuerzas: el sacrificio del venado (Herrera 2012:248-250, 2017). La importancia de inmolar al venado radica, como los explican bien los huicholes, en su profundo sentido de creación y transformación del mundo contribuyendo a asegurar su existencia y continuidad (Gutiérrez 2010:72; Neurath 2013:51).

Conclusiones

Como lo hemos podido apreciar en los sitios de arte rupestre mencionados, la imagen de la mujer con peinado de mariposa no sólo reproduce los mismos elementos iconográficos que la identifican en el Suroeste de los Estados Unidos. Sino que además, se conjuga con temáticas como las vulvas o flautistas, que asemejan el mismo papel que parece desempeñar en escenas también de esta última región. El caso de los sitios de Las Latas y Piedra de Amolar es sumamente ilustrador de cómo la disposición y ordenación de estas mujeres se inspira en un modelo que procede de la cerámica Basketmaker III de Durango, Colorado.

Las imágenes nos confirman que los vínculos entre ambas regiones eran suficientemente estrechos para que personajes como el flautista o la mujer con peinado de mariposa, se adoptaran desde un aspecto meramente formal pero conservando además su función simbólica de origen. Lo anterior parece claramente expresado en la asociación que guardan con otros motivos y en las condiciones naturales y del paisaje de los espacios que son escogidos para pintarlos o grabarlos. Resta desde luego el realizar un registro y análisis a detalle de cada uno de estos sitios para seguir ahondando en el conocimiento de cómo cada una de estas imágenes se inserta en la cosmovisión de sus autores chalchihuiteños.

Agradecimientos. Agradecemos al Dr. William Breen Murray por su apoyo y estímulo. A la Universidad Nacional Autónoma de México y a la Comunidad de Molino: Esperanza Solís, Luis Rocha Solís, Miguel Rocha Solís, Faustina Rodríguez, Natividad Samaniego y Eulalio Rivera. También a Marie Areti Hers y Fernando Berrojalbiz.

Rock Art and Households in Western Mexico: The Case of Chavinda, Michoacán

Kimberly Sumano Ortega, David Arturo Muñiz García, and José Luis Punzo Díaz

Most of the time, rock art is found in sacred places, as a mark on landscape accessible only to members of a certain society, and mostly related to specific rituals or, perhaps, as a discourse readable only by knowing the specific code. Nevertheless, we present a case where rock art seems to be directly related to marking household prestige, more like a social discourse instead of a ritual/sacred one. Chavinda, a small site located in the zone of Ciénega in north-central Michoacán, western Mexico, and dated to approximately A.D. 425–600, could be a case in which rock art represents household narratives in daily life as part of canonical strategies of built environment, a public appropriation of landscape.

Built environment is a concept that serves to give space a humanized sense, but it also provides the possibility of analyzing space as a scenario in which the behavior of people is guided through the use of that environment by the structure of a sociopolitical system (Rapoport 2003). If we agree with that concept (and we do so), we can argue that social space serves as one of the many mechanisms that sociopolitical structure uses to interact with the material world. In this paper we apply these concepts to a study of Chavinda, a small site located in the zone of Ciénega in north-central Michoacán, western Mexico (Figure 1).

The Approach

Several researchers have dealt with the sociopolitical use of space by focusing on architecture and, in fact, we view this as a goal every time we examine some kind of transformation of landscape in order to have better conditions for living. It is obvious that each culture has its own way to get that appropriation in practice, and that is intimately related to the deeply ingrained habits, skills, and dispositions that define habitus as proposed by Bourdieu (1977). What we want to underline here is that all societies use the space where they live, but they also signify it by specific codes that can be understood by members of that culture in particular.

As we know, a *House*, as defined by Levy-Strauss (1969), is a social unit embodied through the *house* as structure, as well as through other elements directly related to it (in our case, rock art). However, an *H-house* would be able to describe several aspects of a society's structure through studies of how it appears in association with its elements. We can also understand a household as a domestic unit in which a social group and a house can be found, a concept that can also be related to lineages (Carsten and Hugh-Jones 1996:44).

In Houses and Households, Blanton (1994) describes two types of strategies that society uses to emit messages according to what is permitted in that

Kimberly Sumano Ortega
Posgrado en Arqueología, El Colegio de Michoacán

David Arturo Muñiz García
Centro INAH Michoacán

José Luis Punzo Díaz
Centro INAH Michoacán

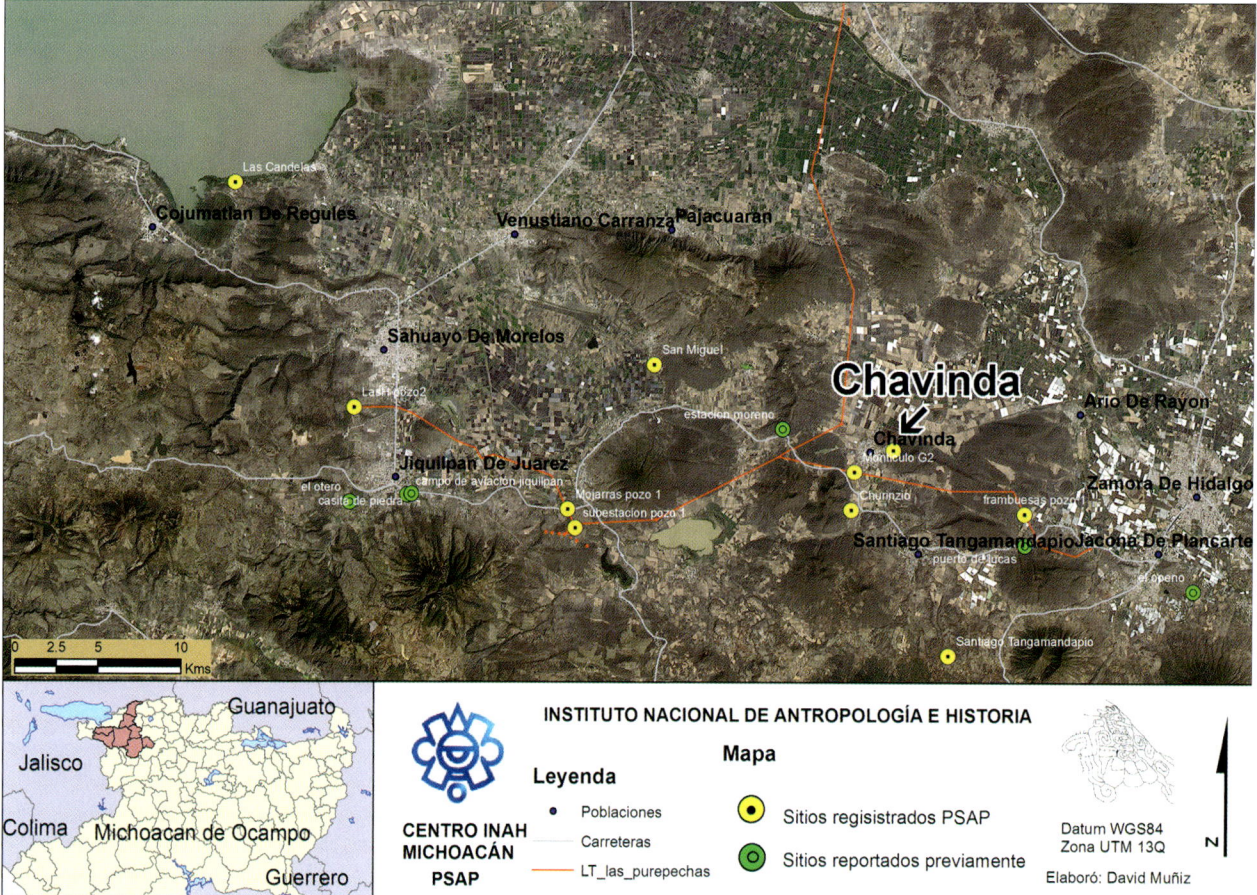

Figure 1. Location of Chavinda in the Ciénega district of northwestern Michoacán. All maps by David Muñiz.
Figura 1. Ubicación de Chavinda en el distrito de Ciénega, al noroeste de Michoacán. Todos los mapas de David Muñiz.

specific culture. He talks about indexical strategies as those presented to members of the family or household, such as interior distribution of activities in the house in which we could detect some kind of stratification, perhaps by gender or age, by activity areas, or by control of access to some spots in the house (such as a modern home office where we may not allow children to enter).

The other type is canonical strategy, which can be understood as that which is presented to the outside world, speaking from the viewpoint of the household. This can be exemplified in factors such as colors chosen to paint houses—like the bright colors seen in Mexican communities—or landscaping as seen in American houses. However, there are restrictions on what is allowed to be shown on the exterior (Bourdieu 1994).

At this point we call attention to one more aspect: landscape archaeology (Seoane-Veiga 2009) appears in our study as an appropriate approach in situations where the regional context is not well known and the site is minimally studied, since we had very little data when we first approached the problem of the possible function of the rock art at Chavinda. Now that we have a lot more information, we still believe studies of household space are viable and useful, and that our interpretation is still valid. Based on Seoane-Veiga's work under this perspective, we registered every design in standard formats, photographing each one and recording them with both digital and freehand drawings in contexts of compositions and "isolated elements" (Figure 2).

In the case that we present in this paper, we propose that Chavinda's inhabitants resorted to prestigious and cosmogonical symbols to denote status in a stratified society in the form of rock art that is directly related to houses, but not to all houses—only to some habitational units belonging to elite families or households (Figure 3).

The Settlement

We were able to study the site in the context of a rescue project supported by Comisión Federal de Electricidad, in agreement with the Instituto Nacional de

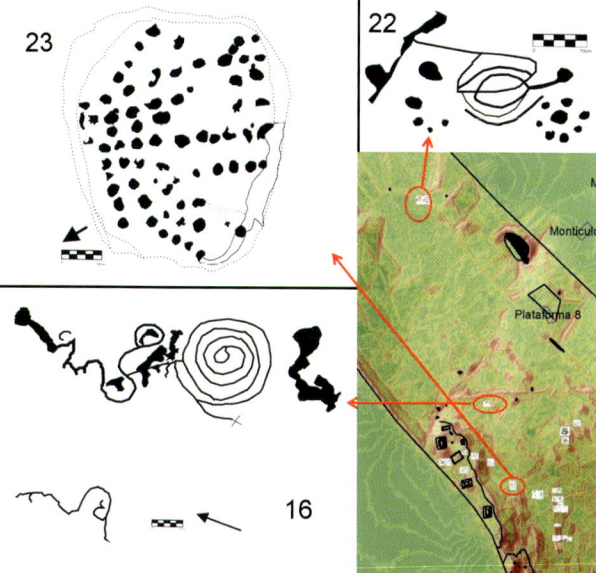

Figure 2. Petroglyphs recorded as isolated elements in site context. All drawings by David Muñiz and Kimberley Sumano, 2015, with the field support of Heriberto Hernandez.
Figura 2. Petroglifos registrados como elementos aislados en el contexto del sitio. Todos los dibujos de David Muñiz y Kimberley Sumano, 2015, con el apoyo de Heriberto Hernandez.

Antropología e Historia, through the Centro INAH Michoacán. All information that we present here was generated during the fieldwork of the team we were part of (Punzo et al. 2015).

Chavinda is located west of the small valley of Chavinda-Ario, Michoacán, that connects with Lake Chapala to the northeast through the valley. We consider it as a medium size site, with 46.5 ha. (115 acres) in total area. The settlement is midway up the slope of Cerro Alto, between 1590 and 1710 m AMSL. The dimensions are 1330 m north-south by 430 m east-west, consisting of three main sectors. To the east is the public civic and ceremonial area with three linear patios surrounded by six structures, all on a 200 m-long platform, as part of the natural slope of the hill. The second section is made up of a few habitational units, all of them built with masonry, and this is the area that presents the main rock art concentration; it forms a second circumference around the main platform. The third space can be described as a large area set aside for agricultural labor, encompassing the two areas first described, even though it also has habitational units, possibly belonging to a non-elite group (the fieldworkers), indicated by its location and the mud and wood materials of which the houses are made (see Figure 1).

To summarize, nine platforms, thirteen terraces, six mounds, and twenty-three abstract style petroglyphs were registered, all divided into four groups. The first, south of the settlement, has five engraved rocks and is directly related to an excavated domestic unit (Figure 4). The second consists of seven engraved rocks, towards the center of the site, associated with domestic unit platforms (Figure 5). The third is made up of three spiral motifs on the east side of Chavinda and is directly

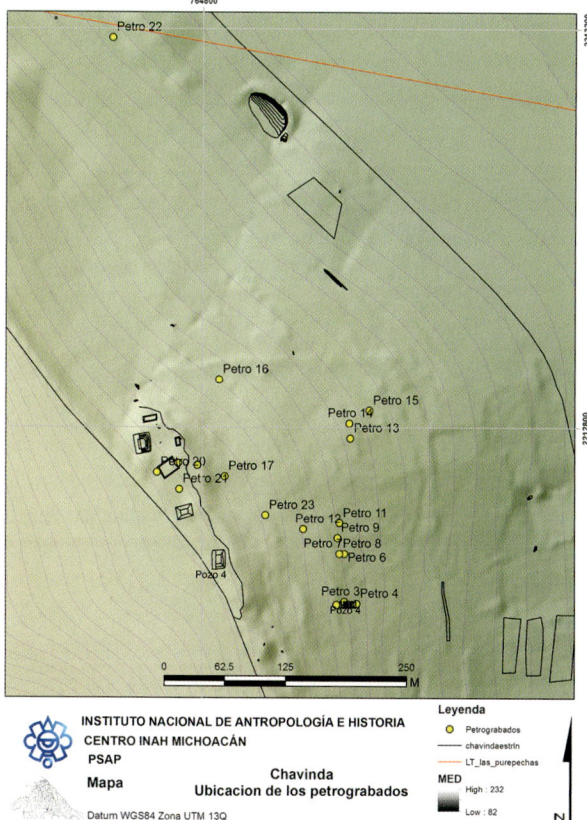

Figure 3. Locations of petroglyphs and excavation units in the site map of Chavinda.
Figura 3. Ubicación de petroglifos y unidades de excavación en el mapa del sitio de Chavinda.

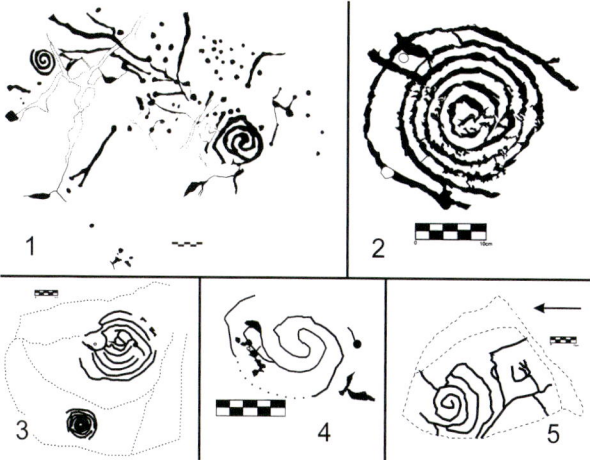

Figure 4. Petroglyphs in Group 1.
Figura 4. Petroglifos en el Grupo 1.

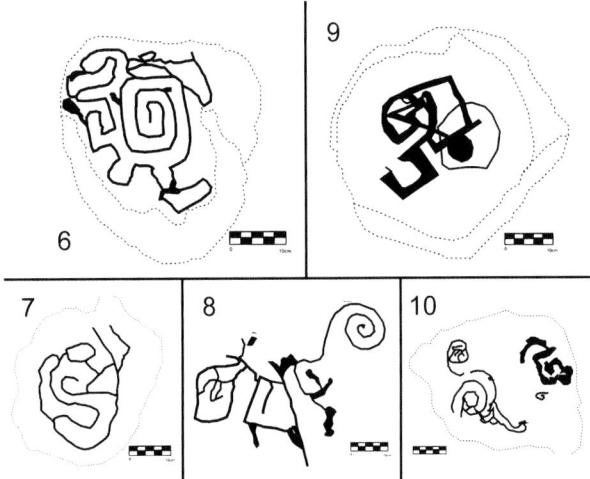

Figure 5. Petroglyphs in Group 2.
Figura 5. Petroglifos en el Grupo 2.

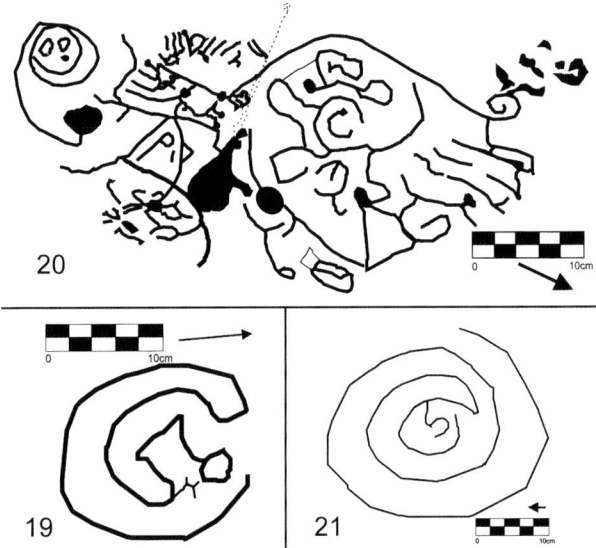

Figure 7. Petroglyphs in Group 4.
Figura 7. Petroglifos en el Grupo 4.

rocks have a more complex formal composition, more motifs, and possibly a more elaborated discourse.

Discussion

We believe that the fact that each petroglyph is totally different from the others could be related to aspects of identity for each family or house, and that possibly most symbols and techniques may be linked to a major lineage. In that sense, we could be talking about a discourse based on social relations revealed in spatial relations through rock art.

It is plausible to consider rock art as both indexical and conical strategies as Blanton (1994) proposed, serving a specific kind of hierarchic social order at least in an intra-site context. We believe that is the case here because every petroglyph is spatially related to a habitational unit, and there is a pattern of a complex design surrounded by other quite simple designs. One rock here deserves special consideration: Petroglyph 12, a large rhyolite outcrop measuring 350 x 250 x 150 cm (Figure 9), located in the middle of a core rock art concentration; it seems to be a spot for sitting, possibly analogous to a throne like those at Chalcatzingo, Morelos. It is also the only rock that has representations of at least three anthropomorphs, possibly two males and a female, all of them facing an open area that could function as a small plaza. If our interpretation is somehow correct, then we may have a strong argument for treating rock art as an important hallmark or emblem for Chavinda's society, a public manifestation of territorial marking as suggested by Sanders (2005:56).

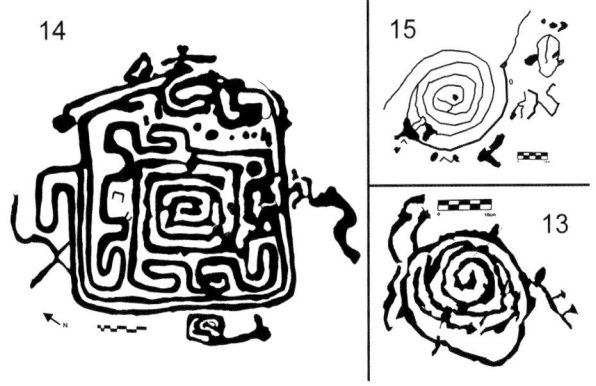

Figure 6. Petroglyphs in Group 3.
Figura 6. Petroglifos en el Grupo 3.

associated with extensive habitational excavations (Figure 6). Finally, the fourth group consists of six engraved rocks associated with a public building (Figure 7).

Rock Art and Architecture

As we mentioned before, most petroglyphs are associated with possible elite households, based on their spatial distribution (Seoane-Veiga 2009). Some designs appear as single motifs, others as small panels; however, we consider that there are two stations or large segments in the overall site, based on the spatial location of the petroglyphs and their relation to architectural structures (Figure 8).

Designs are considerably similar in all cases, spirals, lazy "S," pit-and-groove patterns, vulvas, and a few anthropomorphs, in both rectilinear and curvilinear patterns. Even though there is a repetition of iconographic elements, each petroglyph is considerably distinct from the others. At this point, we should note that some

Figure 8. The "Step Deck" household had a burial in the middle of the house and petroglyphs on the boulder associated with the house.
Figura 8. La casa de "Step Deck" tenía un entierro en el centro de la casa y petroglifos en la roca asociada con la casa.

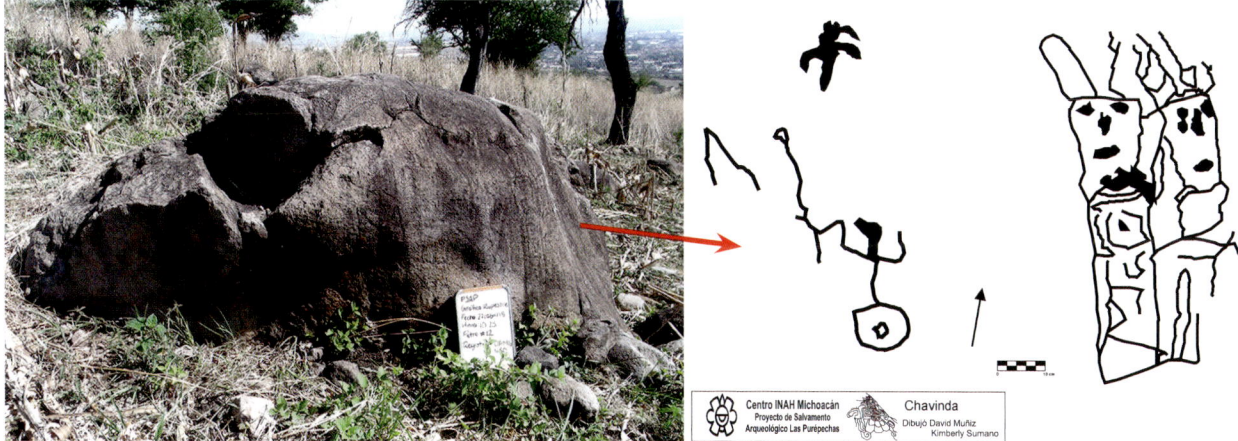

Figure 9. Petroglyph 12, located in the middle of a core rock art concentration.
Figura 9. Petroglifo 12, localizada en medio del núcleo de mayor concentración de arte rupestre del sitio.

Conclusion

What we present here is only a first approach to an area not well known, and we still have a lot more to do. Soon we expect to establish links between rock art and other materials like ceramics, lithics, shell, and bone, for a more solid interpretation of Chavinda's inhabitants. For now, we have preliminary information to suggest a spatial association of domestic architecture with groups of petroglyphs, a rare situation in Mesoamerica.

References Cited

Blanton, Richard
  1994 *Houses and Households: A Comparative Study*. Plenum Press, New York and London.

Bourdieu, Pierre
  1977 *Outline of a Theory of Practice*. Cambridge University Press, Cambridge.
  1994 Stratégies de reproduction et modes de domination. *Actes de la recherche en sciences sociales* 105(1):3–12.

Carsten, Janet, and Stephen Hugh-Jones
  1996 *About the House: Lévi-Strauss and Beyond*. Cambridge University Press, Cambridge.

Lévi-Strauss, Claude
  1969 *The Elementary Structures of Kinship (Les estructures Elémentaires de la Parenté)*. Beacon Press, Boston.

Punzo, José Luis, David Muñiz, Kimberly Sumano, Gabriel Maldondado, Alfredo Salas, Gabriela Arellano, Carlos Gutiérrez, and Mijaeli Castañón
  2015 Informe Técnico Final de Proyecto de Salvamento Arqueológico Las Purépechas. 3 Tomos. Archivo Técnico de la Coordinación Nacional de Arqueología del Instituto Nacional de Antropología e Historia, Centro INAH, Michoacán. Mecanuscrito, Morelia, Michoacan.

Rapoport, Amos
  2003 *Cultura, Arquitectura y Diseño*. Ediciones de la Universitat Politècnica de Catalunya, Barcelona.

Sanders, Ronald
  2005 *Rock Art Savvy: The Responsible Visitor's Guide to Public Sites of the Southwest*. Mountain Press Publishing, Missoula, Montana.

Soeane-Veiga, Yolanda
  2009 *Propuesta Metodológica para el Registro de Gráfica Rupestre en Galicia*. CAPA 23. Laboratorio de Patrimonio, Consejo Superior de Investigaciones Científicas, Santiago de Compostela, Spain.

Arte Rupestre y Sociedades de Casa en el Occidente de México: El Caso de Chavinda, Michoacán

Kimberly Sumano Ortega, David Arturo Muñiz García, and José Luis Punzo Díaz

En muchas ocasiones, el arte rupestre es encontrado en lugares sagrados, como una marca en el paisaje que puede ser accesible a algunos miembros de una sociedad determinada, y generalmente está relacionado a rituales específicos, o bien puede ser leído sólo mediante el conocimiento de un código específico. Sin embargo, presentamos un caso en donde el arte rupestre parece estar directamente relacionado a una marca de prestigio de una sociedad de casa. Chavinda, un sitio pequeño ubicado en una zona de Ciénega en el Centro/Norte de Michoacán en el Occidente mexicano, cuyo desarrollo ha sido datado alrededor del 425–600 d.C., puede ser un caso en donde la gráfica represente narrativas de casa en la vida cotidiana, como parte de una estrategia canónica del entorno construido como apropiación pública del paisaje.

Entorno Construido es un concepto que aparece como una forma de darle al espacio un sentido humanizado, pero también brinda la posibilidad de analizar dicho espacio como un escenario en donde el comportamiento de las personas es guiado a través del uso de ese entorno por la estructura de un sistema sociopolítico (Rapoport 2003). Si estamos de acuerdo con eso (y lo estamos), podemos argumentar que el espacio (social) es susceptible a ser usado como uno de los muchos mecanismos que la estructura sociopolítica tiene para actuar a través del mundo material.

La aproximación

Muchos estudios se han enfocado en el uso sociopolítico del espacio enfocándose en la arquitectura y, de hecho, y consideramos que esto es un acierto en tanto que normalmente se presenta cierta transformación al paisaje para obtener mejores condiciones para morar. Es obvio que cada cultura tiene su propio modo de apropiación en la práctica, íntimamente ligado con el habitus, tal y como Bourdieu lo propusiera alrededor de 1977. Lo que pretendemos subrayar aquí es que todas las sociedades usan el espacio en donde viven, pero también lo significan bajo códigos específicos que pueden ser entendidos por miembros de esa cultura en particular.

Como sabemos, una Casa, como la definiera Lévi-Satrauss (1969), es una unidad social materializada a través de una casa, así como su asociación con otros signos directamente relacionados a esta (en nuestro caso, arte rupestre). De cualquier modo, una C-casa sería capaz de describir múltiples aspectos de la estructura social mediante el estudio de esta asociación de sus elementos. También podemos entender una casa como la unidad doméstica en que un grupo social y una casa pueden ser fundados, relacionándose así con los linajes (Carsten y Hugh-Jones 1996:44).

Blanton, en 1994, publicó Houses and Households, en donde describe dos tipos de estrategias que la sociedad usa para emitir mensajes de acuerdo a lo permitido en determinadas culturas. Habla de las estrategias indéxicas como aquellas presentadas a los miembros de una familia o Casa, tal como la distribución interior de la casa, en donde se pude detectar algún tipo de estratificación (quizá por género o edad), por áreas de actividad o de control de los accesos a algunos puntos del interior (tal como hacemos actualmente al no dejar entrar a nuestros hijos a la oficina en casa ¿no es así?).

La otra estrategia se denomina canónica, que puede ser entendida como aquello que ha de mostrarse al mundo exterior, hablando desde la mirada de la Casa. Podemos ejemplificar esto con los colores elegidos para pintar las casas según las culturas, como los mexicanos que gustamos de los colores brillantes, o como el empeño puesto en los jardines de las casa norteamericanas. De cualquier modo, algunas cosas han de ser mostradas al exterior y otras no deben serlo (Bourdieu 1994).

En este punto cabe aclarar una cosa más: la Arqueología del Paisaje (Seoane-Vega 2009) aparece en nuestro estudio como una aproximación adecuada para incursionar en una región poco conocida y un sitio menos estudiado aún, en tanto que no contábamos con muchos datos cuando comenzamos a pensar y discutir sobre el arte rupestre y su posible función en Chavinda; hemos de decir que actualmente contamos con mucha más información. Aun así, seguimos viendo en los estudios espaciales una herramienta útil para nuestra interpretación. Basados en el trabajo de Seoane-Vega, registramos cada diseño en formatos cerrados, fotografiamos y dibujamos tanto digital como a mano alzada (Figura 2, ejemplos).

En el caso que se presenta en este documento, proponemos que los habitantes de Chavinda recurrieron a símbolos cosmogónicos y de prestigio para denotar estatus en una sociedad estratificada a modo de arte rupestre, mismo que aparece directamente relacionado a las casas. Pero no a todas las casas, sino a algunas unidades habitacionales pertenecientes a familias o linajes de élite (Figura 3, mapa de sitio de Chavinda con la ubicación de los elementos descritos).

El asentamiento

Estuvimos en condiciones de estudiar este asentamiento en el contexto de un proyecto de salvamento arqueológico financiado por Comisión Federal de Electricidad, en acuerdo con el Instituto Nacional de Antropología e Historia a través del Centro INAH Michoacán. Toda la información aquí vertida fue generada durante el trabajo de registro arqueológico del equipo del que, en su momento, formamos parte (Punzo et al. 2015).

Chavinda es un sitio localizado al Oeste del pequeño valle de Chavinda-Ario, Michoacán, que conecta con el río Chapala al Noreste a través del valle y las montañas aledañas. Cuenta con 46.5ha. en sus dimensiones totales. El asentamiento esta en medio de la ladera del Cerro Alto, entre los 1590 y los 1710 msnm. Su distribución aparece como extendida, con 1330m de Norte a Sur y 430m de Este a Oeste, consistiendo en tres sectores principales: al Este el sector público cívico-ceremonial con tres patios lineares rodeados por seis estructuras, todas en una plataforma de 200m de largo como parte de la inclinación natural de la ladera. La segunda sección consiste en algunas unidades habitacionales, todas ellas de mampostería, misma que presenta la mayor concentración de petrograbados, en el segundo radio de la plataforma principal. El tercer sector puede ser descrito como el área de labor agrícola, sirviendo como contenedor de los dos primeros, aunque también cuenta con unidades habitacionales posiblemente pertenecientes a los grupos de no-élite, los trabajadores de la tierra, ello debido a su ubicación y material constructivo (bajareque) (ver Figura 1).

En resumen, nueve plataformas, trece terrazas, seis montículos y veintitrés petrograbados en estilo abstracto fueron registrados finalmente, todo dividido en cuatro grupos. El primero cuenta con cinco rocas grabadas, directamente relacionadas a unidades habitacionales excavadas al Sur del asentamiento (Figura

4). El segundo consiste en siete piedras grabadas, en dirección al centro del sitio, asociadas a plataformas habitacionales (Figura 5). El tercero se conforma por tres motivos de espirales, relacionadas con excavaciones extensivas al Este de Chavinda (Figura 6). Finalmente, el cuarto grupo se compone de seis grabados asociados a edificios públicos (Figura 7).

Arte Rupestre y Arquitectura

Como mencionamos anteriormente, la mayoría de los petrograbados están asociados a posibles Casas de élite por su distribución espacial (Seoane-Vega 2009). Algunos diseños aparecen como un solo motivo y algunos otros como pequeños páneles. De cualquier modo, consideramos la existencia de dos estaciones o grandes segmentos en la totalidad del sitio, basados en la localización espacial de los petroglifos y su relación con las estructuras arquitectónicas (Figura 8).

Los diseños son considerablemente similares en todos los casos: espirales, lazy "s", patrones de pozas y canales, vulvas y unos pocos antroppomorfos, tanto en patrones rectilíneos como curvilíneos. A pesar de haber una repetición de los elementos iconográficos, cada petroglifo es considerablemente distinto a los otros. En este punto podemos distinguir que algunas rocas tienen una composición formal más compleja, con más motivos y posiblemente con un discurso igualmente más elaborado.

Discusión

Consideramos que el hecho de que cada petrograbado sea totalmente distinto a los otros puede estar relacionado a aspectos identitarios de cada familia Casa, y es probable que los símbolos y las técnicas estén asociados a un linaje mayor. En este sentido, podríamos hablar de un discurso basado en relaciones sociales reveladas en las relaciones espaciales a través del arte rupestre.

Es plausible considerar al arte rupestre como parte de las estrategias tanto canónicas como indéxicas según la propuesta de Blanton, al servicio de un tipo específico de orden social jerárquico, cuando menos en un rango intra-sitio. Consideramos esto en tanto de cada petrograbado está espacialmente relacionado con una unidad habitacional, además de que localizamos un diseño complejo rodeado de una serie de motivos más sencillos. Una roca debe recibir trato especial en este estudio, Petro#12, una gran pieza de riolita de 350 x 250 x 150 cm localizada en medio del núcleo de mayor concentración de arte rupestre del sitio; parece ser un espacio para adoptar una posición sedente (¿quizá un trono como en Chalcatzingo?) (Figura 9). Es la única pieza que presenta tres antropomorfos al menos, posiblemente dos masculinos y un femenino, todos ellos mirando hacia un área abierta que podría estar funcionando como una pequeña plaza. Si nuestra interpretación es de algún modo correcta, entonces tendríamos un argumento sólido para pensar en el arte rupestre como una marca distintiva o emblema de la sociedad de Chavinda, como manifestación pública de marca territorial, como sugiere Sanders (2005:56).

Conclusión

Los que hemos presentado aquí no es sino una primera aproximación a un área poco conocida, pero evidentemente aún queda mucho por hacer. Esperamos pronto estar en condiciones de establecer la relación entre diversos materiales como cerámica, lítica. Malacofauna y restos óseos con el arte rupestre, para brindar una mucho más sólida interpretación de los habitantes de Chavinda. Por lo pronto, mostramos los elementos preliminares con los que contamos para sugerir una asociación espacial de la arquitectura doméstica con grupos de petroglifos, una situación pecualiar en Mesoamérica.

A Universalist Taxonomy for Pictures

Livio Dobrez

Over the past decade I have looked for a way of talking about pictures, i.e. for a classification system for pictures, that would cover all art, including rock art, and that would not be based on culture-specific premises. In this article I offer an overview of the investigation, which centers on analysis of the actual perception of pictures—with reference to perceptual situations in real life which might have evolutionary import. I also give consideration to ways in which cognitive psychology and neurophysiology might offer scientific support for the thesis.

After a decade of pursuing a particular set of ideas about rock art and given that most phases of that thinking are represented in *AIRA* publications, I want to offer an overview that places all of this work in proper perspective. This seems especially necessary because the disciplinary basis of the work is unusual. There have been (a few) approaches to rock art guided by phenomenology, the descriptive philosophy outlined a century ago by Edmund Husserl (1970). There has been (some but not a lot of) work done by people with knowledge of Art History. A (very small) number of cognitive psychologists have contributed, as have a (minuscule) number of researchers with some knowledge of neuroscience. Most of the work in rock art around the world has been done by archaeologists and anthropologists (henceforth A&A). The unusualness of my approach is that it combines all of the above. While familiarizing myself with A&A research, I have come to rock art with an interest in philosophy and hermeneutics or interpretation theory in particular, as well as in Art History—and I have added a (soft) scientific line with perceptual psychology and a (hard) scientific line with neurophysiology, in short, with considerations of biology. In an academic context in which specialization is the rule and it seems perfectly reasonable to fence off the disciplines from one another, I have set out to do the opposite.

Ordering the Field of Depiction

This happened because of the nature of the question I wanted to answer. The question being simply this: how to find a way of talking about the whole field of art, i.e., depiction, that would make some ordered sense of the field (but without overly speculative theories, about the origins of art, for example). Clearly anyone wanting to do this must begin with the most ubiquitous art type and the one having the greatest time depth, namely rock art. The task then becomes the devising of a taxonomy for art of all kinds and especially rock art. As it happens my take on this began to shape itself in the United States in the 1990s when, faced with the startling lineup of images at Barrier Canyon, I was prompted to analyze my perceptual response. Attention to ob-

Livio Dobrez
Australian National University, retired

server response, rather than investigation into possible original intentions behind the making of the rock art, marks the difference between a universalist phenomenological approach and a historicist one. Of course direct observation may be good, bad, or indifferent. Hence my desire to give it added weight by appeal to science.

Existing taxonomies for art in general and rock art in particular tend to be historical. Art History has its categories ("Archaic," "Classical," "Hellenistic"; or "Renaissance," "Mannerist," "Baroque"; or "Impressionist," "Post-Impressionist," "Modernist," "Postmodern," etc.) which are, of course, period-bound. Rock art categories, usually proposed on the basis of a combination of archaeological and stylistic sequencing, are likely to be either period- or culture-bound or both:

- Basketmaker II and III; Pueblo I–V (Schaafsma 1980)
- Barrier Canyon, Fremont (Classic Vernal, San Rafael), etc. (Schaafsma 1980)
- "Early hunter," Columbia Plateau, Dinwoody, "pecked abstract," "plains grooved," "foothills abstract," etc. (Keyser 2004)

Alternatively, both A&A and Art History may opt for a more formal categorization of material. Thus the latter divides the discourse of pictures by, for example, categories including "balance," "shape," "form," "space," "light," "color," "movement," "dynamism," and "expression" (Arnheim 1974)—and the former by aspirationally objective binaries such as "zoomorph/anthropomorph," "abstract/representational," "naturalistic/schematic," and "simple/complex."

It may be that some formal categories of the Art History kind are universally applicable, i.e., non-culture-specific. Those rock art conceptual divisions which aim at objectivity, however, turn out on reflection to be very much of the historical present. The "zoomorph/anthropomorph" division clearly makes no sense for hunter-gatherer cultures. The notion of an "abstract" motif probably in part derives from the modern art "figurative/abstract" divide. The notion of "naturalism" is derived from that of "the way things really look" which, again on reflection, is suspiciously like the way things look in post-Renaissance European art and, above all, photography. The suspiciously value-laden "simple/complex" binary brings with it a prejudice in favor of the post-Enlightenment belief in historical "progress" (something the anthropologists may well warn us against). In important respects, then, neither existing Art History nor A&A rock art methodologies offer much scope for breaking the boundaries between art and rock art studies—though it is the case that some formal categories, usually in association with "style," are common to both (provided an extremely hard-edge archaeologist does not enter the discourse with the dire warning that stylistic analysis is subjective).

Perceptual Situations and Evolution

But what about that other dubious divide, the one between "art" and extra-pictorial "life"? After all, I have so far been talking entirely about pictures of things, and not about things themselves. Surely a sound taxonomy for pictures might be expected to apply, if not quite in the same way, to the everyday, non-pictorial context for pictures? I think—and this is critical—that if we take visual perception as a logical starting point (something in any case prompted by the phenomenological starting point, namely analysis of our perceptual responses) all conceptual barriers mentioned above give way. If we examine our visual-perceptual responses to various life-situations, we may expect these to be reproduced, with appropriate modification, in pictorial situations—and, in addition, in *all* pictorial situations, art and rock art included. But which life-situations are we to choose? It seems to me that at this point it is appropriate to co-opt the theory of evolution, i.e., to zero in on certain situations which are likely to have evolutionary import—and which might also have strong representation in art. It goes without saying that here the time depth and geographical range of rock art gives it special relevance.

Before introducing the three perceptual situations that have most preoccupied me to date, a brief aside is necessary. It concerns the objection usually raised against most if not all forms of universalist analysis, namely the idea that we cannot assume that the makers of often very ancient rock art saw the art as we see it now, i.e., that perceptual responses cannot be taken as constant. If by "seeing" we mean knowing the culture-specific significance, say the symbolism, of a given body of rock art, I certainly agree. In this sense, I do not see the art as the makers saw it. Of course this position, if rigorously applied, would rule out not merely my thesis, but all historical studies. So it is rarely rigorously applied. However, those who make this objection, whether in soft or hard form, usually mean something different, namely that "seeing" in the biological sense changes over time. This may be the case in *very* long evolutionary time, but it is not the case in even the longest time spans relevant to the study of rock art. If it *were*, it would make nonsense of everything anyone says about rock art, promptly putting every rock art researcher out of a job.

I have elsewhere used an example from geometry to illustrate the point: if you think that what you perceive as a *square* may conceivably have been perceived by the makers as a *circle*, then there is nothing more to be said about rock art and the researcher may as well go into insurance or retailing. There is another way of clinching the argument, though. For decades the neurophysiology of the visual system was studied with monkeys—who could be sacrificed to science at the end of each experiment. When fMRI became available as a non-invasive means of examining brain structures—in particular the neural structure of the *human* visual system— it emerged that a considerable homology existed between monkey and human. Now we humans diverged from Old World monkeys ca. 20 million years ago, so the visual system has not changed significantly for a time span vastly exceeding any for rock art. The fact is we continue to see the world, pictorial and otherwise, in biological ways laid down long before we became "human," let alone started to make pictures.

With confidence that I do not see a square where rock artists intended a circle and equal confidence that in appealing to visual responses I am not confusing seeing as a biological activity with seeing in the sense of understanding or knowing a cultural/symbolic code, I now turn to three perceptual situations I have sought to analyze in the past decade. Each has its equivalent in depiction; each straddles the divide between different kinds of pictures, in particular the art/rock art divide; and each incorporates elements which should have survival value.

The Category of Canonicals

Patricia Dobrez and I put forward the case for a perceptual/depictive category of images we termed Canonicals in an *AIRA* piece (2013b), at greater length in a piece for *RAR* (2013a) and in a piece for the *Boletín del Museo Chileno de Arte Precolombino* (2014). We envisaged a situation in which the observer notes humans and animals, but animals especially, from a position of safety, possibly for the purpose of hunting. This constitutes a perceptual situation of not insignificant survival value. Its focus is primarily on the recognition of what is being observed and the identification of whatever it is, because it might be either good to eat or potentially dangerous. In this context easy and fast recognition is obtained, with a few well-known exceptions, in profiles facilitating the viewing of what we termed salient features, such as the cervico-dorsal line or horns. These salient points, we argued, encourage part-for-whole apprehension, so that the requirement for speed is satisfied. Of course principles of fast recognition do not guarantee that in any given case recognition is accurate.

Perceptual errors occur and may prompt visual reassessment. I say this because these principles of "canonical form" will not of themselves settle questions such as that of the Sand Island "mammoth." If the Sand Island image is judged to have the canonical form of a mammoth, then what is established is that it *looks like* a mammoth (which, to Dobrez eyes, it does), but not that it *is* a mammoth (hence our wish to remain neutral as regards this debate in American rock art, pending further information). In terms of the canonical thesis, our original claim was that the perceptual situation of observing a real animal had its pictorial equivalent, evident in the animal representations of the European Paleolithic, but equally so in depictions of, for example, macropods (kangaroos and wallabies) in Australia; guanaco in the Andes; capybara in Brazil; horses, sheep, and bison in the United States; deer and cattle in India; eland in southern Africa, etc. "Pictorial equivalent" signifies that the perceptual principles operative in the real situation also operate in the picturing of that real situation. Thus, to take the most obvious principle, salient features of a real animal would be emphasized in a *picture* of the animal.

It is worth noting that "canonical form" avoids the pitfalls of reference to "naturalistic" depiction. It is not a matter of what the animal "really" looks like (whatever that means), nor is it a matter of adherence to a particular style—which would introduce cultural specifics. Images illustrating this article (Figures 1–4), with one exception, are highly conventionalized (some might prefer the term "stylized"). The sheep from St. George, Utah (Figure 1), are primarily represented as rectangles; the guanaco from Cueva de las Manos (Figure 2) as boat-shaped (perhaps to indicate gravity); the wallaroos from Cape York, Queensland (Figure 3), as heavy masses. But all figures, including the horse advertisement from New South Wales (Figure 4), exhibit "canonical form": the sheep via horns and feet (quite distinct from the small dog on the right); the guanaco via the long line of the neck; the wallaroos through their stocky bulk, not least in the tail, which distinguishes them from more aerodynamic macropods. And the appeal to canonical depiction is equally evident in the photograph—equally, not *more* so, because

Figure 1. St. George, Utah.

Figure 3. Giant Wallaroo site, Cape York, Australia.

Figure 2. Cueva de las Manos, Santa Cruz, Argentina.

Figure 4. Advertisement, New South Wales, Australia.

what is at issue here is not a style of presentation (quite different in each of the four cases) but a picture which first and foremost enables perceptual recognition, the conclusion that "yes—it's a sheep…a guanaco…a wallaroo…a horse." The added cultural information, for example the fact that the horse is of the very expensive sort, adds nothing to the status of the image as "best recognition" or canonical.

The Category of Narratives

The second category which concerns me is the one I term Narrative, commonly referred to as the "scene." I have commented on scenes in a number of articles, including two for *AIRA*, but in special detail in a piece for the online journal *Arts* (Dobrez 2007, 2008, 2010, 2010–11, 2011a, 2011b, 2012b, 2013, 2015a, 2015b, 2015c). A scene obtains if, as observers (and here we are always talking about the perceptual situation of the observer), we witness not merely a given X (horse, bison, etc.), but something "going on," an event. This may involve any animal, including the human. It is not important, for my purpose, to name what it is that is "going on." Strictly speaking, that is a matter for cultural specifics, not universals. The universal is simply the perceptual situation of observing an event. Clearly events matter in terms of survival—though, as I stress, an observed scene is not an issue of immediate concern to the observer. Now rock art studies make regular reference to the scene, and I need not labor the point that scenes are found around the world (Red Linear and Biographic in the United States; compositions in the Serra da Capivara, Brazil; in Madhya Pradesh, India; in Arnhem Land and the Kimberley Plateau, Australia; in the Sahara and southern Africa; in the Spanish Levant). In spite of this the concept of the scene has not been adequately analyzed, either in rock art or art studies. I have sought to provide visual markers for it which would apply to any type of depiction and these include (a) compositional imbalance or asymmetry, whether in a single figure (e.g., angled limbs) or a group (e.g., diagonal compositions), in each case indicative of depicted movement; (b) profile depiction, with figures oriented towards each other (for interaction) or towards some common goal; (c) generally small figure size; and (d) spacing between figures that is neither too small nor too great for the perception of cause and effect relations (a point to which I shall return). I have also identified contextual markers for a scene: approach/visibility; placement on the support surface; optimal viewpoint. In rock art, scenes, usually consisting of small elements, will not be visible from a distance. They are more likely to be viewed at eye level and in closeup. This rule applies to comics, graphic novels, Chinese and Japanese figures-in-landscape (in a book or scroll), Thai temple frescoes (eventually set too high on walls or pillars for the eye to read), Persian or Indian miniatures, European paintings of all kinds—and, of course, television/computer-screen images. But the rule may be stretched, as in film, though even here the eye has difficulty reading an "event" if the image is too large, as with IMAX screenings, which are better suited to generating a sense of vistas or ambience.

It must be pointed out that visual markers cannot force the eye, or rather brain, to "see" action, i.e., movement in a still picture. In life we cannot do what is perfectly possible in pictures: to "freeze" the action. Although we can stop depicted action, we will not do so (except for the purpose of perceptual experiment), since it is much easier to go along with markers of depicted action than to resist them. When we follow the markers' prompts we effectively perceive spatial expansions and contractions in the picture, i.e., we participate in the construction of unstable or moving representational space. This is critical, since without such spatial flexibility depicted figures will not register as moving, i.e. they stay "frozen." The other important feature of the scene is that representational space *excludes* the observer, who cannot *enter* the action but is restricted to viewing through something like a "window." This returns us to the real-life perceptual situation described above. In art the feature that most obviously generates this phenomenon is profile depiction; figures in a scene are required to react to each other and not to the viewer of the scene.

All the above points are illustrated in Figures 5–8. Again, it does not matter that these four scenes have specific content, understood or not depending on one's access to relevant cultural knowledge. Figure 5, from

Figure 5. Pressa Canyon, Texas.

Figure 6. Toca da Extrema II, Serra da Capivara, Brazil.

Figure 7. Mt. Brockman, Arnhem Land, Australia (courtesy Judith Hammond).

Pressa Canyon, Texas, may possibly depict a birthing scene. Figure 6, from the Serra da Capivara, appears to depict a sexual ritual focused on a plant. Figure 7, from Arnhem Land, Australia, looks straightforwardly

Figure 8. Breizh (Brittany) Café, Canberra, Australia.

like a hunting scene. But questions of content in rock art are more or less conjectural. With Figure 8, however, we are on solid anthropological ground, as I know the location (the Breizh café in my city of Canberra) and the participants (from left to right, baristas Ollie, Myra, and Jamie). Actually, even here I am not sure about the precise content of the scene, which involves an exchange between Ollie and Jamie (amusing enough to engage the customer behind Jamie). Still, I can be certain of one thing: that this is indeed a scene—the content is of a narrative kind. And this applies to Figures 5–7 too. In each case I register depicted movement (which may be minimal, as in Figure 8), profile figures interacting at just the right distance from each other for me to read cause and effect, and eye-level, closeup accessibility (not least with the photograph). If the Arnhem Land figures (Figure 7) are larger than the ones from Brazil and Texas (Figures 6 and 5), elegant motion would seem to compensate (small figures, according to Gestalt principles, being more intrinsically dynamic). Finally, all four cases, I observe, indeed *generate*, on the prompting of visual markers and not by mere whim, a representational space in which the actors operate—without my being able to intrude.

From the highly varied examples above, it is evident that the response "that this is a scene" is not influenced by "style," in particular by a realist style of presentation which, tendentiously, is usually associated with the camera. Figures 5–7 are just as much scenes as Figure 8. Likewise, they could, if suitably cropped, be just as much scenes with only one figure visible. It happens I have used four examples of *interactive* scenes, but an *action* scene with only one actor, e.g., someone talking, running, throwing a spear, etc., would satisfy defini-

tional criteria listed above. This conclusion goes against received wisdom in rock art studies, but it has analytical logic on its side. Finally there is the question of how many and which visual markers suffice to constitute a scene. As with Canonicals, Narratives are generated by a complex combination of markers, with some having greater, some lesser priority. Again, the absence of some markers will be compensated for by others. Nonetheless, the registering of depicted movement with its associated elements, and of course the larger "viewer-exclusion" principle, would seem essential.

The Category of Performatives

I now come to the third perceptual situation in question, the one which would seem to have the greatest relevance of all for evolutionary survival. It is one thing to observe a profile bison—the situation in which we register its canonical form—and quite another to go from safe observer to threatened participant in an action when the bison turns towards you and charges. Likewise it is one thing to view a scene involving bison interacting among themselves, quite another to join the picture when the bison decide to include you. It must be, and indeed *is*, the case that this shift from the perceptual category of recognition (the Canonical image) or scene (the Narrative image) to a third category, one of greatly heightened tension, has its equivalent in pictures. I have termed this the pictorial category of Performatives (Dobrez 2007, 2008, 2010, 2010–11, 2011b, 2012a, 2013, 2015b, 2015c). Now whereas much has been said, if with insufficient analysis, about scenes, it is astonishing that no one has ever thought of identifying the Performative, though it is everywhere present, whether in rock art or contemporary pop. The Performative is essentially an image that looms at you, i.e., faces you, the viewer, and interestingly, it is unlikely to be that charging bison, at least in art with the greatest time/space depth, i.e., rock art. It may be found in a comic or a movie (especially 3D), of course, where it is as likely to be a monstrous alien as a dangerous beast. In rock art, and not simply in rock art, it will be a *human* animal. With few exceptions, rock art animals are given in profile, whereas humans, other than in scenes, are given as frontals. This suggests to me that we regard our conspecifics as supremely dangerous.

Be that as it may, the visual markers for Performatives or looming figures would seem to be complementary opposites of scene markers. Where the latter generate *representational* space, i.e. space in which some kind of story or narrative unfolds, the former disconcertingly confront the observer, giving an impression of entering or at least being on the point of entering the *real* space of the observer. This is the case with Figures 9–11, all of which, as it were, advance at you—these images from Butler Wash in Utah (Figure 9), Dinwoody in Wyoming (Figure 10), and the Quinkan site in Queensland (Figure 11) are given as frontals, whereas figures in scenes had the requirement of profile. The Quinkan image is very active, though not in a way that might be confused with a scene, since looming action is directed *outside* the picture. The Butler Wash and Dinwoody images may, at a superficial level, seem somewhat static—and initially I made the mistake of analyzing similar images from the great panel at Barrier Canyon along these lines. In fact, nothing could be further from the truth. The undeniable power of the Performative is that, even when given as symmetrical, i.e., without indication of, say, moving limbs, it is more active than any figure in a scene: its activity is concentrated in the fact of its looming, and its unique presentation of pictorial space is *fractured* such that it

Figure 11. Quinkan Shelter, Cape York, Australia.

fails to *contain* the image. This is the principle of the charging bison. Frequently, if not inevitably, the sense of looming is enhanced by a focus on the depicted face and, most tellingly, the eyes, as in Figures 10 and 11. Where no eyes are given, as in Figure 9, frontality does the job. But eye-contact, frequent in religious icons (the Byzantine Christ, or the Hindu deity exhibiting the phenomenon of *darshan* or exchange of gaze between the deity and devotee) has dominance, so much so that it suffices to paint large eyes on a stupa tower, as at Svayambhu, Nepal, to create the effect of looming. However, it should be added that a looming figure need not evoke the religious: Uncle Sam, directly engaging you to call out "Your Country Needs You!" invokes that archetypal looming situation, also unsettling for animals (monkeys are alarmed in looming experiments and, of course, eye-contact is as provocative for a dog as for a human). Add to this the observation that Performatives, especially in rock art, are apt to be large where figures in scenes are apt to be small; and that, accordingly, Performatives are likely to be visible at a distance, often placed above eye level such that the optimal viewpoint is from below, and it comes as no surprise that such images dominate the observer. But this is of itself not essential, and probably not as important as frontality and/or eye-contact. The Butler Wash and

Figure 9. Butler Wash, Utah.

Figure 10. Dinwoody Lake, Wyoming.

Dinwoody hieratic images are indeed some distance up on a cliff, like those at Barrier Canyon. The Quinkans, on the other hand, disturbingly confront you in a more confined space and at your own height—after you have been required to enter by a narrow passageway featuring images on either side that are possibly warning you.

Looming images are found in Australia, not only at Cape York but, notably, as Wandjinas in the Kimberley and Baiames around Sydney. They are prominent in the U.S. from the Pecos to Barrier and Classic Vernal in Utah (and beyond: see Keyser and Poetschat 2017) to Dinwoody in Wyoming (and here we should not omit mention of Tsagiglalal, "she who watches" on the Oregon/Washington border). But they exist in Africa—and in Europe, though less prominently. In formal/perceptual terms they must be regarded as fundamentally incompatible with scenes—indeed as dominant over scenes—for sound evolutionary reasons that take us back to that real-life perceptual situation of the charging bison. A less threatening example might be derived from Figure 8, discussed above. As it is, Ollie and Jamie interact and we look on. Imagine, however, that as Ollie and Jamie continue their conversation, Myra (in the middle) notices the camera and turns her gaze in its direction. The result is that she now looks *out of* the photograph, i.e., directly at anyone observing the photograph. In this situation it would still be possible to see the photograph as the record of a scene, but I suggest eye-contact with you, the observer, would have priority and the scene would be compromised. You could "switch" visual, i.e,. neural attention from the photo-as-scene to the photo-as-Performative—and back again. You could *not* see a scene and Performative *at the same time*. And I think, in the end, the look *out of* the picture would register as primary, at least to the extent of disrupting perception of a scene. An addendum to this discussion of Performatives: the human hand, in rock art usually in the form of a print or stencil, should also be considered as a looming image—and has been so analyzed by Patricia Dobrez (2013). Even without the cultural knowledge that tells us to STOP (rather than, say, "aloha!") this hand at a street-crossing in Waikiki (Figure 12), is, as we say, "arresting."

Art Via Science

There are other perceptual/depictive types I would like to address in the future. Here, however, I want to turn to scientific support for the types discussed above. This not because I do not have confidence in observational logic, but because we may expect experiment

Figure 12. Traffic light, Waikiki, Hawaii.

to shed light on other forms of analysis. Both cognitive psychology and neurophysiology have proved immensely useful to me. With respect to Canonicals, Patricia Dobrez and I referred to the theory of "basic level" categorization of objects, to experimental material on "dominant views" of objects (in this case, profile), and above all to the perception of "salient features." This led us to detailed consideration of (diverse) theories of the relation of "parts" and "wholes," i.e., the issue of seeing the object as whole by the mechanical addition of its parts—or holistically to begin with, this last necessitating a discussion of "saccadic" eye movement during perception of both real and pictured objects. It was then a matter of investigating how the whole-first or parts-first debate in cognitive psychology plays out in the neural structures of the visual system, in particular the object-processing area of the inferior temporal lobe (inferotemporal). That in turn led to focus on neurons sensitive to the precise orientation of objects ("viewer-centered" neurons) to feed-forward processing mechanisms and the role of memory (after all, you cannot recognize the canonical form of an animal you have never seen before).

With respect to scenes and their vital component—movement—I have made particular use of Johansson's "point-light" experiment (1973) which showed that we see motion before we see what is moving, a finding consistent with the fact that the visual processing path at the back of the brain divides in two, with a faster pathway (the "dorsal") to the motion-processing area V5 in the visual cortex, and a slower pathway (the "ventral") to the object-processing of the inferotemporal mentioned above. So, while we quickly recognize a bison part-for-whole simply because we have glimpsed its hump, something which might require a feed-forward mechanism, we spot its movement (in V5) *before* we properly focus on it in the inferotemporal. So insofar as it involves pictured movement, a scene should be perceived with greater urgency than a canonical form. In connection with movement in a scene I have especially referred to the work of Freyd (1983, 1987), who was actually able to *measure* the displacement of a figure in a picture, i.e., its perceived motion. Since this was motion in a *still*, it showed we do not merely *infer* such motion: we really *see* it. Along comparable lines the psychologist Michotte (1963) showed that we directly perceive cause and effect relations between objects—something I could readily apply to depicted scenes. Most important of all—and this has bearing on all three type-situations I am outlining—neurophysiology clearly indicates that there is fundamental similarity in our perceptual processing of the real and the depicted. It seems that real and depicted register in the same neural areas, i.e., the same areas fire for both. More than that: some *individual* neurons fire for both, making no distinction between real movement and movement in a picture!

There is, to my knowledge, less precise neural evidence in connection with the phenomenon of looming, though I have made some modest predictions in relation to this. There is material from perceptual psychology I have been able to use. For example, experiments have been made involving shapes (projected on a screen) which gradually increase in size. Tellingly, subjects do not see the shapes as getting bigger: they see them as *coming closer*, i.e., as looming (Gibson 1979). Some, including Freyd, have examined aspects of the looming/Performative effect, notably the fact that we actually *see* looming images as being in motion (Kelly and Freyd 1987). There have been animal-response experiments involving perception of faces and eyes—and there is also a lot of neurophysiological information relating to face-processing, all of which I have been able to use so as to balance phenomenological observation ("looking at our looking") with science. Overall, it seems to me science has offered solid support for the thesis I have presented. At the same time it must be stressed that there is little material available that specifically combines art with science, and scarcely any that does this with focus on rock art. Alpert (2008) produced the only published book-length study I know of in the latter category, and in the former there are, most notably, Zeki (1999), Ramachandran and Hirstein (1999), and Livingstone (2002). Where I confidently part company with neuroscientists who have entered the field of Art History such as Zeki and Ramachandran, as well as with some rock art scholars who, like Bednarik (1984), want to promote a scientific approach, is in the fact that I do not regard science—in the present context, the hard data of neurophysiology—as "explaining" either art in general or rock art in particular. Of course any perceptual activity (my three type situations: a canonical bison, or a narrative bison scene, or a bison charging in your direction) necessarily has neural substrates or correlates. But it does not follow that these correlates constitute *the* explanation for the perceptual act. It is just that they entail a "bottom-up" explanation matching an equivalent "top-down" one.

In summary, we have here a coherently-structured case for a particular way of making sense of pictures, *all* pictures, whether rock art or art in general—and this by grounding the phenomenon of pictures in real-life situations. The key lies in the analysis of our visual perception in (a) real situations having survival value, and (b) their pictorial equivalents. Such an approach incorporates elements of disciplines such as A&A, Art History, and philosophical hermeneutics and makes ready use of experimental work in psychology and neuroscience. Its premises and conclusions are necessarily universalist rather than historicist, and to that extent they depart from the historical concerns which have traditionally been and continue to be the basis of art studies. Nonetheless I am far from advocating replacing historical studies with biological ones. In line with the inclusive nature of the argument I have advanced, I regard universalist approaches as complementing historically-oriented analysis.

Acknowledgment. I am grateful to my anonymous reviewer for reminding me that a figure with large eyes (typically neonate) should trigger the "performative" effect, also with evolutionary import.

References Cited

Alpert, Barbara
  2008 *The Creative Ice Age Brain: Cave Art in the Light of Neuroscience.* Nyehaus/Foundation 20 21, New York.

Arnheim, Rudolf
  1974 *Art and Visual Perception: A Psychology of the Creative Eye.* University of California Press, Berkeley.

Bednarik, Robert
  1984 On the Nature of Psychograms. *The Artefact* 8:27–31.

Dobrez, Livio
  2007 The Reception of Visual Representations. In *XXII International Valcamonica Symposium*, edited by Mindi Bloom, Piero Giorgi, and Genny Pietroboni, pp. 115–121. Centro Camuno di Studi Preistorici, Edizioni del Centro, Capo di Ponte, Italy.

2008 A Rock Art Typology: Narrative and Non-Narrative Figural Representation. In *Aesthetics and Rock Art III Symposium*, edited by Thomas Heyd, and John Clegg, pp. 29–33. Proceedings of the XV UISPP World Congress (Lisbon), Volume 10, Session C73. Archaeopress, Oxford, United Kingdom.

2010 "Good to Think" Representational Modalities. In *Global Rock Art FumdhaMentos IX*, pp. 284–294. Fundação Museu do Homem Americano, São Raimundo Nonato, Brazil.

2010–11 What Representations Tell Us About the Way We See (with Commentary by R. Bednarik and Reply). *Purakala: The Journal of Rock Art Society of India* 20–21:23–41.

2011a Rock Art, Perception and the Subject/Object Binary. *Rock Art Research* 28(1):71–83.

2011b Looking at Our Looking: A New Approach to the Definition of a Rock Art Scene. In *American Indian Rock Art, Volume 37*, edited by Mavis Greer, John Greer, and Peggy Whitehead, pp. 251–264. American Rock Art Research Association, Glendale, Arizona.

2012a American Ikon: How to Choose an ARARA Logo. In *American Indian Rock Art, Volume 38*, edited by Eric W. Ritter, Melissa Greer, and Peggy Whitehead, pp. 145–164. American Rock Art Research Association. Glendale, Arizona.

2012b Towards a More Rigorous Definition of Terms: Are There Scenes in European Palaeolithic Art? In *L'Art Pléistocène dans le monde*, edited by Jean Clottes, pp. 316 (abstract), 1837–1851. Actes du Congrès IFRAO, Tarascon-sur-Ariège, septembre 2010, Numéro spécial de Préhistoire, Art et Sociétés, Bulletin de la Société Préhistorique Ariège-Pyrénées, LXV-LXVI, Ariège, France (CD).

2013 The Perception of Depicted Motion. *Arts* 2(4):383–446. Electronic document (doi:10.3390/arts20403837), http://www.mdpi.com/2076-0752/2/4/383, accessed March 8, 2017.

2015a Depicted Motion, Interaction and Causality in Rock Art. In *American Indian Rock Art, Volume 41*, edited by James D. Keyser and David A. Kaiser, pp. 57–68. American Rock Art Research Association, San Jose, California.

2015b Evolutionary Perceptual Constants in Rock Art Motifs. In *XXVI Valcamonica Symposium*, edited by Federico Troletti, pp. 101–106. Centro Camuno di Studi Preistorici, Edizioni del Centro, Capo di Ponte, Italy.

2015c Making Sense of Pictures. *Bollettino del Centro Camuno di Studi Preistorici* 40:31–47.

Dobrez, Livio, and Patricia Dobrez
2013a Rock Art Animals in Profile: Visual Recognition and the Principles of Canonical Form. *Rock Art Research* 30(1):75–90.

2013b Canonical Form and the Identification of Rock Art Figures. In *American Indian Rock Art, Volume 39*, edited by William D. Hyder, pp. 115–129. American Rock Art Research Association. Glendale, Arizona.

2014 Canonical Figures and the Recognition of Animals in Art and Life. *Boletín del Museo Chileno de Arte Precolombino* 19(1):9–22.

Dobrez, Patricia
2013 The Case for Hand Stencils and Prints as Proprioperformative. *Arts* 2(4):273–327. Electronic document (doi:10.3390/arts2040273), http://www.mdpi.com/2076-0752/2/4/273, accessed March 8, 2017.

Freyd, Jennifer
1983 The Mental Representation of Movement When Static Stimuli Are Viewed. *Perception and Psychophysics* 33(6):575–581.

1987 Dynamic Mental Representations. *Psychological Review* 94(4):427–438.

Gibson, James
1979 *The Ecological Approach to Visual Perception*. Houghton Mifflin, Boston.

Husserl, Edmund
1970 *Logical Investigations*. Translated by J.N. Findlay. Routledge & Kegan Paul, London. Originally published as *Logische Untersuchungen*, Max Niemeyer, Halle, Germany, 1900/1901.

Johansson, Gunnar
1973 Visual Perception of Biological Motion and a Model for Its Analysis. *Perception and Psychophysics* 14(2):201–211.

Kelly, Michael, and Jennifer Freyd
1987 Explorations of Representational Momentum. *Cognitive Psychology* 19(3):369–401.

Keyser, James D.
2004 *Art of the Warriors: Rock Art of the American Plains*. University of Utah Press, Salt Lake City.

Keyser, James D., and George Poetschat
2017 Uinta Fremont Rock Art in Southwestern Wyoming: Marking the Fremont Northern Periphery. *Plains Anthropologist*, in press.

Livingstone, Margaret
2002 *Vision and Art: The Biology of Seeing*. Abrams, New York.

Michotte, Albert
1963 *The Perception of Causality*. Translated by T. R. and E. Miles. Methuen, London.

Ramachandran, Vilayanur, and William Hirstein
1999 The science of art: A neurological theory of aesthetic experience. *Journal of Consciousness Studies* 6:15–51.

Schaafsma, Polly
1980 *Indian Rock Art of the Southwest*. School of American Research, Santa Fe, and University of New Mexico Press, Albuquerque.

Zeki, Semir
1999 *Inner Vision: An Exploration of Art and the Brain*. Oxford University Press, Oxford.